6433

Words and Images

For Duncan, Susannah, and Sophie.

Words and Images

Australian Novels into Film

Brian McFarlane

Heinemann Publishers Australia
in association with Cinema Papers

HEINEMANN PUBLISHERS AUSTRALIA PTY LTD
85 Abinger Street, Richmond, Victoria, 3121, Australia.

© Brian McFarlane 1983.
First Published 1983.

Typeset in Baskerville by B-P Typesetting.
Printed in Hong Kong by Dah Hua Printing Press Co Ltd.
Designed by Ernie Althoff.

National Library of Australia cataloguing-in-publication data:

McFarlane, Brian, 1934-.
   Words and images.

ISBN 0 436 27600 3

1. Australian Literature — Film and Video adaptations —
History and Criticism. 2. Moving-pictures — Australia —
history and criticism. I. Title.

791.43′09′09357

Contents

Author's Note

Though there is not yet, as far as I can tell, a definitive work on the film-literature connection, among the books I have read on the subject none seems to me to have surpassed George Bluestone's *Novels into Film* which first appeared in 1957. I would like to acknowledge my indebtedness to this work.

As well, thanks are due to: Scott Murray for his enthusiasm for the project, and his vigorous and unfailingly helpful editorship; Helen Greenwood, Arthur Salton and Anne Sinclair of Cinema Papers, who helped in the preparation of the manuscript; Val Grinblat, who did most of the typing; Australasian Film Hire (Barry Hall), The Film House, and L.J. Promotions (John Gauci) for making films available; and The National Library, Canberra, for permission to reprint the photographs from **Wake in Fright**.

1. From Page to Screen

Everyone has at some time had the experience of leaving a cinema after seeing the film version of a well-known novel and of over-hearing comments like: "Why did they change the ending?" or "I liked the book better" or "Fancy leaving out . . . [this or that character or incident]". On a slightly more sophisticated level, one may hear something like, "I thought they were quite faithful to the *spirit* of the novel", hinting at name-less violations of the letter. Such common responses to films derived from novels are usually based on an implied sense of the primacy of the novel. Complaints that characters and episodes have been altered or omitted usually suggest that the novel has been "tampered with", as if such a process were vaguely indecent. There is a widespread assumption — among general readers and more specifically literary people — that it is the job of film-makers to "capture the spirit" of the original and to avoid "unnecessary" distortions of its detail, as if the novel were in some sense sacrosanct. Further, there are those who believe that filming inevitably takes away the element of imaginative involvement which the novel-reader feels, without suggesting that the film might offer a comparable if different form of involvement. And there is also the common complaint that the film has missed the novelist's unique "tone". The latter comment will almost certainly be true, because a film — whether adapted from a novel or not — is essentially a *new* act of creativity.

It is of course fascinating to consider how particular novels have been transposed to the screen; a close study of the process can throw new light on both novel and film, especially if the emphasis is on how the trans-position has been effected, rather than on labelling one text as "better" than the other. The kinds of comments referred to above are, it seems to me, all posited on a quite extraordinary assumption: that is, an un-examined belief that one could *ever* take the essence of one art form and recreate it in another *without* serious alteration. Such comments assume that there is something removable from a book which can be translated without loss to the screen. They do not take into account the crucial differences in the conventions governing each medium or the different circumstances of authorship and response in each case.

The more, in fact, one considers the basic idea of adapting a work of art in one medium to the demands of another, the more one is struck both by the inherent strangeness of the idea, and by the wide prevalence of the custom. Chaucer and Shakespeare wrote poems and plays respectively based on old prose stories or histories; operas have been made from *Macbeth* and *Othello*, from Walter Scott's *The Bride of Lammermoor*; there is a series of remarkable paintings by Geoffrey Dance based on Herman Melville's *Billy Budd*; and Benjamin Britten's "War Requiem" offers a

1

composer's response to Wilfred Owen's poem, "Strange Meeting". This list hints at the *range* in the curious process of adaptation, and yet no efforts at transposition seem to provoke the sorts of outrage one hears in relation to films made from novels. Even films made from plays seem to escape more lightly, perhaps because in one sense theatrical "performance" seems closer in spirit to a film screening and there is, consequently, less of a gap to be closed between the two. I do not actually endorse this point of view, believing that the novel and the film — the narrative fiction film — are more alike in certain crucial ways than any other two of the art forms mentioned above.

Nevertheless, one must stress the sheer improbability that an illusion of reality created in one form (i.e., the novel) could be recreated in another (i.e., film or television) without major change. The nature of such major changes will be central to any comparative study of texts in the two media. Films may try to be "faithful" to the original author's incidents, characters and point of view; they have tended to be much more so in the past dozen or so years than they were in the 1930s and '40s. However, if the film is to have any value of its own, it will need to have its *own point of view*, its own sense of the significance of what it is presenting. The lively film version of a novel will not necessarily be the most literal rendering of the original but the one which has responded to what has excited the film-maker in the original and which has succeeded in capturing this excitement in the new medium. There is no sense in which a written account and a visual realization can ever have been the *same* thing, however closely the film adaptation may aim to follow its predecessor. Reverent to the point of discipleship, the BBC's production of **Brideshead Revisited** cannot be a replacement for reading Evelyn Waugh's novel, or even a comparable experience; Peter Bogdanovich in general opts for the "faithful" treatment of Henry James' *Daisy Miller*: both might have been more exciting projects if their makers had taken a more vigorously individual approach to what had stirred them in the original works.

The question at issue is less "Is this being true or untrue to the original?" than "Does this make for a coherent and persuasive narrative in its own right?" As far as this book is concerned, it is likely that my personal evaluation of each in relation to the other will emerge. This is nevertheless not its chief aim. Its purpose is to arrive at understanding of how each member of the pairs of texts examined — novel and film — works to create its own meaning, its own impact, rather than to work towards finding one superior to the other. It is essentially a study of how the various elements in each combine to create a unique formal structure, each drawing as it does on certain common narrative elements; and of how each element relates to another and to the total structure of the film or novel concerned. It is also a study of the major changes that have taken place as that narrative is transformed to meet the demands of the other medium. With **The Getting of Wisdom**, for example, film director Bruce

Beresford has quite strikingly altered aspects of the narrative created by Henry Handel Richardson's novel. My central question, having examined Richardson's seventy-year-old text, is whether the new text created by Beresford establishes a dramatically interesting life of its own.

Some Problems of Adaptation

Given the inherent differences in the ways novels and films work to make their meanings and to engage their audiences, and given the different conventions governing the production, distribution and reception of each, it is scarcely surprising that the process of transposition from one medium to the other should be fraught with difficulties. The film-maker who seeks to adapt a well-known novel, whether a "classic" or merely popular, is immediately up against the fact that its readers already have firm ideas on how the project should be realized. At very least, these readers will have firm ideas about how it should *not* have been handled: this actor was "unsuited" to the role, the setting was "wrong", a favourite scene was "omitted". These words "unsuited", "wrong" and "omitted" suggest that a good deal of negative criticism of film adaptations derives from a prior attachment to the novel. The American novelist, John Hersey, has spoken on the matter from the writer's point of view, claiming that the author has little chance of being satisfied with a film made from his novel:

> There's a basic conflict of visions here — and I do mean, exactly, visions. The author of the novel has seen in his mind's eye for many months, or for years, the faces, the gestures, the mannerisms of his characters. Then on the screen appear total strangers displacing those images, asserting new characteristics, outward and inward. The writer almost can't help being outraged.[1]

If the adaptation is deemed successful by large numbers of film-goers, it may well be the case that those "total strangers", the actors, *have* "displace[d] those images" originally created by the novelist. If in re-reading Jane Austen's *Pride and Prejudice* one inevitably sees Greer Garson and Laurence Olivier as Elizabeth and Darcy, then that act of displacement has occurred. Whatever reality they had, for the contented viewer of the M-G-M film version of the novel it has given way, at least as far as those two characters are concerned, to their screen incarnations.

Hersey's comment points to what is perhaps the chief problem in the process of adaptation: the differences arising from single and multiple authorship. The author of the novel is the sole creator of his work with complete control over selection and omission, over the emphasis in every unit of his work: from the choice of one word rather than another, to how an episode works so as to gain our sympathies, to shock or amuse, or to achieve whatever effect he has in mind, to the over-all effect of the novel in which his tone will be the governing factor. The reader may not always respond as he intends but at least he does not have to defer to anyone else's point of view and is not at the mercy of other influences. Charles Dickens, we know, chose to offer an alternative ending to *Great Expectations* on the basis of advice from Bulwer Lytton, but the choice to accept this advice was wholly his own. John Fowles may choose to suggest that various possibilities are open to his characters in *The French Lieutenant's Woman* but it is disingenuous of him to suggest that anyone other than he is the creator of these possibilities. Within the constraints of having his work published, the novelist is subject to no one's influence on, or interference with, his work. Nothing, that is, comes between his "vision" and its realization but his own capacity to effect that realization.

Following the pioneering work of certain French critics in the influential journal *Cahiers du Cinema* and their *politique des auteurs*, certain directors became known as *auteurs*. By this term, itself a metaphor borrowed from literature, these directors were regarded as stamping their films with their own personalities, a notion that was extended by the American critic, Andrew Sarris. The implication was that these directors — for example, John Ford, Nicholas Ray, Vincente Minnelli — had the kind of control over their films that the author of a novel has, that they were in fact the authors of their films. This was a useful and stimulating idea at the time (the late 1960s), particularly in regard to the mass of American films made in the studio system. It was, and is, nevertheless a misleading notion: however powerful a director may be in carrying out his wishes, in trying to secure his vision on film, he is inevitably part of a collaborative enterprise. He may be the most important collaborator[2]; his may be the over-all

John Wayne as Ethan Edwards in John Ford's **The Searchers**.

shaping intelligence at work; but he can never be more than the most important among a number of other co-workers on whose sensitivity to his wishes and capacity to carry them out he must depend for the effecting of his intentions.

Even a great director will be dependent on actors who will look, sound and move as he wants them to, on set designers and art directors who will create the material aspects of the world in which the film is set, on a cameraman who will know how to light and photograph the staged action — the *mise-en-scene* — to record and complete the experiences being created on the set or on location by those other collaborators. The kind of controversy the American critic Pauline Kael sought to inflame over the "authorship" of **Citizen Kane**[3] — how far was Orson Welles or Herman J. Mankiewicz responsible for its unique quality — is unthinkable for a novelist. Kael's essay, "Raising Kane", and books like Richard Corliss' *Talking Pictures* have sought to rehabilitate the screenwriter's status in the question of authorship. Even when the director has acquired the mystique of *auteur*, he can have done so only by orchestrating the contributions of many others. The magnificent skyline shots of the U.S. Cavalry that are regarded as personal signatures in John Ford's westerns are joint achievements with distinguished cameramen such as Winton Hoch. If one thinks of screen "characters" indelibly stamped on the mind, can one separate the contributions of actor and others from that of the director? Think of Martita Hunt as Miss Havisham in the David Lean film of *Great Expectations* or John Wayne as Ethan Edwards in Ford's **The Searchers**, to pick two examples at random. These performances depend enormously on the physical appearances of the actors concerned, on the ways they are dressed, lit and photographed, on other aspects of the *mise-en-scène* of which they are a part, as well as on the guiding intelligence and visual sense of Lean and Ford. When one studies novels and films together, the enterprise will be distorted and defeated if the gulf between the nature of authorship in each case is not kept firmly in mind. The idea of a co-operative authorship's achieving results comparable in tone and meaning to those achieved by a single author ought not, then, be lightly held.

Though both novel and film are essentially concerned with narrative-making, the difference in the means at the disposal of the novelist and film-maker is so marked that one should be surprised when a film version does "feel like" the novel from which it is adapted rather than when it does not. That the novelist makes his narrative wholly through the use of verbal language and the film-maker through visual and aural means is so obvious as to be almost unnecessary to state. However, though the difference in means is clear, some of the implications for the adaptor may need to be noted. A word and a picture (or visual image) are, in the language of semiotics, both "signs" which convey meanings. This "sign" may be seen as having two aspects: the "signifier" (the means by which the meaning is conveyed, whether word or image); and the "signified" (the meaning or associations conveyed). This is not the place for a full discussion of this

5

theory, of which James Monaco gives a clear, summarizing account in his valuable book *How to Read a Film*.[4] It is enough to note here that, whereas in language systems there is a great difference between signifier (e.g., the word "school") and signified (i.e., an actual school), there is much less gap between the visual signifier (e.g., a picture of a school) and its signified (i.e., the school represented in the picture). Whereas words work almost wholly in a *symbolic* way, film has a much higher *signific* content. A sign in a film — whether a person, place, or thing — will have a much closer resemblance to an actual person, thing or place than a word or words can ever suggest. The implications of this brutally simplified account and the problems they cause in adaptation from novel to film are immense.

One of the pleasures of novels is that they do engage one's active, imaginative co-operation in completing, as it were, the act of creation set in motion by the novelist. The novelist in this sense has much less control than the film-maker over how his audience receives his signs. He has immense control over the signs — that is, words — he chooses to offer but comparatively little over how they are received. The visual nature of film on the one hand tells one much more than a novel possibly could of the physical nature of places, things, and people, but on the other hand greatly reduces the audience's capacity for diverse interpretation of the signs it offers. The film-maker is more constrained than the novelist in the images he gives but has much more control than the novelist over how the audience receives such images. What an audience makes of, for instance, Laura's school in the film **The Getting of Wisdom** is dictated by the visual image of it which the film keeps offering in shots of echoing corridors, in overhead shots emphasizing its oppressiveness, etc.

More significant still, what the actress, Susannah Fowle, brings to the role of Laura in the same film, in terms of appearance, voice and movement, offers certain clearly limiting factors in the viewer's response to Laura and her situation. One does not have to imagine what Laura looks like when she is inventing her tale of vestry seduction, or when she is angry, because her face is up there on the screen recording these responses and feelings, thus underlining what the dialogue is saying. The adaptor's inevitable problem is to find actors who will disturb readers' responses to a novel's characters as little as possible — that is, if the film-maker is anxious to make a "faithful" film version. An actor's face is possibly the single most important sign with which the film can work; where meaning is concerned in the matter of adaptation, it is a source of immense power *and* a severe limitation. After seeing a film version of a novel, try re-reading the book and imagining a different face for the leading character. Nevertheless, in both cases — novel and film — an active process is required of the reader or observer. Monaco sums up this requirement in these words:

> The reader of a page invents the image, the reader of a film does not, yet both readers must work to interpret the signs they receive in order to complete the process of intellection.[5]

There is, though, a marked distinction between the two media in their degrees of directness of appeal. The film comes to the audience directly through perception; it is a direct evocation of reality. Words must be translated into images of things, people, and places, into patterns of thought and feeling, through the reader's own intellectual processes. The greater directness of the film's appeal perhaps accounts for the way in which film — either in the cinema or on television — has in this century superseded the novel as popular entertainment. On the level of immediate response to phenomena, the film works faster and makes fewer demands.

The difference between viewing time for a film and reading time for a novel has some very obvious implications for the film-maker adapting a novel. On the simplest level, a film rarely takes longer than two uninterrupted hours to watch whereas most novels, for averagely fast readers, could be expected to take up to three or four times as long. The film-maker adapting the novel must address himself to the problems of *emphasis* and *selection*; because he can't include everything (even the extraordinarily inclusive and slow-moving **Brideshead Revisited** serial couldn't quite), he must make choices. He will need to decide what are to be his central emphases and the over-all shaping narrative pattern, and then choose which characters, incidents and backgrounds will be most important in achieving this central goal.

In a 1938 film version of *Wuthering Heights*, producer Sam Goldwyn, director William Wyler, or scriptwriters Ben Hecht and Charles MacArthur, or all four, have chosen to omit the second half of Emily Brontë's novel, thus eliminating the processes of Heathcliff's revenge and the reconciliation of important conflicting emotional elements. I do not know exactly whose choice this was or why it was made. Perhaps the decision was dictated by so external a matter as what would work best to promote its leading lady Merle Oberon (Cathy); perhaps it was felt unwise to kill off the film's major star half-way through. The point is that, while the film is a handsome romantic melodrama, in certain crucial ways it can scarcely be regarded as a serious version of the Brontë novel. The emphases, the governing narrative motifs, of the original have been replaced by others, in the interests — it can be argued — of the inner consistency and coherence of a commercial film.

On a very simple level, mere running time may have been a determining factor when filming almost half the novel has taken 103 minutes. The question of how long an audience will be willing to give unbroken attention to a film is a vexing matter to the film-maker. When a reader's concentration span is exhausted in reading a novel, he simply puts the book aside for a while, secure in the knowledge that he can go on from the exact place of stopping. Further, the reader can stop to consider what has happened or to reflect on turns the narrative might take. I think that taking this kind of pause happens in a wide range of novel-reading: for example, from detective fiction when the reader may want to consider the clues provided to, say, D. H. Lawrence's detailed explorations of

*Above: Miss Havisham (Martita Hunt) and Pip (Anthony Wager) in David Lean's **Great Expectations**.*
*Below: Charles Ryder (Jeremy Irons) and Lady Marchmain (Claire Bloom). **Brideshead Revisited**.*

character which often require reflection to assess what they add up to. The film-viewer obviously does not have this time at his disposal (the situation is somewhat different for the viewer of the television serial)[6]; key narrative elements must be clearly indicated since the audience cannot go back to check on them; the spacing of events is important to create an acceptable narrative rhythm (i.e., to avoid a sense of undue rush or sluggishness); narrative information must be highlighted by skilful use of *mise-en-scène* and editing (i.e., put crudely, of what is in the frame and what links the frames). All narrative has a powerful linear component but nowhere does this linearity need to exercise such remorseless control as it does in film.

A great deal of time spent in reading novels may be taken up with description of place or character. With the best novelists, such description is never merely decorative or a matter of setting; it will have been integrated with other elements for the purpose of furthering the narrative. The sense Dickens gives of a physically and socially constricting world in the opening chapters of *Great Expectations* is certainly vivid in itself, but, more important, it helps the reader to understand the sorts of forces which help to push Pip away from the forge and the village. The film-maker can economize in adapting descriptive elements, especially in regard to description of place, when a couple of carefully planned shots can give as full a sense of setting as several pages of description might do. David Lean's film of *Great Expectations* deals with the matter suggested above in — as I recall — a strikingly composed overhead shot at the Gargerys' Christmas-dinner table with Pip oppressed by the presence of his grotesque elders, played by some very distinctive-looking British character actors. As to description of character, it can, up to a point, be replaced by facial expression, gesture, camera angle and so on, but this may be an area which the novel, read at our leisure, will always be able to do more amply than film. A good example is the last paragraph of Chapter 1 of *Pride and Prejudice* in which Jane Austen offers a summarizing account of Mr and Mrs Bennet:

> Mr. Bennet was so odd a mixture of quick parts, sarcastic humour, reserve, and caprice, that the experience of three and twenty years had been insufficient to make his wife understand his character. *Her* mind was less difficult to develope. She was a woman of mean understanding, little information, and uncertain temper. When she was discontented, she fancied herself nervous. The business of her life was to get her daughters married; its solace was visiting and news.

The reader's pleasure in that paragraph is not just in the information it gives; it could even be argued that as *mere* information it is scarcely necessary since the novel at large shows all the named qualities in action. What it particularly offers, and what a film cannot (short, perhaps, of having the paragraph read on the soundtrack), is the author's own evaluation of the two lives encapsulated there. This evaluation is felt in the way the prose works: in its contrasting lists of qualities; its satirical emphasis on *her*; in the rhythms set up in the structure of the sentences; in the irony that is not merely a literary device but a way of looking at people. Whatever else Aldous Huxley and Jane Murfin's screenplay provided for the M-G-M film, it did not find a visual equivalent for that kind of coolly assessing, descriptive account.

Nor could it find one for Chapter XXXVI which is wholly given over to Elizabeth Bennet's "perturbed state of mind, with thoughts that could rest on nothing" as she reads Darcy's letter of explanation of his behaviour following her rejection of his proposal. A novel can render thought processes much more directly than a film can. We allow an omniscient novelist simply to tell us what a character is thinking, or, better still, her prose to enact those processes of mind. At the start of Chapter 12 of *The Getting of Wisdom*, we know exactly the kind of conflict Laura is experiencing, not because it is presented in action (though this is the case elsewhere), but because Richardson takes a paragraph to show us Laura's thoughts:

> You might regulate your outward habit to the last button of what you were expected to wear; you might conceal the tiny flaws and shuffle over the big improprieties in your home life, which were likely to damage your value in the eyes of your companions; you might, in brief, march in the strictest order along the narrow road laid down for you by these young law-givers, keeping perfect step and time with them: yet of what use were all your pains, if you could not marshal your thoughts and feelings — the very realest part of you — in rank and file as well? . . . if these persisted in escaping control? Such was the question which, at this time, began to present itself in Laura's mind. (p. 102)

That paragraph dramatizes accurately Laura's relentless attempts to be like her companions, to conform to the deadly predictabilities of the codes of behaviour of "these young law-givers"; and the intensity of the effort she makes is felt in the prose itself. The repetition of "you might" enacts the strict efforts she makes to adjust the surface of her life; the "if"'s and broken clauses at the end dramatize the thought processes that indicate why she can't conform. Richardson very often seems to hide her author's voice behind Laura's words, as she does here, so as to give the sense of Laura's mind at work. Can film really do this? A look, a gesture, a movement may tell us a good deal but I doubt if it can create the sense of sustained thought that can come from the interior analysis which is one of the tools of the omniscient author. This incapacity is, in adapting many serious novels, a major problem for film-makers; of the Australian novels considered in this book, *The Getting of Wisdom* poses the main difficulties, in this respect, for the film-maker. The directness of the appeal of film accounts for much of its power but, inherent in this power, is also the limitation that the film-maker must always find concrete images to convey his meaning, and the intricacies and abstractions of thought processes are peculiarly unsusceptible to such images.

It is a truism that some novels adapt more readily to the screen than others and I suspect that one of the chief discriminating factors is whether the novelist has a distinctive narrative "voice". The more distinctive it is, the more the narrative is shaped and coloured by that *tone*, the more difficult will be the film-maker's work in finding a cinematic equivalent for it. It is not claiming too much to say that great novels are distinguished chiefly by their tone, by the quality of the controlling intelligence which not merely presents an action but persistently judges it as well. Whatever the excellences of the screenplay for **Pride and Prejudice**, it did not achieve the ironic viewpoint that makes Jane Austen's account of the Bennet family so peculiarly her own. By a word or phrase, as well as in her novel's narrative structure, she can make clear her attitude to a particular character (e.g., her description of the insinuating Miss Bingley as Darcy's "faithful assistant"); in the film, this can never be done quite so tersely nor perhaps so consistently. That is to say, an actor's gesture or inflection, or the way he is positioned in the frame, may reveal much about attitude and may guide audience responses considerably, but the viewer can never be sure that the director, the cast and the other key collaborators are adequately attuned to a point of view in the way the single novelist may be. The reader discerns a novelist's point of view essentially through attention to his use of the language: it is this which dictates where our sympathies will fall.

Whereas the novelist, as discussed earlier, is a single artist with complete, unquestioned control over meaning, emphasis and selection of details, the film director, however influential, is only the most important creator in a communal activity. If he emerges as a distinctive voice, as an *auteur*, it will be remarkable. It *does* happen but the ways in which it happens will be different from those available to a novelist. Such a director may establish his point of view through a series of images (as Fred Schepisi does in **The Chant of Jimmie Blacksmith**: he does not imitate the tone of Thomas Keneally's source novel, but establishes his own) or through certain revealing juxtapositions (like French director Claude Chabrol's placing of violent crime in a calmly bourgeois setting). In this book, I have tried to emphasize the film-maker's achievement in creating his own point of view on the material of his film, rather than his degree of success in capturing the tone of the novel on which it is based.

The dissimilarities between novel and film are so great that it is surprising how many films — and successful ones, too — have been derived from novels. One writer summed up the dissimilarities by saying: "Film is a multi-sensory communal experience emphasizing immediacy, whereas literature is a mono-sensory experience that is more conducive to reflection."[7] The successful adaptor will have been excited or challenged by various aspects of the original and will have succeeded in recreating these in the new medium, overcoming the problems that have been suggested here. Linked by a common concern for narrative, the two media are nevertheless widely divergent in their deployment of the ideas of "narration" and "narrator", a matter to be touched on shortly.

The sorts of problems of adaptation considered so far have to do with the inherent difference in the way novels and films make their meanings. There are as well other *external* factors which account for some problems. For instance, because of the enormously greater cost involved in the production of a film as compared with the publication of a novel, the film must find a much larger audience. A novel which finds a reading public of, say, 10,000 will be a modest success; a film which reaches such a number of people will be a financial disaster. This means that the film which aspires to profitability will need to take into account what a large, heterogeneous audience will be willing to accept. In adapting C. J. Koch's novel, *The Year of Living Dangerously*, the film-makers have, in my view, chosen to stress the romantic element at the expense of the political, moved no doubt by the fact that politics have been "box-office poison" whereas romance has a proven track record. The fact that film types tend to come in cycles — like the science-fiction cycle launched by the success of **Star Wars** — is evidence of film-makers' anxious need to tap a widespread public response. Public taste is constantly on the move so that an art form which requires large numbers of paying customers will need to be aware of its fluctuations.

It is much more important to the film-maker than to the novelist to be

*Bruce Beresford directs his cast for **The Getting of Wisdom**.*

responsive to the prevailing standards of public morality in those societies in which he most relies on selling his film. Novelists have, for instance, been more honest about sexual matters than film-makers have been able to be. Only since the late 1960s has the popular film been able to suggest that there were answers other than death or an unwanted pregnancy (or both) available to the girl who "loved not wisely but too well". In novels, certainly since D. H. Lawrence, it has been possible for unmarried people to engage in sexual relations without the certainty of retribution. The fact that film seems to lag behind the novel in these ways has several possible explanations. Partly, the greater explicitness of the visual image has led film-makers to adopt a self-imposed censorship; partly, it is a matter of historical development. The cinema and the novel both have their roots in popular narrative entertainment, in melodrama specifically; they both are essentially realist forms, heavily dependent on the mimetic mode for meaning. The novel, however, in the course of its longer history, has in this century taken other directions and gone beyond realism. Because it is no longer *the* popular art form it was in the nineteenth century, it has been able to take more risks with its public than film can. This difference in assessment of its audience's requirements is nowhere better seen than in the incidence of the happy ending in each mode. It was a bold film in the 1940s, at least from Hollywood, the chief source of mass cinema entertainment, that would risk an unhappy ending. The happy ending is more than just a convention; it has clearly fulfilled certain deep-felt needs at various stages of Western cultural history. It represents a triumph of aspirations, a confirmation of the power of good over evil. Both Bruce Beresford's **The Getting of Wisdom** and Gillian Armstrong's **My Brilliant Career**, though made in the 1970s when the happy ending was no longer as predictable as in earlier decades, offer more optimistic, more determinedly up-beat endings than the novels from which they are derived.

These matters relating to the different expectations of the mass audience — receiving the film text in the public, communal setting of the cinema, as opposed to the relatively small novel-reading public, receiving the text singly and privately — are here presented as mere suggestions. In this chapter, I want to do no more than indicate that the different circumstances in which we respond to novels and films, as well as those in which they are produced, constitute at least a challenge, if not indeed serious problems, for the film-maker adapting the written text to the screen.

Why Study Novel and Film Together?

In spite of the major dissimilarities between the two media and the problems involved in adaptation, it is still worth considering the two together, partly because of the light it may shed on the processes involved in each and partly for the interest of the way the act of transposition has been made from page to screen. And, further, in spite of their dissimilarities, the two media have some important features in common. Above all, both are concerned with narrative, with the relating of a series of events in a cause-effect chain of relationship, these events acting as the particular manifestations of an over-all controlling narrative pattern. As will become apparent in the chapters on individual texts, the film-maker's narrative may offer a marked shift in emphasis from that of the corresponding novelist; all of them, though, novelists and film-makers, are inescapably concerned with narrative. (I am of course speaking of fiction film-makers here, though even some documentary films depend strongly on a narrative line.) The shift in emphasis, even when basically the same events are being presented, may well be the product of a different choice of view-point.

Film-viewers and novel-readers share certain expectations with regard to the text before them. They expect narrative to be presented in such a way as to produce a logical sequence of events: that is, the $A \rightarrow B \rightarrow C$ effect. If this sense of sequence is broken, they will expect a good narrative reason for the apparent break with the anticipated development. When, in *Great Expectations*, Dickens suddenly brings Uncle Pumblechook with news that the eccentric Miss Havisham wants a boy to come and play, nothing in the preceding sequence of events prepares the reader for this intervention, but as the reader pursues the narrative it becomes clear what function this break performs. In Alfred Hitchcock's **Psycho**, there is no revealed cause leading to the famous and grisly shower murder; it comes as the narrative shock it is meant to be and its function in the film's pattern of events becomes clear only when the rest of the film is considered. Aside, however, from such calculated playing with readers' anticipations, what readers of both film and novel expect is a narrative in which a situation changes, through a series of cause-effect links, until it has become demonstrably a new situation. The creation of the expectation of change — how will Laura react to leaving home and going to school? — and the presentation of those events that effect the change — her actual experiences at school — are at the heart of the narrative procedure in both media.

Our expectations of narrative films are based partly on our experience of other films, and of other narrative forms like novels, partly on our experience of life. Life teaches us, for instance, that leaving the security of home for the unknown environment of a distant boarding school is likely to be disturbing, and this knowledge has as much to do with how we receive Laura's responses to the College in **The Getting of Wisdom** as our recollections of the novel. Essentially, we expect narrative to be concerned with *human* causes and effects, even if it may initially be set in motion by some arbitrary, non-human element (as in "disaster" movies).

Both novel and film are wholly artificial systems of meaning: everything in them has been the result of a conscious decision; both, therefore, are responsive to an approach based on a criterion of function. One of the clearest accounts of narrative form is that given by David Bordwell and Kristin Thompson. In the following passage, they are writing about narrative film but the comment might just as easily apply to novels:

> A narrative is not a natural object; its events do not take place in the same real world in which we exist. Instead, a narrative is a human artifact, a construct. Therefore, we should avoid saying, 'It is *natural* that X happens in that narrative.' Events that occur in narrative films have a function in the over-all system of the plot. Therefore we should ask, 'What is X doing in this narrative? How does X function?'[8]

In **Picnic at Hanging Rock**, film and novel, the function of the scientifically-based statements of Miss McCraw, the mathematics teacher later lost on the Rock, is to contrast with the more romantic responses of the girls, and to make more striking the fact that this most rational of women will later succumb to the mysterious, *ir*rational lure of the Rock. Both novels and films seem to me more responsive to an approach which considers how one element works in relation to another, or what its function is in the whole, than to questions like, "Is it true to life?"

Though novel and film have a common concern with narrative, there are nevertheless some crucial distinctions in the way each goes about creating the narrative process. The narrative in a novel is conveyed through two kinds of voices: those attributed to various characters in direct speech and that of the author's narration. Colin McCabe has described the first of these, the characters' dialogue, as the "subjective discourse", which is surrounded by an "apparently objective meta-language"[9], the voice of authorial narration. In the film adaptation, actors can be given the words of characters, either direct from the novel or in some modified form; it is considerably more challenging for the film-maker to render that other voice, that of authorial narration, which, in the novel, will be our guide as to what we make of the words spoken by the characters. McCabe claims that the camera assumes the role of the objective narrator: "The camera shows us what happens — it tells the truth against which we can measure the discourses" (p. 10). This is too large a claim to consider in detail here, but, clearly, certain functions of this narrative voice, such as establishing setting and physical appearance of characters, can be achieved through the film's *mise-en-scène*. Other functions, such as those which enable us, through the writer's tone, to evaluate a character's speech, seem less immediately amenable to the camera's eye. The camera in this sense becomes the narrator by, for instance, focusing on such aspects of *mise-en-scène* as the way actors look, move or gesture, or on the ways in which they are positioned in a scene or on how they are photographed: in these ways the camera may catch a "truth" which comments on and qualifies what the characters actually say.

If the narrative interest of plots and characters is the chief formal parallel between the novel and the film derived from it, it is at once a very

*Above: Sarah Woodruff (Meryl Streep) in Karel Reisz' **The French Lieutenant's Woman**. Below: Ashley Wilkes (Leslie Howard) and Scarlett O'Hara (Vivien Leigh). Victor Fleming's **Gone with the Wind**.*

important piece of common ground and not the *only* similarity. It is not surprising that people should be interested in studying together two obviously "popular" art forms. Even in the great theatrical centres of the world (London, New York), the live theatre does not begin nowadays to compete in popularity with film (including as it does television, which is not to imply that they are the same thing). The novel was the great popular art form of the nineteenth century and, if its pre-eminence has been ceded to film in the twentieth century, its popularity has survived in certain genres such as the detective story, science fiction, the best-selling romance or melodrama. The "serious" novel, having to some extent abandoned realism before the challenge of modernism, has no doubt lost ground with the rise of the film as the chief satisfier of the narrative impulse. But this impulse which substantially accounts for the popularity of film and novel is a persuasive reason for considering together the two forms which most exploit and gratify it. Their shared interest in plot and character and their different ways of rendering these offer a rich field of study.

Such a study seems an obvious extension of the habit of people interested in one art form who frequently find themselves referring to others. Art forms do not exist in a vacuum; they emerge from a particular state of culture, reflect and/or criticize aspects of the ideology of that culture, and they exist in relation to each other. It is not surprising, then, that one form is likely to be influenced by developments in another, and there are obvious links between film and theatre, film and painting, and film and literature, with special reference to the novel. Given that film has clearly a good deal of shared background with the novel and caters to many of the same interests, it is likely to be rewarding to consider them together.

Given also that so many critically and financially successful films have been based on novels, it is worth considering what makes the latter attractive to film-makers, in spite of all the obstacles to adaptation. Morris Beja claims that, since the inception of the Academy Awards in 1927-28, "more than three-fourths of the awards for 'best picture' have gone to adaptations . . . [and that] the all-time box office successes favor novels even more."[10] The reasons for the preponderance of films adapted from novels are not wholly based in the aesthetic appeal of the original; as Beja suggests, "they are financial, perhaps, or derive from the sheer need to come up with material to be filmed" (p. 77). In the case of best-selling novels like *Gone with the Wind* and *The French Lieutenant's Woman*, to choose two filmed roughly forty years apart, the producers have the inestimable financial advantage of a pre-sold title. They also have the daunting prospect of a large number of readers with pre-determined responses to the illusion of reality created by the original work. There is in fact, in spite of the problems both inherent in the differences between the two forms and external, like that suggested in the previous sentence, almost a reliance by film-makers on literary sources — on novels, *novellae*, short stories, plays, and even poems. Apart from the financial attraction to film-makers, there is clearly something inviting about the prospect of transposing a reality created in one medium into that of another. And, equally, many novelists, famous and obscure, have been willing to have the transposition made; at the very least it has made the names of their books more widely known. Certainly, there seems at present to be no danger of the process diminishing.

Australian Novels on Film

In the Australian film revival of the past decade, there has been a striking number of adaptations, some of them from plays (e.g., David Williamson's *Don's Party*) but mostly from novels. These have ranged from "classic" novels like *The Getting of Wisdom* and Miles Franklin's *My Brilliant Career* to modern novels like Helen Garner's *Monkey Grip* and C. J. Koch's *The Year of Living Dangerously*. It is true to say that a notable proportion of the most distinguished Australian films since about 1970 have literary origins of some kind. This being so, it is interesting to note that some major works of Australian fiction have so far been avoided by film-makers: for instance, Henry Handel Richardson's *The Fortunes of Richard Mahony*, Patrick White's *The Tree of Man* (film-makers are perhaps daunted by the doomed efforts of Joseph Losey to film *Voss*), and, a television version of *Outbreak of Love* to one side, the "Langton" novels of Martin Boyd.

Peter Weir (white hat) directs actors Mel Gibson and Linda Hunt on the set of **The Year of Living Dangerously.**

The reasons for some reliance on literary sources in the renaissant Australian film industry are no doubt mixed. There is certainly some sense of a pre-sold title in relation to, say, *The Getting of Wisdom*, a book that has been, and continues to be, widely prescribed in senior secondary school. In relation to modern novels such as *Monkey Grip*, *Picnic at Hanging Rock* and *Wake in Fright*, it appears that, whatever their qualities, their sales were considerably increased by the success of the films. They had been scarcely in the "runaway best-seller" class; there was, that is, nothing inevitable about their being transposed into film.

However, while Australian films of the past ten or twelve years have thrown up some very talented directors (Peter Weir, Gillian Armstrong, Fred Schepisi) and cameramen of world class (Don McAlpine, Russell Boyd, Brian Probyn), there has been a marked shortage of original screenplays and of reliable script-writers. The only original screenplays I recall with special pleasure are those written by Everett de Roche for Richard Franklin's **Patrick** and **Roadgames**, and by David Williamson for Peter Weir's **Gallipoli**. Perhaps in the absence of script-writers equal in talent to other collaborators, producers have deemed it safer to stick to stories of proven quality. This can be no more than a speculation, and directors interviewed in relation to particular films have usually spoken about what has attracted them to the relevant novel. Fred Schepisi, asked this question in an interview about **The Chant of Jimmie Blacksmith**, said:

> The subject matter. I think it is *a great story* [my italics], one that is extremely relevant today. I believe it is the kind of story that can reach people on a mass level, and also say something that needs to be said in this country.[11]

In view of Schepisi's earlier claim in the same interview that adaptation "is normally against my principles", the two notions of "a great story" and "extremely relevant today" are revealing. Great stories have been rare in modern Australian films from original screenplays and so, with a few notable exceptions such as John Duigan's **Mouth to Mouth**, has much relevance to contemporary life.

There has also been a strong element of nostalgia, an almost deliberately anti-"ocker" element in many of the films of the period as if to establish a cinema at odds with prevailing myths of Australian life. Not surprisingly, this has led film-makers to novels of an earlier period, or at least novels *set* in an earlier period. One of the marked qualities of such films (e.g., **Picnic at Hanging Rock**, **My Brilliant Career**, **The Mango Tree**) has been a very careful, loving attention to *mise-en-scène* in recreating past eras. The effect has sometimes been very impressive in locating narrative impulses in aspects of the *mise-en-scène*; Sybylla's progress in **My Brilliant Career** may be charted in terms of the changes in the superbly realized settings in which she is successively placed. On other occasions, the films have looked decorous, as if all the care has gone into recreating an authentic physical surface at the expense of more crucial dramatic elements; this, I think, has happened in Don Crombie's **The Irishman** (based on Elizabeth O'Conner's novel) and to a lesser extent in Kevin Dobson's **The Mango Tree** (from Ronald McKie's novel).

One result of so much reliance on novels — and other literary sources — has been an undervaluing of the screen-writer's function. In the quoted interview, Fred Schepisi says:

> What I did was to read the book again and again until I found what he [Keneally] was about. I then put that aside and tried to find my own justification for it, treating it as if I was writing it myself.[12]

This may account for his film's having a coherence of its own; his screen-play does have the marks of a new act of creativity whereas too often the effect has been, instead, of translation. There has been a failure in some cases to come to grips with what adaptation means and a consequent growth of a surprisingly *literary* cinema, characterized by a pervading sense of unadventurous carefulness. What one wants is not a literary cinema which runs the risk of sounding like an illustrated novel, but, rather, a "literate" cinema. By this I mean films which sound, whether based on novels or not, true to the lives they present and this involves the film-makers, especially director and scriptwriter, in immersing themselves in the creation of a new experience, not in the re-heating of one already completed.

The Texts Chosen

The nine central chapters of this book focus on nine Australian novels which have been made into films. The choice is inevitably somewhat arbitrary but in each case the decision was based on the reputation and/or popularity of either the original text or its film version, and in some cases of both. I have included *The Night the Prowler*, a long short story rather than a novel, because it is the only work of Patrick White to have been filmed to date, even though it seems far short of his best work and even though the film was scarcely the "major motion picture" the Penguin reprint claimed. The other eight novels offer, I hope, a balance between established literary titles and newer novels, between films that have "improved on" the originals and those which seem to have lost something important in the transposition without finding a new significance of their own. In each case, there was a major source of interest to me in one or both texts in the pair. In those cases where I have previously published articles or reviews, I have sometimes referred to these where it has seemed appropriate. However, on several occasions where my readings of the texts have been modified by time, I have indicated this, either in the body of the relevant chapter or in a note.

The chapter on the Martin Boyd novels adapted for television — *Lucinda Brayford* and *Outbreak of Love* — is there because, in my view, Boyd is the only major Australian novelist so far ignored by film-makers. The problems of novels adapted to make television series are in many cases different from those involved in adapting novels to film, but the opportunity to consider the Boyd series seemed worth taking in view of some of the special difficulties these novels offer the adaptor.

This is not intended as a reference book, though I hope the lists given in the Appendices may prove useful. Nor is it intended as a definitive critical study, sorting out literary sheep from cinematic goats (or vice-versa). It draws attention to some of the main changes the original text has undergone in the transposition and speculates on the reasons and effects of those changes. This book grew out of an interest in the way films have drawn on novels for their source material and an increasing fascination with what happens in the process.

Notes

1. In answer to a questionnaire from James R. Messenger who summarizes the results from nineteen authors in "I Think I Liked the Book Better: Nineteen Novelists Look at the Film Version of their Work", *Literature/Film Quarterly*, Vol. 6, No. 2, Spring 1978, p. 134.
2. Though not always so: for instance, can anyone regard the directors of the Fred Astaire-Ginger Rogers films as being more significant *auteurs* of the films than the stars themselves?
3. Pauline Kael, *The Citizen Kane Book*, Paladin, St Albans, 1974.
4. James Monaco, *How to Read a Film*, Oxford University Press, New York, 1977. There are of course much ampler discussions of this theory to be found elsewhere.
5. Monaco, *Op cit*, p. 125.
6. One should perhaps note here that the potential for stop-start viewing on video will almost certainly change traditional ways of viewing films.
7. William Jinks, *The Celluloid Literature*, Glencoe Press, California, 1971, p. 15.
8. David Bordwell and Kristin Thompson, *Fine Art: An Introduction*, Addison Wesley, The Philippines, 1979, p. 54.
9. Colin McCabe, "Realism and the Cinema: Notes on Some Brechtian Theses", *Screen*, Summer 1974, Vol. 15, No. 2, pp. 7-21.
10. Morris Beja, *Film and Literature*, Longmans, New York, 1979, p. 78.
11. "Fred Schepisi: Producer/Director/Scriptwriter". Interview by David Roe and Scott Murray, *Cinema Papers*, No. 15, January 1978, p. 244.
12. *Ibid*, p. 244.

2. Wake in Fright

Kenneth Cook's *Wake in Fright* was first published by Michael Joseph, 1961, and by Penguin Books, 1967 (page references to the latter). Cook, born in Sydney in 1929, has worked as a journalist, and as a scriptwriter for radio and television. His other novels include *Blood Red Roses*, *Wanted Dead*, and *Play Little Victims*.

Wake in Fright was directed by Ted Kotcheff, for producer George Willoughby, from a screenplay by Evan Jones. The director of photography was Brian West, the editor Anthony Buckley and the composer John Scott. Running 109 minutes, it was released in 1971.

Kenneth Cook's short, evocative novel *Wake in Fright*, is, like *Picnic at Hanging Rock*, an Australian novel with a modest publishing history which was given a fillip by the production of a successful film. Reissued by Penguin in 1971 to coincide with the release of the film (known elsewhere as **Outback**), it has since been prescribed as a text for senior secondary students on several occasions and gone through at least seven reprints. What it offers is an unusually savage picture of a certain kind of Australian life, redressing the unbalanced and sentimental picture of outback life which has been part of Australia's literature since the days of Henry Lawson. Mateship, easy hospitality, unpretentiousness and a casual approach to the law: such qualities have had their share of celebration in Australian novels (and poetry) which have directed attention to the outback. Cook subjects the outback to the scrutiny of realism and offers a disturbing picture of empty, enforced camaraderie, interminable boozing, mindless brutality, and a contempt for the law that is all but invited by its chief exponent. His adaptors — director Ted Kotcheff and scriptwriter Evan Jones — have captured the tone of Cook's novel in cinematic terms with remarkable fidelity. The film's *mise-en-scène* achieves a precision of detail that matches, and in some ways surpasses, the novel's generally spare, occasionally overwrought prose.

The essential narrative line of the book is paralleled in the film. John Grant, the teacher at the tiny railway siding of Tiboonda in western New South Wales, sets out for Sydney on the last day of the school year, relieved to be leaving the broiling heat and emptiness, and eagerly anticipating six weeks of surf and a girl called Robyn. The first night of the journey is to be spent at Bundunyabba, a mining town (based on Broken Hill), from where he plans to fly to Sydney the next day. The night in The Yabba, as the hideous town is affectionately known to its chauvinistic inhabitants, changes all that.

Opposite: Doc Tydon (Donald Pleasence) and John Grant (Gary Bond).

There is an almost classic simplicity in the narrative: a man glad to be leaving one place and very sure of what he is heading towards is almost certain, in fiction, to have his plans interrupted. Grant, to pass the evening in The Yabba, joins in a two-up game, encouraged by the local policeman. At first he wins, then loses disastrously, so that the prospect of Sydney, surf and Robyn is wiped out. The narrative interest is now deflected, through this unexpected turn of events, to questions of how Grant will survive the six weeks ahead and how his character will respond to the despair he now feels. If he had spent the night quietly at his hotel, boarded his plane for Sydney the next day, and enjoyed the six weeks as planned, there would scarcely have been a narrative at all. As always, narrative interest arises from a change in situation, the chief motivating element for the change being some aspect of human character. Here the motivating element is Grant's succumbing to the lure of gambling and, thereby, being shaken out of his bored contempt with The Yabba and subsequently out of his complacent view of himself and his plans.

Next day, broke and despairing, he falls in with some of the locals: Tim Hynes, who invites him home for a boozing afternoon with a pair of yahoo miners, Dick and Joe; Tim's daughter Janette who all but rapes Grant; and Doc Tydon, an alcoholic ex-doctor, who lives in a filthy shed owned by the mining company. After a heavy night's drinking, Grant wakes in this shed, much worse for wear, to find himself committed to a kangaroo hunt with Tydon, Dick and Joe. A day of mindless butchery, maniacal driving, and continuous drinking finishes at the lowest point of Grant's degradation: an obscure sexual assault by Tydon back at his hut.

A last, desperate bid to leave The Yabba, with a dollar and a rifle bequeathed to him from the previous day's expedition, is foiled when he begs a lift in a truck he believes is heading for 'the city' but which deposits him back in The Yabba. Utterly destitute, he returns to Tydon's hut and tries to kill himself. The attempt fails and, after a spell in Bundunyabba Hospital, he returns to Tiboonda, a sadder but presumably wiser man.

Though this is a simple narrative, and though it is very short (143 pages), it is surprisingly resonant in what it suggests about a certain kind of character and powerfully so in its evocation of some aspects of Australian life. In reviewing the film version, Gillian Hanson writes of "the script's shallow and largely unmotivated characterization of John Grant".[1] Hanson seems to me to have missed the film's *and* the novel's point about Grant: he is presented in both as a curiously unformed character, a touch complacent and superior, both complacency and superiority seen as the result of an untested and unconsidered attitude to life. He does his work competently enough as far as one can tell, but it is no more than something which has to be got through until he can get to Sydney for the holidays and, at the end of his bonded period of service with the Education Department, leave for good. He is entirely uncommitted in professional terms and perhaps so in personal matters. The girl Robyn about whom he fantasizes — in a short white tennis dress in the novel, emerging from the surf in the film's visual image — is not an object for real emotions. At most, she will be a pleasant diversion. As he is about to succumb to Janette Hynes' unmistakable invitation, he thinks of Robyn, but "Robyn wasn't here. Robyn was a long way away. And what was Robyn to him anyway?" (p. 61). Grant is in effect a blank page for real experience to be written on, and his time in The Yabba finds him utterly unready to cope with the temptation and the horrors he finds there.

For the thematic concern that gives coherence to *Wake in Fright*'s savage picture of a certain kind of Australian life is the testing of his character. Arriving in The Yabba with no thought profounder than relief to be out of Tiboonda, he is shaken into an awareness of possibilities within himself that have hitherto lain dormant. One feels a mild sympathy for him dumped as he is in the physical and intellectual desolation of Tiboonda, though Cook does not stress this. The Yabba, whose possibilities he believes he has exhausted during term holidays, is the merest stop-over to him. "He wished there had been an aircraft flying eastwards that evening", Cook writes, adding with a casually dropped irony as Grant stows the return half of his rail ticket to Tiboonda in his wallet, "He consciously ignored the torn scrap of the cardboard's silent statement that he had not seen the last of Tiboonda" (p. 14), an irony whose full extent is not felt till the novel's last pages.

Grant is contemptuous of the prevailing ideology of The Yabba: "Best place in Australia" and "Nobody cares who you are or where you come from; as long as you're a good bloke you're all right" (p. 15), as the taxi driver tells him. He finds the "friendly habits" of the locals "crude and embarrassing", as each one asks him if he is "new to The Yabba", and his observation of the hotel receptionist — "a faded facsimile of girls behind reception desks all over the world" — has an unpleasing superiority about it. It is not that Cook presents these people as the salt of the earth or even as *meaning* anything valuable by their friendliness; in fact, it is not clear whether he sees any more in these people than Grant does. The receptionist "returned to the vacuous contemplation practised by her kind" (p. 16), a narrative comment near the edge of nasty patronage. And at the hotel where Grant later goes to drink, the narrative gloss to the licensee's greetings is "False good fellowship struggled with satisfied avarice to make up the expression on his hot, wet, mobile face" (p. 17). Cook builds up a grim picture of The Yabba and its inhabitants, but doesn't, in the process, present Grant as being markedly sensitive or perceptive. Grant's scepticism of the local friendliness and the fervour for The Yabba grows out of the easy complacency of one who sees himself merely passing through, as much as from realizing its potential nastiness.

Grant is ripe for waking and his meeting with the venal policeman, Jock Crawford, initiates this process. In Crawford's company, with its overbearing hospitality, he drinks more than he is used to and finds his way into the two-up game. In rapid succession he experiences three new emotions: "the strange passion that gamblers know" (p. 30); "the remorse of the gambler who has not put all his money on a successful wager" (p. 31); and, after some initial wins and as he leans forward to gather up his winnings, "his third strange emotion that night — the mysticism of gamblers" (p. 33). Having lost two hundred pounds as quickly as he had won it, he gambles his entire holiday salary cheque, "being forced forward by a decision, made, it seemed now, forever ago . . . He had no hope of winning, but he would not have recalled his bet even if there had been time . . ." (p. 39), and his entire cheque is wasted. A thought of Robyn has flickered through his mind without being able to detain it; it makes scarcely any greater impact than Crawford's earlier reference to The Yabba's high suicide rate, a reference which will resonate later on.

Up against the strongest emotion he has ever felt — the gambler's passion — he has been seen to have no defensive resources. The novel then traces with some power and fluency (both qualities more than equalled in the film) Grant's rapid fall from disdainful observation to enmeshment in compulsion, desolation and degradation. Now that he has no money, no means of completing his proposed journey, the narrative must take another turn as Grant considers his prospects. As he reflects on his situation — "All right, now it had to be faced: what was he to do?" — there are the first signs of a stiffening of his character:

> The contrast between what lay before him now and what he had planned the night before swept across him with physical violence, but he jammed his thoughts back to the immediate problems. (p. 43)

There is, too, a bruising sense of the physical setting as an adversary, and, despite his reflections and determination to focus on the problem, the narrative does not move inspiringly in the direction of self-help. There is not yet enough *to* Grant to avert the dismal possibilities of his situation, and he is thus in no position to ward off Hynes' hospitality ("There's no strangers in The Yabba"). Besides, The Yabba, having first made him a gambler, is now well on the way to making him a drunkard through its tyrannical hospitality, but his lack of resistance is wholly his own.

Having decided "there was a limit to the humiliation he could stand" (p. 56), he tries to shake himself into reality and out of the liquored blur of Hynes' hospitality, but the limits of humiliation are shortly to be reached: his vomiting bout as he is being seduced by Janette; his role in the mind-less brutalities of the kangaroo hunt; his drunkenness; and, clinchingly, whatever it is that has happened between him and the repulsive Tydon. The novel is rhetorically elusive about what did happen; Grant associates it next morning with a "little bright flashing light . . . Oh God, that light! But what had happened before was terrible. It should not have happened: It could not have happened. It had happened twice" (p. 95). Whatever the nature of the presumably homosexual act, Cook makes it clear that, drunk as he was and remorseful as he may now feel, Grant was compliant enough for "it" to happen twice. Grant, who "had never had a woman before" (p. 61), as he drunkenly reflects in his abortive bout with Janette, is in sexual matters, as in most others, an unformed person. Because of a lack of firmness within, he is a ready prey for Janette or Tydon, as he is for those whose friendliness consists of filling him with beer.

Grant's degradation is not just in his view of what happened with Tydon but in his response to the kangaroo hunt. The spotlighting to dazzle the animals and make them easy targets, at ranges too close to miss, ought, the reader feels, to repel him. Instead, "as Grant's eager fingers worked to reload he could hear the tearing thump the bullets made as they hit flesh" (p. 86). The author's point of view on this disgusting and cowardly sport is clear enough: the fact that Grant's fingers were "eager" gives equally clear information about what is happening to him. So clear, perhaps, that a statement like the following seems redundant, spelling out what has already been made clear about the corrupting process at work in him: "Grant was surprised that he did not feel particularly upset at the mass carnage. They were, after all, only kangaroos" (p. 87).

Grant (centre) squanders all his holiday pay in a two-up game, experiencing for the first time the gambler's passion.

As he moves towards the nadir of his degradation, with his horror at the gashing of the small, blinded kangaroo, there is also the beginnings of a process of self-awareness:

> Oh God! What was he, John Grant, schoolteacher and lover, doing out here under the contemptuous stars butchering this warm grey beast? (pp. 92-3)

And later in the night, after killing many kangaroos and after a disastrous attempt to eviscerate one before it was dead, "Everybody laughed, and they laughed again because Grant was covered in blood and they drank all the whisky and they drank all the beer and their shooting became wilder" (p. 93). Cook's prose in this section dramatizes with chilling accuracy the processes of Grant's mind: odd moments of self-awareness and self-disgust; alertness to some appalling physical sensation (as when he is knifing the kangaroo); and the pulling down of "the blanket of drunkenness" to make him feel better. Once or twice Cook's aspirations outstrip his prose (there is too much "Oh God!", "Dear God!"), but over-all there is a convincing sense of nightmare as Grant slips into a brutalizing vortex.

The process is not quite finished yet. The narrative pushes Grant a little further: foiled in his attempt to get to Sydney, he is confronted with the sheer hopelessness of his situation. "There was nothing he could do": he could neither stay in Bundunyabba for five weeks nor had he the means to

Grant, alone in the scrub around Bundunyabba, with his suitcase and the rifle given to him for the kangaroo shoot by his mates.

leave. Worse than the fact of this *impasse*, he is brought face to face with its absurdity:

> But what was so fantastic was that there had been no element of necessity about it all. It was as though he had deliberately set about destroying himself; and yet one thing had seemed to lead to the next. But he needn't have done any of it. (p. 127)

Finding one cartridge left in his pocket, and having no belief in any other life, he decides to kill himself. The failure of the suicide attempt (recalling the early conversation with Jock Crawford about The Yabba's "accidental death" rate) ushers in, in the novel's last pages, the suggestion of a new John Grant. In this short final chapter, by means of a cinematically conceived flashback technique, he is seen returning in the train to Tiboonda, recalling scenes from the past few weeks. He looks "with satisfaction at the glass in the window", having lately "developed a deep affection for the normal, simple trappings of being alive" (p. 134). The first stage of his regeneration is a value for life itself, a positive step from the John Grant who has previously been so easily dismissive about so much of life. If there is nothing especially subtle in Cook's treatment of Grant's new self-awareness, and awareness of the life around him, it is sufficiently persuasive as a means of pulling together the thematic significance of the narrative.

It is curious that the film eschews the obvious invitation of this final sequence in favor of a more direct, linear treatment of these last scenes in which Janette Hynes and Jock Crawford appear at Grant's hospital bed. In failing to do so, it misses the effect, which skilful cutting might have achieved, of the sense of Grant's regeneration growing out of the miracle of his escape from death. For, in general, the film has not merely adhered closely to Cook's central narrative, retaining its cohering interest in Grant's exposure to convulsive experience, but it has consistently used the resources of film — *mise-en-scène* and cutting especially — to achieve what Cook's prose has done in the novel. The choice of Gary Bond for the role of Grant is very apt: in his conventional good looks, in the Englishness of his voice (Bond is of course English) contrasting with The Yabba's cruder tones, in his way of holding himself slightly aloof from human contacts until he is caught in the whirlpool that starts with the two-up game, in the suggestions of (upper-) middle-classness unglimpsed elsewhere in the film. All these — essentially visual or behavioural qualities — work very much in favour of Cook's conception of Grant and to delineate him against the physicalities and the mental set of The Yabba. Evan Jones' adaptation preserves the novel's sense of Grant as essentially unformed; Bond's playing of the role and Kotcheff's direction of him and of his cameraman (George Willoughby) preserve that sense of his separateness and its giving way to bitter involvement.

   The film's use of its actors is strikingly apt, both in capturing what Cook appears to have had in mind and, more important, in establishing them as part of the film's brilliantly conceived and executed *mise-en-scène*. In his last film role, Chips Rafferty's all-but iconic status in Australian films is both subjected to its first serious scrutiny *and* confirmed. That is, the sort of film *persona* Rafferty has been projecting for nearly 30 years — leathery, laconic, heart-of-gold — has been slightly re-arranged and re-appraised so as to bring its darker underside into the light. As Crawford, he quite powerfully suggests the corruption that lies just beneath the easy good-fellowship of the surface. The role is extremely well-written, drawing very closely on Cook's original dialogue. In one small divergence, Crawford, instead of merely calling Grant by his first name at the moment of meeting (a fact Cook allows Grant to register with faint distress), at once diminishes him to Jack. Rafferty quite brilliantly suggests the falseness and held-in-check bullying attitude, in gestures, movement and inflection. He first appears in the film, as his arm shoots out from the left of the frame to light Grant's cigarette, establishing at once his authoritative presence; in the novel, Grant asks for the light. The effect of the film's small change here is to sharpen one's expectation of Crawford and to "motivate" the way Grant is later led by Crawford to The Game. Everything in Rafferty's physical appearance — the tall thickening body, the uniform with tie, his way of effortlessly moving through crowds to the bar or wherever, his sudden narrowing of the eyes as he suspects an irony he doesn't understand — feeds into the concept of the Crawford character.
   Crawford is very important to the film's narrative and thematic concerns. It is he who, perhaps unconsciously recognizing something malleable in Grant, gives him the crucial push in the direction of The Game from which his troubles chiefly spring. Crawford is also the official spokesman for all that "progress-association" perception of The Yabba ("Best little town in the world this is") and dismissive of anything else ("Did three months' training in the city. Didn't like it"). He is very interesting in his function as policeman. He speaks of the town's "quite a few suicides" as being "a bit of trouble" (p. 22), causing Grant to remember "the local custom of declaring the most blatant act of self-destruction 'accidental death'". Crawford gives a hard joking edge to this discussion in the film and in both media he is seen as distorting the truth in the case of Grant's attempted suicide, writing it off as an accident caused by dropping the rifle. "That'd be about it, wouldn't it?" Crawford asks Grant, his authority in the film accentuated by his looming over Grant's bed, viewed in a low-angle shot. And yet, film and book, Rafferty's performance and Cook's prose, don't quite work to convict Crawford of mere venality: though he obviously doesn't want to register a suicide attempt ("so many suicides give the place a bad name", p. 23), there is also no doubt that his suppression of the truth works in Grant's favour. On another level, he allows the illegal two-up school to continue, partly

because it suits him to and because of the clout it gives him over many people, but there is also a suggestion that he knows it to be the town's favourite sport and therefore part of its unique appeal.

The film's actors, by their physical presences as well as through Evan Jones' dialogue, fill out some of the novel's insights into the nature of "western" friendliness and mateship. These qualities obviously have a near-mythic status in The Yabba territory and this status is seen as being almost wholly unearned. But in Rafferty's Crawford, in the performances of Jack Thompson (particularly) and Peter Whittle as the miners Dick and Joe, and of Al Thomas as Hynes, there are discomforting suggestions that stop an audience from categorizing them too quickly. About all three, as in Crawford, there is a kind of bullying note to the friendship they offer: they *insist* on buying Grant drinks or taking him home in Hynes' case or on the disgusting 'roo-shooting expedition. They are loud, boring, crude, witless and devoid of any sensitivity of thought or feeling — or are they? Dick and Joe, Grant finds out next day when he has sobered up, have left him as a present the rifle they had lent him for the shooting. Hynes has in fact taken him home for a meal when he had no money to buy one. They brush aside as irrelevant Grant's talk of being unable to pay or of later payment. The fact that their insistent hospitality helps to bring Grant to the edge of self-destruction is something the viewer/reader obviously responds to, but this response is complicated in the way I have suggested. The casting of an actor like Thompson (not in 1971 well-known as he is today) is in itself a complicating factor. With his cheerful, open looks and despite the entrenched male chauvinism of his role, it is hard to dismiss the character of Dick as merely a brutal, ocker hedonist. Dick *is* all those things (he wonders "what's wrong with [Grant]? Rather talk to a woman than drink?" in a line from the screenplay, though not from the novel), but there is also the refusal to consider Grant's inability to pay for drinks. Neither Cook nor Kotcheff values this camaraderie much but it is there and it is forced on our attention by the now-familiar, likable *persona* of Thompson.

Donald Pleasence, on the other hand, is a British character actor with an honourable career in playing mad-eyed villains of a particularly insidious corruption, and the resonances he brings from these roles stand him in good stead as the repulsive Tydon. He may be repulsive, however, but apart from Grant he is also the only educated man in the narrative, and he both repels Grant and acts as a warning to him in his downward course. The point is underlined by casting British actors in both roles, forcing the viewer to consider them together and forcing Grant to do so. "Tydon was a foul thing. But so was John Grant (p. 95)", he agonizes in the novel. The film seems to insist on Grant's link with Tydon even more firmly than the novel. For one thing, it introduces Tydon earlier. Whereas in the novel he slips in unobtrusively at Tim Hynes' house on the Satur- day afternoon, the film introduces him the night before as Grant sits down to his nasty meal at the restaurant attached to The Game. The viewer is suddenly arrested by Tydon's face in profile at the left of the screen observing Grant as the latter eats. Tydon offers the first variant on the idea of Bundunyabba's perfections but claims it could be worse: "The supply of beer could run out." Grant complains about the arrogant hospitality and the stupid people "who want you to be as stupid as they are", but Tydon is kept by them in return for feeding them information about The Game.

Again, at the end of the film, Tydon appears with a persistence that forces the viewer to consider his significance in a way that the novel does not. Tydon is not, for instance, mentioned in the last two chapters of the novel. In the film, it is at his hut that Grant makes his suicide attempt just as Tydon enters, and in the preceding montage of images, of regret and disgust and self-disgust, Tydon appears several times as if to emphasize how large he looms in Grant's despair. More revealing still, as Grant steps out of the hospital at the end, Tydon emerges from the right of the frame; he had originally appeared on Grant's left in the restaurant, so that there is a kind of "framing" effect, as if Grant's bad experience of The Yabba has been enclosed by Tydon. Tydon is neatly dressed in a black suit and tie, at variance with the squalor in which the film has presented him, and he picks up Grant's case and farewells him at the station. His dress, now more nearly approximating Grant's conventionally suited appearance, makes a final, subtle and entirely cinematic reminder of what Grant has

Grant at Tiboonda station before setting out for Sydney, but becoming entrapped in The Yabba.

escaped from. The gap between his situation and Tydon's may seem superficially wide; Tydon's appearance at this stage, in this way, suggests that that kind of formal show of respectability is no guarantee against the sorts of degeneracy that characterize his life. The potential correspondence between them is more subtly made in terms of film than in Cook's more explicit statement of it.

My point in considering these performances in some detail is to indicate that, though the film is extremely impressive as a *milieu* study, this is not the source of its coherence or its power. These derive from Grant's response to specific aspects of that *milieu* as embodied in these key characters. His interaction with them — and this is achieved through the performances as much as through the screenplay — is the result of an essentially unprepared character being worked on by influences of a kind and strength of which he has hitherto had no knowledge.

This said, it is also true that the film realizes certain ugly aspects of Australian outback life with a vigour and exactness rare to the point of uniqueness in Australian films. This may be partly due to the fact that the film is being seen through the eyes of a foreigner, Kotcheff being a Canadian. He had previously shown himself an astute observer of *milieu* and of a weak character under pressure in the British-made **Life at the Top**, but it did not require of him the raw power he achieves in **Wake in Fright** nor did it call on him to respond, in its view of urban infidelities, to anything as strange as the world encompassed by Tiboonda and The Yabba. It is interesting to compare his response to the harshness of the physical scene with that of Nicolas Roeg, another "foreign" director working here at roughly the same time. Roeg, in **Walkabout**, found poetry, and fascination with the supernatural forces at work in this challenging landscape, whereas Kotcheff's task is to capture its emptiness and the mindless viciousness of some of its inhabitants.

The opening sequences establish the desolateness of Tiboonda with remarkable authority. In a pre-credits sequence, the camera pans over the empty landscape, gradually revealing the railway line, with a dirt track beside it, two small buildings viewed from a distance, then the railway siding with the name Tiboonda. The school is glimpsed through the rails of the siding and Kotcheff cuts to the inside of the school, on the last day of term, with the clock ticking, and the children all sitting ready to leave, intently watching the teacher seated out the front. The camera tracks behind him so that the audience can share his view of the class. The time to leave comes and, behind the credits, he quits the school, in swirling dust goes out the gate, and crosses to the pub. Kotcheff has in these first minutes created a powerful sense of the unresonant emptiness of the scene, utterly at odds with the mystery and poetry with which Roeg imbues — or perhaps finds in — the setting in **Walkabout**.

Kotcheff's control of the *mise-en-scène*, including as I have suggested his deployment of actors, extends effortlessly to include his evocation of the

Above: The Game, with the "spinner" tossing the coins. Below: Grant watches as Janette (Sylvia Kay) unbuttons her dress, her invitation unequivocal.

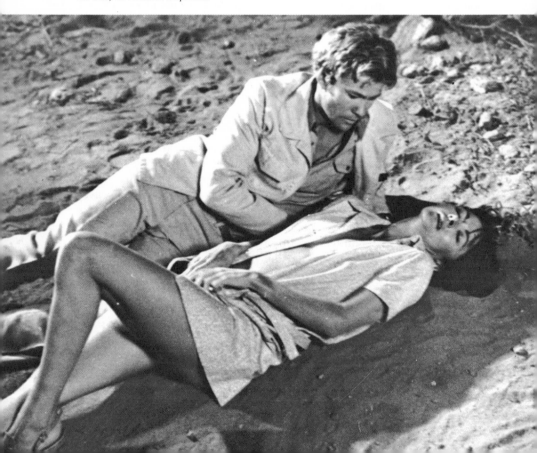

film's other settings, beginning with the Tiboonda pub. John Meillon plays the scruffy-looking barman, Charlie, sly, cadging, and, at heart, malicious; the pub itself is a hideous corrugated-iron affair, with a low-angled shot of a verandah that is a mockery of a Fordian porch, and its long bar recalls the Western saloon, but shorn of all attempts at character. The pubs that figure so prominently in the rest of the film are models of suggestive realism. At the hotel where Grant stays, the unsmiling receptionist cooling herself in front of a fan is scarcely able to tell him how to get to his (unlovely) room. When he goes to another pub for a drink, someone shouts at him "Shut the door mate, we're closed" as he enters a crowded bar, a seething scene of noisy, meaningless male camaraderie, created swiftly in a wide-screen shot of the crowd, followed by a montage of hands pulling beer and grabbing glasses. Here, as at the scene of The Game, Grant stands back observing the swarm with a sense of his own distance from it. The little outback pubs visited on the kangaroo shoot are sketched in a few lethal strokes. Kotcheff has created — much helped by Dennis Gentile's art direction — a convincing picture of some of the world's squalidest drinking habits.

Kotcheff knows where he wants the camera placed and how he wants his film cut in order to create his meaning. Once or twice his effects are a trifle showy but more often they work to promote narrative concision and intensity. In the virtuoso sequence of The Game, the camera circles Grant to vertiginous effect, accentuated by the next shot of him in the low left of the frame which is dominated by the overhead light. This is followed by an overhead shot of Grant as "spinner", blinking into the light. All the camera movements in this sequence work towards stressing Grant's vulnerability and enmeshment, just as, a little later at Hynes' house, a montage of drinking, swirling lights, and stupid faces signals Grant's collapse into oblivion. This gives way to his waking in Tydon's filthy hut where a beam of light shines in his eye, flies buzz round the light, and Tydon is preparing food while an operatic soprano is incongruously heard on an ancient gramophone. The music in the filth is a somewhat obvious signifier for the idea of educated-man-sunk-low, which Tydon is and Grant may be, but it makes its point.

The kangaroo hunt itself is the film's climax, both as an expression of the simple brutality that underlies all the surface cheeriness and as the occasion where Grant loses not only control but, almost, sight of his civilized self. The whole episode is brilliantly shot by a tracking camera as the battered car races over the empty dusty plain, to the accompaniment of wild, mindless laughter and pot shots at road signs. The camera records fleetingly the beauty of the kangaroos about to be destroyed by the yahoo invasion. There are again elements of the Western genre, as the red land seems to move in billows, the whooping noise of the intruders intensifying the suggestion. But it is distinctly the image of the de-romanticized West that is evoked here, Ralph Nelson's **Soldier Blue** rather than John Ford's

My Darling Clementine, for example. After another montage — and the montage is an essential element of this film's "prose" — of falling 'roos, rifles cracking and flashing lights, the sequence finishes on the ultimate brutality, that of killing the 'roo with a knife. There is a close-up of Joe and Dick's stupid faces laughing, of Tydon just looking and drinking, and the soundtrack registers and reinforces the de-humanizing horror of the incident.

I hope to have suggested that Kotcheff and his collaborators have not merely been "true" to Cook's central narrative, but that their exercise of cinematic resources has given the viewer a richer sense of the prevailing ideology of which Grant is at first scornful and to which he then succumbs, almost fatally. *Mise-en-scène* cannot always achieve what prose can; as I have claimed in Chapter 1, there are aspects of the narrative "meta-language" of great writers that resist the fixed explicitness of film. Nevertheless, in the case of **Wake in Fright**, a very competent, terse little narrative on the page has been enriched by the way the film works on Cook's suggestions. Some may find Kotcheff's use of montage more distracting than I do; it seems to me to work very aptly in the visual depiction of mental states, achieving what in fact Cook's prose on occasions merely strains toward (e.g., in his account of Grant's contemplation of suicide).

The novel sketches its female characters quite surely — the receptionist, a barmaid called Joyce, Janette Hynes and Robyn — placing them firmly in a male-dominated world. The first two are seen only at the beck and call of men in various stages of drunkenness; Janette, a trained nurse but, at home, her father's reticent servant; and Robyn, an ideal of soft brown girlhood in a short white skirt. Cook makes clear that their functions are marginal in the narrative and in the boorishly masculine *milieu*. It is not always the case that visually presented images will be more potent than verbal ones; the suggestive capacity of the latter can often work more productively on the reader's co-operative mind than the bold statement of a film's image on the relative passivity of the viewer's mind. In **Wake in Fright**, though, the images of femininity imply a spectrum of male insensitivity and exploitation about which the novel is both more and less explicit: *more*, in the sense of spelling out, through Tydon's comments on sex, the double standard at work in relation to Janette or the diminishing clarity of Robyn in Grant's mind; *less*, in that film can, through a glance or a posture, signify a range of cultural/ideological meaning. The way Robyn appears in Grant's day-dream, emerging from the surf in provocative swimsuit to lean teasingly over him, is a man's view of allowable, respectable female appeal. Janette, on the other hand, who lies down on the dusty ground, her invitation unequivocal, and who unbuttons her dress, is the subject for crude jokes. As played by Sylvia Kay, she has a touching moment. After Grant has thrown up just as he was about to mount her (and the metaphor is apt), she turns away sadly, does up her dress and then wipes his face. The film invests this gesture with honesty and compassion before an ugly experience that causes the viewer to re-assess Janette's apparent sexual readiness. In the end, neither has really touched his untried manhood; but the film, especially, does acknowledge objectively in Janette some sense of generous life which is character-istically misunderstood even as it is exploited.

Wake in Fright, in both the prose and celluloid texts, has a clearly plotted narrative which offers in some ways a model of narrative construc-tion: for instance, in its setting up of and frustrating of expectations, in its careful motivation of sequences, in its firm opening and symmetrically firm, slightly but significantly different, closing sequence. Kotcheff's film has picked up the suggestions of Cook's original text, rendered some of them more concisely and fleshed out others very persuasively. The film was not really part of the Australian film revival of the 1970s, but the indigenous directors who created the "revival" might well have learnt from its virtues. It has a narrative control and visual authority which few, if any, Australian films have matched since.

Notes

1. Gillian Hanson, "**Outback**", reviewed in *Monthly Film Bulletin*, The British Film Institute, December 1971, p. 244.

3. Picnic at Hanging Rock

Joan Lindsay's *Picnic at Hanging Rock* was first published by Cheshire, 1967, and by Penguin Books, 1970 (page references to the latter). Married to the artist, Sir Daryl Lindsay, she travelled extensively overseas before settling in Australia. She has also written a reminiscence, *Time Without Clocks*.

Picnic at Hanging Rock was directed by Peter Weir, for producers Hal and Jim McElroy, in association with Patricia Lovell, from a screenplay by Cliff Green. The director of photography was Russell Boyd, the editor Max Lemon and the composer Bruce Smeaton (who incorporated Gheorghe Zamphir's "Pipe de Pan" and Beethoven's Fifth Piano Concerto). Running 116 minutes, it was released in 1975.

The publishing history of Joan Lindsay's novel is revealing: first published in 1967, and for the first time in Penguin in 1970, it was then reprinted more than a dozen times in Penguin between 1975 and 1982.[1] There was, that is to say, very little interest in it until Peter Weir's seductive film appeared in 1975, and reading it again one sees why. What Weir has done is to take a banal text in the prose medium and transform it into a film text which, if it does not entirely avoid banality, uses the resources of its medium imaginatively and intelligently.

The novel's central narrative strategy is to try to deceive its readers into accepting its fictional mystery as fact. The author's comment at the end of the list of characters — "And many others who do not appear in this book" — is clearly aimed at feeding this uncertainty. So is the disingenuous succeeding gloss:

> Whether *Picnic at Hanging Rock* is fact or fiction, my readers must decide for themselves. As the fateful picnic took place in the year nineteen hundred, and all the characters who appear in this book are long since dead, it hardly seems important. (p. 6)

There is a conscious attempt to lull the reader into believing the story at least *may* be true, though why, one wonders, should everyone be "long since dead" in 1967 when the novel first appeared? There are other ways in which Lindsay seeks to maintain the fact/fiction tease: she "transcribes" Mr Hussey's apparently verbatim police statement about the day's events at Hanging Rock, to which the girls travelled in his drag (pp. 48-51); his later statement to Sergeant Bumpher about taking Mrs Appleyard to the Rock (pp. 208-9); the letter of Mademoiselle de Poitiers, the French mistress, to Sergeant Bumpher with her suspicions about Mrs Appleyard's treatment of the orphan Sara (pp. 201-2); the extract from

Opposite: Miss McCraw (Vivean Gray) and schoolgirls at the foot of the Rock.

the statement of Mr Whitehead, the gardener, about Sara's death (pp. 206-8); the "Author's Note: Edward Whitehead actually lived to the age of ninety-five years", this given in an authenticating footnote (p. 207); and the final "Extract from a Melbourne newspaper, dated February 14th, 1913" which recalls the events of 13 years before and refers to the later lives of some of the participants (pp. 212-3).

Weir's film begins and ends with statements which seem to take up the novel's blurring of the line between fact and fiction, but, because the film is much less interested in the "College Mystery" aspect of the story, he is not concerned to develop the idea. He creates imagistically a coherence both thematic and tonal that the novel never begins to find. If Lindsay's aim in the use of police statements, etc., is to persuade the reader that the events at Hanging Rock really happened, then certain aspects of the narrative and other stylistic elements work against this effect. Much of the writing is clichéd and stilted, belonging to very inferior novelistic modes, and the attempts at philosophizing are threadbare. Weir wisely drops the fact/fiction tease as a narrative motif, though not so wisely retains some of the novel's penchant for aphorism. I say *Weir* rather than Cliff Green who wrote the screenplay[2] because the film's coherence, insofar as it achieves one, is essentially a visual rather than a verbal achievement.

The film keeps quite closely to the bones of Lindsay's narrative. There are perhaps nine main stages in the book's central narrative chain;

First: the expedition. Amid excitement and warnings, the girls from Appleyard College set out on their journey to Hanging Rock for the St Valentine's Day picnic. A sense of potential delight and danger is created.

Second: the picnic itself. This includes the climbing of the Rock as observed by the young Englishman, Michael Fitzhubert, and Albert Crundall, his uncle's coachman.

Third: the establishment of the mystery. Edith returns screaming with terror to the picnic party which returns late to the College with three girls and the maths mistress, Miss McCraw, missing on the Rock.

Fourth: Sergeant Bumpher's investigations of the mystery. These signally fail to generate much interest or suspense.

Fifth: Michael and Albert's search of the Rock. This leads to the finding of Irma, one of the missing girls. (This occurs half-way through the book and the rest is taken up chiefly with disintegration and red herrings.)

Sixth: the falling apart of Appleyard College. Parents take to withdrawing their children; Mrs Appleyard takes to brandy — and to victimizing the orphan Sara.

Seventh: Irma's recovery, which does nothing to dispel the mystery, and her farewell visit to the school, which produces a scene of hysteria in the school's gym.

Eighth: a series of straggling events. These include Mademoiselle's departure; the death in a city fire of Miss Lumley, a teacher who has left the College; Albert's reward for his part in Irma's discovery; and the death of Sara.

Ninth: the collapse and death of Mrs Appleyard.

Now this is a far from strong narrative line; owing little to character or to any unifying idea, its events too often seem arbitrary and improbable. The idea of the "College Mystery" is used in the latter half of the novel as if to provide a narrative rallying point for a set of events which do not otherwise hang persuasively together. These events include the gratuitous deaths of Miss Lumley and her brother; the connection between Albert and Sara, hinted at but not disclosed; and Mrs Appleyard's persecution of Sara when the school is collapsing around her. It is as though Lindsay is aware of the thinness of her central narrative line and has sought to strengthen it by associated mysteries, without having the art quite to integrate them. She wholly lacks the thriller-writer's capacities for using the police investigation and the search parties as means to intensify the sense of mystery, and thereby stiffen and complicate the narrative's grasp of our attention.

The mystery at the heart of the novel — that of the girls' inexplicable disappearance — also founders on one's sense of its central improbability. Why are Edith and Irma unable to give any account of what happened on the Rock? Why, despite the apparently intensive search, is no sign of the others found? Such "realistic" objections would matter very much less if the novel seemed not to be so concerned with maintaining an air of factual authenticity. As long as it wants the reader to believe that these events really happened, it is bound to pay more attention to details and probabilities than it does.

These objections scarcely arise in relation to the film because Weir has clearly not been much interested in such verisimilitude. Quibbles about probability in narrative vary directly with the author's concern for realism. It is possible for a narrative to hang on a quite outrageous improbability if the author can persuade us to direct our attention elsewhere. Alfred Hitchcock's masterpiece, **Vertigo**, depends on the audience's acceptance of the extremely unlikely and wholly unexplained fact that his hero did not fall to his death in the first few minutes. The reasons are simply not important; Hitchcock's drama of romantic obsession distracts and holds the attention by other means. Or to take another example from literature: in *Great Expectations*, Dickens creates Miss Havisham in a single, sweeping, imaginative act and her function in the novel is so imagistically powerful that one does not bother to speculate on the realistic probability of anyone's living as she does. Dickens relates that she has never removed her wedding dress or cleaned the bridal table in the many years since she was jilted. The potent suggestiveness of the idea is enough to dispel such quibbles. But Lindsay's novel does not work like either of these two great fictions. Given her overt concern with authenticity, she has only herself to blame when the reader stumbles over obstacles to belief.

An intermittent thematic connection *is* suggested but it is not really developed. By this I mean the adumbrated notion that repression, especially perhaps sexual repression, is a likely source of disaster. (Weir's film takes up this suggestion more amply.) In the early chapters, there is a sense of excitement held under (cf. the sexual undertones of St Valentine's Day, Sara's "crush" on Miranda), of muffled danger and delight in the journey. There is a generalized suggestion of the ordered, repressive environment of the school's having an essentially frail grasp on reality: a grasp in fact so frail that, in the crisis of hysteria following the picnic, the school will disintegrate and so will all but the most wholesomely-adjusted of its inhabitants (Mademoiselle, Minnie the maid). Throughout, this pattern of repression/disintegration seems hinted at but, perhaps because Lindsay is shy of the sexual implications, it is never developed. Are, for instance, latent lesbian feelings indicated in Mrs Appleyard's recollection of Miss McCraw?:

> It was inconceivable that this woman of masculine intellect on whom she had come to rely in the last years should have allowed herself to be spirited away, lost, raped, murdered in cold blood like an innocent schoolgirl, on the Hanging Rock. (p. 195)

As for the nature of Irma's feelings for Michael Fitzhubert, who rescues her, the novel drops in the following lush dollop of romantic writing:

> Again she sees the flash of the creek, the wagonette under the blackwood trees and a fair-haired young man sitting on the grass reading a newspaper. As soon as she sees him she turns her head away and doesn't look at him again. 'Why? Why? . . .' 'Why?' screeches the peacock on the lawn. Because I knew, even then . . . I have always known, that Mike is my beloved. (p. 146)

It is hard enough coping with the punctuation here, let alone the question of the passage's significance in the novel. Is it meant to suggest that, for Irma, the experience of the Rock has somehow freed her from the school's sexual repressiveness? Possibly; but Lindsay does nothing further with the idea.

It is not as though the narrative is full of tantalizing ambiguities. It is not that Lindsay has gone to school with the Henry James of *The Turn of the Screw*. The problem is that she has not even gone to school with, say, a competent mystery writer such as Marjorie Allingham. The dangling threads of her narrative remain obdurately that: loose ends, not fascinating riddles. One suspects one is meant to find them "intriguing", as they say. What is the point of the long-lost-sibling idea associated with Albert and Sara? Is it just to touch us with the pathos of their being physically so near, after years of separation, and yet unaware of it? Has it to do with the general elusiveness of human relationship? As it stands, it is less a matter of tantalizing ambiguity than of feeble-minded plotting.

The most perversely interesting aspects of Lindsay's narrative are there without, one guesses, her being wholly aware of what she is doing. Certain ideas relating to class and sexuality make themselves felt in ways that reflect on the author and on certain middle-class perceptions of experience. *Picnic at Hanging Rock* is an extremely — and instinctively — snobbish book. The snobbery is seen in the patronizing treatment of the lower orders (with their vulgar speech patterns and habits of mind) and in the admiring treatment of, say, Fitzhubert of ancient and impeccable lineage:

> There was only one conscious thought in his head: *Go on*. A Fitzhubert ancestor hacking his way through bloody barricades at Agincourt had felt much the same way; and had, in fact, incorporated those very words, in Latin, in the family crest: *Go on*. Mike, some five centuries later, went on climbing. (p. 92)

Blood, Lindsay clearly believes, will out. In the Mike-Albert relationship, though Mike comes to appreciate Albert's qualities, he is invariably seen as superior in his sensitivities, language and responses. Albert is at best a rough diamond with a heart of gold (to mix mineral metaphors) and the banalities about the relationship between class and true warmth and

Albert Crundall (John Jarratt), a rough diamond, and Michael Fitzhubert (Dominic Guard), of ancient and impeccable lineage.

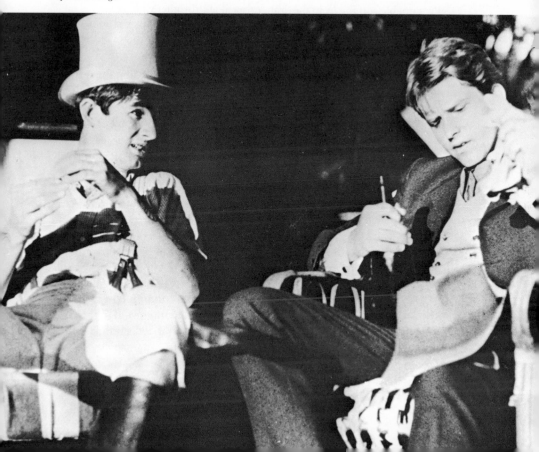

goodness are almost more offensive than overt snobbery would be. For instance, when Mike goes to visit Albert in his room above the stables, he "thought there was an air of welcome, even of comfort, unknown in his Aunt's drawing-room" (p. 173). This simplistic observation is reinforced by Mike's later, sentimental reflection on Albert's worth:

> Mike glanced affectionately at the brick red features, more honest in the flickering candlelight than the faces of many of his Cambridge friends who let their tailors' bills run on for years and had never passed a night behind bars. (p. 174)

The novel is at its most banal when it is *obviously* talking about class. Lindsay seems even to believe that the upper classes actually *look* better than the lower orders, implicitly comparing Mike's fair handsomeness with Albert's brick-red bullet-head. Clichés about class proliferate, sometimes superficially as in the way Colonel Fitzhubert is always "spluttering" or "snorting" and saying "What the deuce!", sometimes in revealing a proletarian heart of gold. More unattractively snobbish, because more carefully embedded in the narrative, is the quite brutally condescending treatment of lower-middle-class characters, such as Miss Lumley and her brother, or even Mrs Appleyard. Indulging a post-Yeatsian peasant-and-aristocrat sentimentality, Lindsay clearly despises those between. They are characteristically stupid, grasping, opinionated and mean-spirited. On St Valentine's Day, Miss Lumley had produced a card:

> Presumably coming from the drab, unspeakable brother who had called on his sister last term. Who else, reasoned the budding girls, would adore the myopic junior governess, eternally garbed in brown serge and flat-heeled shoes. (p. 10)

Callowly characterizing the Lumleys in terms of their passion for respectability, Lindsay clearly shares to the full the young ladies' view of them. They are finally — and, the novel suggests, appropriately — burnt to death in "a respectable small hotel in a respectable city street" (p. 170).

The novel's views on sexuality are also invariably conditioned by the social level involved. Mike's longing for the lost Miranda is plaintively romantic ("Oh, my lost, lovely darling, where are you?", p. 92), finding a tonal echo in Irma's one-off utterance, "I have always known, that Mike is my beloved" (p. 146). The lower classes, sentimentally seen as being much earthier, more instinctive about sex, are represented by "Tom and Minnie, locked in each other's arms, murmur[ing] endlessly of love" (p. 123); that is, getting on with it. The film glances at these conventional depictions but is more pervasively concerned with the idea of a whole institutionalized, smothered sexuality, symbolized in the St Valentine's Day rituals, which is there in the novel as no more than a barely apprehended sub-text. Weir has said: "I was never really interested in that side of the film."[3] Maybe; but trust the tale rather than the teller: much of the film's superior narrative coherence derives from the way it picks up this suggestion from the novel and explores it in terms of some very potent images.

As a novel, *Picnic at Hanging Rock* would not be worth talking about at such length. Its chief interest now — to me, at least — is in the way in which it has been used as the source of one of the most popular Australian films. In figures adjusted for inflation, as of January 1, 1982[4], it appears as the second-highest-grossing Australian film. As well, it seems — and this is of course only an impression — to be the film which stays in most people's minds as the finest flower of the local film renaissance of the 1970s. The film undoubtedly created a stir of a kind the novel simply did not.

Despite the comments of Weir, Green and Pat Lovell (executive producer) in a "Dialogue"[5] that introduces the published screenplay, and, despite the euphoric over-valuation at the time of its release, the film appears to me enormously more interesting than the novel. They (i.e., Weir, Green and Lovell) seem all to have *extrapolated* from the novel rather than been taken by it as an entity. To Green,

> The book seemed . . . to have two major themes, and both of them excited me . . . First of all there was the theme of the environment; of these Europeans intruding into this timeless environment and being rejected and in some cases destroyed by it . . . And the other theme that deeply interested me was the one concerned with the way adults treat children . . . We think of this sort of subtle cruelty to children as something that died with the Victorian age, but I don't believe this is so.[6]

For Weir, "The great power of the story lies in its ability to unlock your own ghosts"[7]; I am not entirely clear what he means by this and the fact that "you'll never get Joan Lindsay to talk about [it]" suggests reasons other than reluctance to discuss "the deepest power of the story". And Lovell comments:

> I was so stunned by the visual quality of the book. I seemed to be able to *see* all those people, and the places. And you could almost feel the under-currents.[8]

Without sharing the enthusiasm of any of the three for the original, I find their "Dialogue" instructive in relation to the finished film. Green's thematic interests certainly do surface in his screenplay and in the film, and so do what I take to be Weir's metaphysical preoccupations. Further, where the film is at its best, these interests and preoccupations are realized in images of remarkable beauty and suggestiveness. At its worst, it swallows the novel's pretensions as if in the presence of higher thought; but, even at its worst, that is when it is indulging its whim for vapid philosophizing, the film, by its visual grace, is lifted out of the novel's shallows. The affection and respect that Weir, Green and Lovell have shown for Lindsay is touching but their misplaced sense of responsibility to the book leads them to accept its lacunae as if to tamper with it were

Above: Miranda (Anne Lambert) leads the girls up the Rock. Below: at the College, Miss Lumley (Kirsty Child) says grace for the St Valentine's Day breakfast.

irreverent. I mean particularly the way they accept inconclusiveness —
e.g., the Sara-Albert connection or the did-she-fall-or-was-she-pushed
aspect of Sara's death — as simply "leav[ing] a lot to be thought about".
"And this to me is the magic of the story", claims Lovell.[9]

Lindsay devotes considerable space to descriptive writing aimed at
making one aware of those two monoliths — Appleyard College and
Hanging Rock — both incongruously set down in the Australian bush.
Between these two contrasted outcrops, the drama (of both novel and
film) takes place, physically and metaphorically. Lindsay writes that
"Appleyard College was already, in the year nineteen hundred, an archi-
tectural anachronism in the Australian bush — a hopeless misfit in time
and place" (p. 8), with gardens in which "Heavy-headed dahlias flared
and drooped in the immaculate flowerbeds, the well-trimmed lawns
steamed under the mounting sun" (p. 7). As for the Rock, it is introduced
in full-view as the school party gets its first sudden glimpse of it: "Directly
ahead, the grey volcanic mass rose up slabbed and pinnacled like a fortress
from the empty yellow plain" (p. 19). *Its* incongruity is spatial rather than
temporal. A little later, Lindsay offers a novelist's "close-up" of the Rock:

> On the rocks and grass the diligent ants were crossing miniature Saharas of
> dry sand, jungles of seeding grass, in the never ending task of collecting
> and storing food. (p. 23)

Against the background of this natural wonder, "the drowsy well-fed girls
lounging in the shade were no more a part of their environment than
figures in a photography album."

In the light of these descriptive passages, it is easy to see the basis for
Green's interest in the theme of environment, and human incongruity in
it, and it is perhaps not too much to claim that the film's meaning is organized around its presentation of these two basic images: the Rock and the
College. The two come together in the adventure of the picnic: the College
is "tested" by the Rock, and disintegrates under the strain while the Rock
remains wholly unmoved by the College's venturing upon it, and yields
no secrets.

Picnic certainly has one of the most evocative opening shots in an Australian film. A bird call is heard over a pale wash of trees and mist from
which Hanging Rock emerges: at first distant and then close-up, always
ominous, in the way that John Ford makes great rock faces threatening
and mysterious in **The Searchers**.[10] The film, that is, chooses to begin
with the Rock, and one has that haunting image (emphasized by the pan
pipes on the soundtrack) in mind through the subsequent scenes at the
school. The Rock, from the outset, constitutes a threat to the school, and
the point, made visually, is much more potently felt than it is in the novel
which chooses to begin with the school. The sense of threat and allure-
ment posed by the Rock is emphasized by the way the brooding rock face
is replaced by an exquisite girl's face on a pillow. This is in turn succeeded

by a susurration of sexual excitement, imaged in shots of girls washing, dressing in flimsy white, reading their St Valentine's Day cards, the banal verses of which provide a romantic focus for their suppressed longings. The film's other chief icon — the school — is introduced quite explicitly as a scene of adolescent sexual yearning. Very astutely it picks up this sentence from the novel — "Edith Horton, plain as a frog, had smugly accounted for at least eleven [i.e., cards]" — and uses it dramatically as the novel does not. Whereas the other girls are swooning over the cards, fat Edith (Christine Schuller) is merely counting them as possessions; their romance is lost on her. And one remembers this as, later, she escapes the pull of the Rock and returns screaming to the rest of the school party.

In establishing his centrally significant images, Weir has the advantage of one of Australia's finest cameramen, Russell Boyd, whose camera again and again catches the danger and massive inscrutability of the Rock's faces, contrasting these with the lushness of the surrounding foliage and the soft, billowing whiteness of the girls' dresses. Together, Weir and Boyd do equally well in capturing the oppressive Victorian facade and interiors of Appleyard College, whose incongruity is established at first by the oddly exotic palm trees that flank it. Whereas striking overhead shots of the girls climbing through narrow passes on the Rock reinforce the threat and enticement it offers, low-angled shots of the school's facade, with the girls being addressed by Mrs Appleyard (Rachel Roberts) prior to their leaving on the picnic, emphasize its repressively authoritarian influence. Barred from the picnic, the orphan Sara's (Margaret Nelson) isolation from the picnic party is intensified by the low-angled shot which follows Miranda's (Anne Lambert) gaze to Sara standing on the College's parapet.

Within the film's first few minutes, then, both Rock and school have been clearly imaged, as described in Green's screenplay: "Shot 2. Very Wide Shot: The Rock — strange, haunting — standing up out of the fog-blanketed plain" (p. 1) and

> Shot 14. Long Shot: The College, glimpsed through the dusty gold and grey-green gums. Foursquare and incongruous. An island of hard stone and English garden, marooned in the bush, dreaming of Europe. Hopelessly. (p. 4)

Working impressionistically, suggesting where the novel describes, the film charges both of these images with a much more potent significance than the novel does, and in each case that significance is felt as inimical to human life. Further, by the dozen brief shots between the two above, so brief as almost to constitute in their totality a montage, the film seems to enunciate the connection between the two. Miranda's whispered voice-over — "What we see, and what we seem, are but a dream. A dream within a dream . . ." — establishes, through the dissolve from Rock to school, *her* connection with the two. What is being achieved is not so much "truth" to the original as a "truthful" expectation in regard to the new creation.

What links these two images of Rock and school is something more than a mere parallelism of incongruity, parallelism being no guarantee of coherence. In spite of Weir's disclaimers, I believe the link is the notion of sexuality, smothered at Appleyard College, in some undefined way both threatened and liberated at Hanging Rock. In the interview referred to previously, Weir replied to a suggestion that the film "is very interesting in its exploration of a sort of smothered sexuality, of sexuality in an environment which represses it . . .",

> I was never really interested in that side of the film. I didn't see it as a part of its theme. I remember when I went to London for the promotion, that that was the area which most interested the British critics. Comments ranged from talk of repressed sexuality to the less subtle, talking about lesbianism and so on. But it didn't interest me. For me, the grand theme was Nature, and even the girls' sexuality was as much a part of that as the lizard crawling across the top of the rock. They were part of the same whole; part of the larger question.[11]

Maybe. However, that last phrase "part of the larger question" remains vague, as does "the grand theme was Nature." Weir emerges in interview as more analytically intelligent than he wants to be given credit for. He may well be more interested in "other areas: sounds, smells, the way hair fell on the shoulder, images — just plain pictures"[12], but whatever he was *conscious* of doing I should still want to insist on the pervasiveness of the film's sexual references and the cohesive way in which they work. Weir may well think primarily in terms of images but in adapting a novel or, for that matter, interpreting an original screenplay he must constantly consider how those images will work to create a meaning and a response. Unless he is to make a work of amorphous surrealism, he must, one feels, have some notion of where those images are heading.

On the basis then of the film itself, the sexual motif works controllingly in making those visual images *mean*. Whatever happens to the girls and the teacher who disappear on the Rock, the film insists on a sexual connection of some kind. What we have seen at the College — St Valentine's Day: Sara's "crush" on Miranda; the girls in their virginal white, who are like sympathetic, romantic Mlle de Poitiers (Helen Morse) and unlike the other teachers — has encouraged the reading of a sexual sub-text. Scarcely even "sub-" in fact. The Rock, on the other hand, is presented as alluring as well as ominous, as inviting a release from sexual inhibition. The three girls who disappear, leaving Edith behind, seem almost to float through the trees as if to the embrace of a lover. The young English aristocrat, Michael Fitzhubert (Dominic Guard), and the Australian groom, Albert Crundall (John Jarratt), who observe them, respond — the one with quivering sensitivity, the other with crude realism — to the sexual challenge of the fleeting image.

And this response has been prepared for. Mrs Appleyard has told the girls, "You may remove your gloves after the drag has passed through Woodend", inadvertently hinting at the loss of inhibition which will follow at the Rock itself. Her warning about the dangers of the Rock passes unheeded, but that earlier remark about the gloves is echoed in the genuinely erotic moment in which the girls remove stockings and boots as they begin to explore the Rock. The notion that the Rock is somehow associated with sexual release is reinforced later when Edith prudishly recalls that, as she was rushing down from the Rock, she passed the missing teacher, Miss McCraw (Vivean Gray), running up without her dress. Miss McCraw, in severe brown costume and veiled hat, had been the most thoroughly dressed of the party, contrasted with the rest in flimsy white. If the experience of the Rock, which she has earlier talked of in terms of geology, can so have released *her* from the inhibitions of respectability, its powers are considerable indeed. The film does not show Miss McCraw in *déshabillé*: to do so would have risked misplaced giggles: but what it means in thematic terms is sharply felt in Edith's smirking revelation.

Edith is by now back at the school where such sexually-associated detail is either suppressed or euphemized. When one of the girls, Irma (Karen Robson), is found by Michael, Mrs Appleyard asks the doctor whether she had been "molested", but the doctor assures her that "She is quite intact", and mutters the comment twice again — to the sergeant and to the Fitzhuberts' housekeeper. The maid at Colonel Fitzhubert's home, where Irma is convalescing (significantly, perhaps, not at the school), confides to the housekeeper that Irma was wearing no corset when found, and the housekeeper tells her she was quite right to suppress this information.

The climax to this persistent use of the sexual motif as the link between Rock and school comes in the scene in which Irma, recovered from the ordeal, visits the school gym to say goodbye to her fellow pupils. This scene also represents one of Green's thematic interests, that of "the way adults treat children". Miss Lumley (Kirsty Child) is at the piano, "hammering out 'Men of Harlech' — hideously", enjoying the authority of her position on the dais and her function (that is, directing the girls as they "listlessly dip and rise in time to the music, performing a lunatic ritual . . ."[13]). Into this oppressive scene comes Irma, clad in long crimson cloak and crimson hat, a striking figure as she appears in the doorway, flanked in the frame by the two rows of girls doing posture exercises. Whatever has happened to Irma on the Rock — and she has refused or been unable to tell — it has changed her from romantic schoolgirl to assured woman. The girls sense a new — sexual? — knowledge about her and crowd around hysterically, demanding explanations.

The film has at this point drawn fairly literally on the novel in making this scene the occasion for the eruption of the girls' suppressed fears about what happened on the Rock. But the film does it more powerfully and suggestively. Partly this is because Lindsay's prose drifts into romantic cliché at crucial moments: "the monotonous thumping was inhuman, almost unendurable" (p. 152) as the girls get on with their exercises; the film enacts the aching tedium in a brief shot that takes in their bored movements and Miss Lumley's enjoyment of her authority. A little later, instead of the vivid image of crimson-clad Irma in the doorway, the novel gives access to Mademoiselle's point of view:

> Oh, dear Heaven, what do these unhappy children see that I do not? So the communal vision unfolds before them and Mademoiselle dare not pierce the taut gossamer veil by a spoken word. (p. 153)

This purple-patchiness is replaced by a tense visual control, established in the contrast between Irma and her still-oppressed former schoolfellows, in the aural contrast between the threatening silence that greets Irma's arrival and the hysterical outburst of questioning that follows.

The same large thematic interest relating to the treatment of children is present in both book and film, but in the film there is a firmer stress on *sexual* repression's being let loose here. One sees this in the slight but significant re-wording of Edith's line about the missing girls: "All dead as doornails in a nasty old cave full of bats on the Hanging Rock" (p. 156) is transmuted in the screenplay to "They're dead! All dead as doornails in a

Irma (Karen Robson) is attacked by her schoolfriends on visiting the school gym for the first time since her rescue on the Rock.

filthy dirty cave full of bats on Hanging Rock. Dead — and going rotten" (p. 91). Edith's denunciatory use of "filthy" and "rotten" is the culmination of a series of instructions in the screenplay in which the girls crowd around the newly mature Irma: "A snub nose hugely out of focus with an exposure of bristling hair", ". . . a cavernous mouth agape on a gold-tipped tooth", ". . . the moist tip of a drooling tongue", ". . . heated bodies pressed against Irma's sensitive breasts", ". . . hot fetid breath on Irma's face" (p. 91). Further, the girls' words intensify the sexual over-tones indicated in the images which the camera catches: "Tell us! Men did it, didn't they? It was a man! Tell us! Tell us!" The hysteria is there in both novel and film but the sexual component is rendered explicit in word and image in the film in such a way as to make this scene the film's climax.

In stressing this aspect of the film, whether intentionally or not, Weir has given the film another sort of narrative interest. The "College Mystery" aspect, which hovers between fantasy and melodrama and which seems to interest Weir and Green less, is given a richer texture. That there is something unwholesome in the sexual repression is given a double context: first, the disappearance is perhaps a direct function of sexual release (cf. the erotic detail of removing shoes and stockings); and, second, the lower orders — Minnie (Jacki Weaver) and Tom (Anthony Llewellyn-Jones), and Albert — are unpatronizingly shown to have a more straightforward sexual interest, unencumbered by polite education. These three, less inhibited about sex, are less likely to be victims of Rock or College. I am aware that Weir would probably consider such a discussion too analytical, and should add that the major visual context for the theme of repressed sexuality is the brilliant and dangerous luxuriance of nature. The film's visual style heightens by contrast with all this effortless efflorescence the sense of what is smothered.

In this light, the Rock may perhaps be seen as a symbol of ancient knowingness as compared with the superficial learning and accomplishments the school offers. Again, the Rock, by being so wholly itself, organic and primitive, more of a contrast to than a parallel with the recently-erected stone pile of the College, excites a loosening of the moral corsets: it is alluring and terrifying, tempting the girls to behave instinctively, and exacting an awesome price for their succumbing to this temptation.

The sexual motif represents the film's most coherently pursued interest, but elsewhere the film is left with a number of dissatisfying elements. As in the novel, it is not clear what one is to make of the situation of the orphan Sara, either in regard to Mrs Appleyard's victimization of her while the school is crumbling around her, or in the suggestion that she is Albert's sister. The latter remains a curiously undeveloped tangent to the film's main action, and Sara's death seems merely gratuitous.

As to the notions of class, unconsciously informing every page of Lindsay's novel, I believe the film to be much more intelligently aware of what it is up to. Its adumbrations of class-consciousness are clear enough and plainly *intended*. They are seen in, for example, the town's attitude to the school (to the picnic party pursued by the town's children as it passes through Woodend; to the school group, curiously eyed at church, after the fateful day); in Tom's class-based resistance to Minnie's sympathy for "them kids"; in the fossilized Fitzhuberts whose picnic scene is critically placed as a still life by contrast with the school's noisy party; and especially in the exchanges between Michael and Albert. But though these manifestations are all quite perceptively observed, and a marked advance on the book's instinctive snobbery, they nevertheless fail to add up to much. In the cross-class friendship between Michael and Albert, for instance, their different approaches to sex and to the whole episode of the Rock are quite clear, as are the sources of the difference. What is not so clear is where the film stands in relation to either of them. Is the film more committed to Albert's wholesome realism or to Michael's romantic-chivalric view, or perhaps to neither? Lindsay's views on these two approaches is clear: Albert's down-to-earthness is critically "placed" by Michael's superior sensitivity. The matter is complicated in the film by John Jarratt's more detailed and attractive performance as Albert, whereas Dominic Guard's stiffly aristocratic Michael, bending somewhat under more relaxed colonial mores, is nearer to stereotype.

The last part of the film — following the scene in the gym — needs to be dramatically tighter. The film adopts the novel's equivocal approach to the death of Sara and has no more success in integrating it into its narrative. What might have strengthened these last sequences is a sharper focus on Mrs Appleyard's collapse under the strain of the girls' disappearance and the loss of the teacher she had relied on:

> So much masculine intellect . . . How could she allow herself to be spirited away? . . . Lost. Raped, murdered in cold blood like a silly schoolgirl. On that wretched Hanging Rock. (screenplay, p. 100)

The camera has frequently stressed her heavily repressive dominance as when, on the top of the school steps, she warns the girls of the dangers of the Rock, or when she hovers threateningly over Sara who has not learnt the prescribed poem (by "Mrs Felicia Haymans, one of our finest English poets") but has written one herself. Mrs Appleyard's appearance — upholstered rather than dressed, hair sculpted — has been a striking aspect of the film's *mise-en-scène*, and no symbol of disintegration is more shocking than the grey wisps of hair that later threaten the fearful symmetry of her coiffure. Rachel Roberts plays her with a grim gentility that commands attention as it maintains control by an iron exercise of the will. But the film's treatment of her, often locally very telling, is in the end too scrappy for the announcement of her death, at the foot of Hanging Rock, to have the impact it might have had.

Then there is the question of the film's metaphysical preoccupations which it wears on its exquisite sleeve, rather than locating them more centrally. "What we see, and what we seem, are but a dream. A dream within a dream." This is the opening sentence on the soundtrack; it sets up expectations that the rest of the film does little to gratify. Perhaps we assume that the episode of the Rock (strange things happening, if not emerging) is merely a dream within the larger dream of life itself, but the notion is too romantically vague to engage the mind. The same might be said for Miranda's gnomic utterance that "Everything begins — and ends — at exactly the right time and place." This precedes the much more sharply cinematic insight caught by Miss McCraw's worried looking up from the ascertainable truths of the geometry text she is reading to the Rock which yields no answers. Irma, much later pondering the end of the summer, quotes Miranda's words about the right time and place as though they meant something. If they do, the film does not make its audience privy to that meaning.[14]

Green's screenplay is often shrewdly right, especially in its dealings with Mrs Appleyard, but, in the end, it is undiscriminating. It does not focus sharply enough on the facts of the disappearance; it does not compel attention firmly on what exactly happened at Hanging Rock. Not that the audience requires him to offer an answer to the riddle, but that the nature of riddle and after-effects should be kept more clearly before it. As Adrian Martin writes in his intelligent analysis of **Picnic at Hanging Rock**: "The film suggests meaningful connections but only to frustrate the audience."[15]

Mrs Appleyard (Rachel Roberts) becomes increasingly distraught as the College falters in the wake of the tragedy at Hanging Rock.

Nevertheless, though there are undoubtedly some ill-digested elements in the film, a good deal of it works very persuasively. If one reads it as essentially a narrative of the dangers of repressed sexuality, set in the larger context of the dangers of a way of life at odds with natural instinct and natural environment, I believe that it offers a coherence not yielded by the novel. It is the film's achievement to be more alert to the possibilities of the central situation than the novel is. If its makers had respected the original less than they did, they might have been more ruthless in pruning some of its extraneous aspects. As it is, Weir, immensely assisted by Boyd's glowing images and by the eeriness of Gheorghe Zamphir's pan pipes, has created a lushly ominous cinematic world which accommodates itself to a variety of unsettling interpretation. The reply to the question, "What happened on Hanging Rock?", is never given, but the film's visual power, the intelligent suggestiveness of its images and sounds, transforms the original text into a wholly new creation, and one that is much more worth discussing. The art form which depends on a mass audience — a fact often adduced to account for its crudification of written texts — has in this case produced a new text that not only pleased many more people than the original but is a more satisfying, if more uncomfortable, experience than its source.

Notes

1. Publishing history: Australia — Cheshire, 1967; Britain — Chatto and Windus, 1968, Penguin — 1970, 1975 (five times), 1976 (three), 1977 (two), 1978, 1979 and 1982; U.S. — Penguin, 1977.
2. Cliff Green, *Picnic at Hanging Rock: A Film*, Cheshire, Melbourne, 1975.
3. "Peter Weir: Towards the Centre", interview by Brian McFarlane and Tom Ryan, *Cinema Papers*, No. 34, September-October 1981, p. 325.
4. Compiled by Ross Lansell, *Australian Motion Picture Yearbook 1983*, Four Seasons Publications, Melbourne, 1982, p. 305.
5. "Of Ghosts Unlocked: A Dialogue", in Cliff Green's *Picnic at Hanging Rock: A Film*.
6. *Ibid*, p. xvi-xvii.
7. *Ibid*, p. xvii.
8. *Ibid*, p. xv.
9. *Ibid*, p. xix.
10. This comparison first appeared in my monograph, "The Films of Peter Weir", Special Supplement, *Cinema Papers*, No. 27, April-May 1980, p. 10. In the discussion that follows I shall draw on some of the material from that monograph, though my present opinion of the film, several viewings later, is, in some key respects, higher than it was then.
11. *Cinema Papers*, No. 34, September-October 1981, p. 325.
12. *Ibid*, p. 326.
13. Green, *op cit*, p. 55.
14. For those interested in more fanciful interpretations of the book (and the film), I draw attention to Scott Murray's review in *Cinema Papers*, No. 7, November-December 1975, p. 264; Phillip Adams' article in *The Age*, 1 November 1975, p. 6; and Yvonne Rousseau's witty, intelligent *jeu d'esprit*, *The Murders at Hanging Rock*, Scribe, Fitzroy, 1980.
15. Adrian Martin, "Fantasy", Ch. 6 in *The New Australian Cinema*, Scott Murray (ed.), Thomas Nelson Australia-Cinema Papers, Melbourne, 1980, p. 99.

4. The Getting of Wisdom

The Getting of Wisdom, by Henry Handel Richardson (born Ethel Florence Lindesay Richardson), was first published by William Heinemann, 1910 (page references to the 1968 reprint). After an Australian girlhood, described in *Myself When Young*, Richardson spent the rest of her life in Europe. Her other novels are *Maurice Guest*, *The Young Cosima* and her famous trilogy, *The Fortunes of Richard Mahony*.

The Getting of Wisdom was directed by Bruce Beresford, for producer Phillip Adams, from a screenplay by Eleanor Witcombe. The director of photography was Don McAlpine and the editor William Anderson. The music score included the works of Franz Schubert, Sigismund Thalberg and Arthur Sullivan. Running 100 minutes, it was released in 1977.

Since Henry Handel Richardson's is the first name to appear on the credits of Bruce Beresford's film of *The Getting of Wisdom*, one anticipates a respect for the informing spirit of the book. Further, it is perhaps reasonable to ask: how far is this a faithful film version of the novel? And, further still, this is not just any novel: it is a distinguished work by one of the two or three most universally esteemed of Australian novelists. That is to say, the viewer is all but encouraged to think of **The Getting of Wisdom** as the "film-of-the-book" rather than as "a-film-as-a-film". What I want to suggest is that the film, though often perceptive and amusing, goes most wrong when it does most violence to Richardson's view of life; in relinquishing the essentially grim view of her square-peg heroine and the limited success she grants her, the film loses coherence. That sounds as if I mean to criticize the film as inferior because it departs from the novel in certain important ways; in fact, it is inferior because it does not, having made such departures, find a coherence of its own. Insofar as it fails, the film fails *as a film*, not merely as an adaptation; its own creative impulses, working on an artwork in another medium, prove unequal to the occasion.

It is not that Beresford or his scriptwriter Eleanor Witcombe[1] have elected to play fast and loose with Richardson from the word go. In fact, for much of the film's length, it has preserved the shape of the novel's episodes and a good deal of its dialogue. Beresford and Witcombe have clearly been interested in certain aspects of the novel — Laura's adjustment to changing circumstances and the growth that derives from that, the ambience of the school and its repressive habits and effects — and like many Australian film-makers they have been drawn to earlier times. There is a certain nostalgia in Beresford's approach to his famous subject,

Opposite: Laura (Susannah Fowle) and her sister (Karen Sutton).

which is necessarily lacking from Richardson's 1910 novel; "necessarily" because she was so much closer in time to the events she (remembers and) creates but also, even allowing for that, because Richardson's book is a much tougher-minded piece of work. The things that have attracted Beresford seem to have been mainly superficial. He has missed the element that gives it not merely narrative coherence but also accounts for its tonal consistency: that is, Richardson's controlling irony.

It is not as though, with Richardson, Beresford was dealing with a novelist who, such as Jane Austen or Henry James for instance, has a dazzling verbal style. Richardson's lightest touch as a stylist is far from delicate; her novelistic skills lie elsewhere. She controls her narrative through the patient accretion of details — physical, psychological, social — submitting these to an ironic scrutiny that depends less on verbal facility or felicity than on sharply intelligent juxtapositions. She would, for example, be incapable of that line from *Pride and Prejudice* with which Jane Austen's subtle, ironic phrasing places Miss Bingley's malice about Elizabeth Bennet: "Miss Bingley was not so entirely satisfied with [Darcy's] reply as to continue the subject."[2] Richardson's irony works characteristically through the building and subversion of narrative expectations by a reality that both furthers the narrative and offers a comment on the expectations. For example, Laura's imagined arrival at her city boarding school, herself the cynosure of admiring eyes, is ironically undercut a dozen or so pages later with: "She felt forlornly miserable under the fire of all these unkind eyes, which took a delight in marking her slips" (p. 40). Perhaps Richardson's chief technical skill as a novelist is in the careful organizational procedures that enable one episode (sometimes just an image) to offer an ironic comment on what has gone before.

This irony is at the heart of Richardson's narrative structure, not just in small, individual episodes but in the shaping of the entire novel. She repeatedly described *The Getting of Wisdom* as a "merry little book"[3], but though many of its episodes are comically intended their implications are essentially painful. The author's pervasive irony casts doubt on apparent triumphs and warns that success and happiness are usually fleeting. The "wisdom" that Laura "gets" is the novel's central irony: she learns that an instinctive honesty of response is a dangerous attribute; to be wholly yourself is apt to make you disagreeable to others and a trial to yourself; to learn to cope with the world is found to be largely a matter of learning to deceive others. In an essay in 1977, I wrote:

> that, despite Laura's exhilarating run down the avenue at the end, *The Getting of Wisdom* is at heart grim in its view of life; that the run is, in the over-all view of the novel, not much more than a gesture on the author's part — and a misleading one.[4]

Misleading, that is, in the sense that it leaves one feeling that the book is "merrier" than has been the case. Virtually everything Laura has learnt has been presented ironically so as to evaluate its worth: she wins accept-ance from that pillar of aseptic rectitude, Mary Pidwall, by a toadying piety quite at odds with her own instincts; her religious fervour eventually founders on the shabby role God has played in her history exam, meanly letting unlearnt Cromwell appear at the expense of, say, the Eureka Stockade ("She could not go on loving and worshipping a God who was capable of double dealing", p. 228). Above all, education is presented not as opening out intellectually and morally but as a process of hammering in information and received standards without questioning them.

The prickly, likable oddity who is Laura at the beginning of the novel quickly learns the wisdom of conformity. This wisdom involves her in subterfuges large and small to win favour, and the suppression of her individuality when it seems likely to run counter to the prevailing *mores*. She becomes jealous, sly, unkind and hypocritical as the occasion demands (e.g., joining in the laughter against a girl whose uncle runs a newspaper, p. 69). But what inevitably separates Laura from her school-fellows is that she *knows* what she is doing: she both conforms and knows she is doing so, or, rather, that she is *trying* to do so: and she *knows* this because of what Richardson intends her to be in the novel. By that, I mean an incipient artist, who must always aspire to distinguish the true from the false in her society. Richardson has written that, though *The Getting of Wisdom* was intended as

> a more or less subtle story of a young girl's growth, . . . [Laura is] a girl with a difference. For this particular one was a writer in the making; and, even thus early, the taint of her calling was in her, marking her off from the rest of her schoolmates.[5]

The phrase — "the *taint* of her calling" — is revealing: Richardson does not at heart see Laura's situation as a happy one, "merry little book" notwithstanding.

Viewed in this light, not because Richardson tells us that that is what she meant but because it proposes a convincing account of the novel's coherence, I believe everything important in the novel works towards creating a "portrait of the artist as a young girl". And Laura is to be a particular kind of artist — a maker of conscious fictions of a very specific kind to which the experiences of the novel gradually and firmly direct her. If irony is the novel's dominant tonal element, its most prominently recurring narrative motif is the making of narrative itself. The novel — the film, too — begins with Laura's telling her younger sister and brothers a fanciful tale of a prince and beautiful lady, interrupted by sibling quibbling of a realist nature ("But what about the marks of travel?", etc.); the imagining of her arrival at school involves Laura in the dramatic aspects of fiction-making (e.g., the relation of character to setting, the effect of one striking character on others); and three of the book's major episodes — the expulsion of Annie Johns (Ch. 12), Laura's account of the curate's passion for her (Chs 16-18), and her dealings with the Literary

Society (Ch. 21) — all work towards establishing Laura's potential as a particular kind of writer. The only other narrative element of comparable power in the novel is Laura's passionate feeling for the older girl Evelyn Souttar, and even here the novel suggests that this capacity for emotional commitment is also crucial to the sort of artist Laura will be. She will — like her creator — be an artist whose work must be firmly rooted in auto-biographical "fact".

What I am suggesting here is that everything that happens in the book can be seen — *is* seen, I believe, by the author — as contributing to the growth of a mind which will ultimately seek to express itself in the writing of a certain kind of fiction. Laura is still far from clear at the end just where this will lead her, but perhaps the single most crucial piece of "wisdom" she gets is the one she gleans after her third — successful — attempt with the Literary Society. Rebelling against her "first bluff contact with realism [i.e., Ibsen]" and anxious for the recognition of the Literary Society, she first writes a wildly romantic tale of Venetian assassins. Chided for its patent falsity, she goes to the other extreme for her second attempt, and presents a disastrous 20-page account of "A Day at School" in which she "consistently set down detail on detail" and which bores her audience to madness. Like Richardson, Laura has to learn exactly how *much* fact is necessary to produce the effect of verisimilitude. And in her third — successful — narrative, she gets the balance right. Describing an imaginary excursion to the hills near her home, she arrives at what will be the secret of her narrative art:

> . . . neither this particular excursion, nor the exciting incident which she described with all the aplomb of an eye-witness had ever taken place. That is to say: not a word of her narration was true, but every word of it might have been true. (p. 196)

This episode ties together, is in fact the climax of, the recurring threads and motifs that have to do with the making of narratives, which is one of the book's sources of coherence. The dealings with the Literary Society illuminate the significance of those episodes referred to earlier.

The film, however, eliminates all reference to the Literary Society (a brief allusion to Laura's winning the Literature prize is inconsequential) and one sees why: the image of budding authors reading their juvenilia aloud is not one to rivet the eye. Nevertheless, Beresford and Witcombe's decision to omit this episode proves a dangerous and costly one for the film because they have not been able to find a cinematic equivalent. Without this key episode, the film leaves one wondering about the significance of the expulsion of Annie Johns or the invention of the curate's passion in the pattern of Laura's development. These remain isolated and not very meaningful episodes unless — as Richardson does and Witcombe's script does not — they are drawn together by a persuasive over-view of what they mean in Laura's growth as an artist.

Richardson is an essentially episodic novelist — a bricklayer rather than an architect, often working with superior bricks — who relies on the controlling irony of her vision to make those episodes cohere. The film treats these two episodes for more than their intrinsic value and for less than their representative importance. Their treatment in each medium calls for closer inspection.

In the novel, the expulsion of Annie Johns is central to the getting of Laura's wisdom; that it is Laura on whom Richardson wants us to focus is borne out by the fact that Annie Johns is never heard of before or after the event. The episode is central because it dramatizes both Laura's desperate efforts to conform to the behaviour of her fellows *and* her utter inability to do so. At the same time, *she* comes to recognize this fact. The Annie Johns episode makes her isolation clear to her; makes its source clear to her and to the reader; and, perhaps incidentally though I doubt it, offers the first important suggestion as to how Richardson goes about her work and the kind of artist Laura will be.

If there is something cruel in Richardson's curt dismissal of Annie Johns as "a very ugly girl of fourteen with a pasty face, and lank hair that dangled to her shoulders" (p. 105), it is because she wants to keep the reader's attention fixed on Laura and does not want it to be distracted by ready sympathy for the hapless Annie. Snarled at by Tilly for staring at Annie, "she tried to do what was expected of her: to feel *a decent unconcern*" (p. 106 — my italics, to stress the fact that the sort of conformity the school

At boarding school: Maria (Sigrid Thornton), Tilly (Jo-Anne Moore) and Laura.

enjoins and endorses precludes the inner activity of real feeling). Afterwards, having desperately tried to outdo her friends in revulsion at the crime, Laura is forced to admit to herself that:

> . . . her feelings *had* been different — there was no denying that. Did she now think back over the half-hour spent in Number One, and act honest Injun with herself, she had to admit that her companions' indignant and horrified aversion to the crime had not been hers, let alone their decent indifference towards the criminal. No, to be candid, she had been deeply interested in the whole affair, had even managed to extract an unseemly amount of entertainment from it. (p. 109)

The source of Laura's differentness is her much more vivid apprehension of Annie's plight and this apprehension is to be explained in two ways. First, "She understood what it would mean to lack your tram-fare on a rainy morning . . . because a lolly shop had stretched out its octopus arms after you" (p. 105). There is thus an autobiographically-rooted empathy with the thief. The next sentence — "She could imagine, too, with a shiver, how easy it would be, the loss of the first pennies having remained undiscovered, to go on to threepenny bits, and from these to sixpences" — offers the second explanation. Laura's *imagination*, fired by Mr Strachey's factual account, leads her easily to construct in her mind the likely development of events, to sort out the culprit's motives, and it is this which makes it impossible for her to respond with the "decent unconcern" of the others. It is not pity she feels, nor any other of the common reactions, but, rather, a sense of passionate excitement at the drama of the occasion. Richardson uses the scene to crystallize the peculiar sharpness of Laura's perceptions, to prepare the reader for the intensity of her later feeling for Evelyn ("Laura was shot through by an ecstatic quiver, such as she had felt only once in her life before", p. 107), and, perhaps most important, to show us the relationship between what an artist knows and feels *and* how she articulates this. Laura does not yet know how to value her response to Annie's situation, but she has made a first — and wholly unwilling — step towards knowing that she is different and has arrived at some explanation of the fact:

> The real reason of her pleasurable absorption was, she supposed, that she had understood Annie Johns' motive better than anyone else . . . And her companions had been quick to recognize her difference of attitude, or they would never have dared to accuse her of sympathy with a thief, or to doubt her chorusing assertion with a sneer. (p. 109)

The cool assessment implied in "pleasurable absorption" suggests the conscious artist's appraisal of her degree of emotional involvement *after* the event: it hardly tallies with "Laura's heart began to palpitate" and "the ecstatic quiver" of the page before. I labour this point because I think it shows in embryo a real insight into Richardson's methods. It is important for her to have felt an emotion truthfully or to have observed a situation accurately before she can *make* anything. Laura, pretty clearly the Artist as a Young Girl, has felt the ecstatic quiver, has "watched lynx-eyed, every inch of Annie Johns' progress", and now, at a remove from the incident, is assessing her own part in it. She has been a passionately committed observer, and as she tries later to sort out her responses she is profoundly disturbed at what she finds in herself. Strength of feeling and honesty in facing this invariably brings no joy to Richardson's protagonists.

As I have said, one of the major narrative preoccupations of this novel is in fact the making of narratives: fictional accounts based variously on factual material, both Richardson's and Laura's "facts". A moment's thought suggests how little "filmable" such a notion is, and of course Bruce Beresford has recognized this difficulty. However, recognizing is not the same as finding a way out. In my view, the film wholly mishandles the "Annie Johns affair", milking it for the wrong kind of melodramatic *frisson*, and building to the wrong kind of climax — wrong, that is, not because the episode moves away from its function in the novel, but because it fulfils no legitimate criterion of function in the film. By making Annie a friend of Laura's (Susannah Fowle), through conflating Chinky (Amanda Longman), Laura's hero-worshipper, with Annie, and by making the motive for Annie's theft her adoration of Laura, the film seeks to involve Laura in the incident on a much more conventional level than the novel does. The value of the episode in the novel — as a stimulus to Laura's creative imagination by showing how detachment and empathy work together — is lost and nothing replaces it. Laura's outburst afterwards to Evelyn (Hilary Ryan) — "I know how it feels . . ." — is too little, too late, and too sloppy-minded. Chinky's feeling for Laura adumbrates Laura's later passion for Evelyn, suggesting how little earlier experience guides people in emotional matters, but by using Chinky as Annie Johns the film obscures this function.

It is not just in the writing that the scene seems adrift from the rest of the film. Barry Humphries' otherwise well-controlled performance as the austerely Victorian headmaster has also been allowed to succumb to broadly melodramatic effects. There is enough melodrama in the "burst of eloquence" Richardson has allowed Mr Strachey ("Herewith, Miss Annie Johns, I publicly expel you from the school! Leave it, now, this minute, and never darken its doors again!") without this needing the emphasis of low-angled camera or of the close-up of Humphries' pointing hand or of the assembled girls' parting like the Red Sea to let Chinky/Annie through. Whereas Richardson tells us, "Laura suddenly grew calm, and could take note of everything that passed" (p. 104), the Witcombe screenplay's instructions point to a quite different sort of involvement: "Laura is horrified", "Laura drops her head as Chinky starts coming down towards her . . . Laura notices that one of her laces is undone, and her shoes are very worn", "Laura closes her eyes, not in prayer, but in horror" (pp. 71-2). The episode is directed and played as if it were some kind of climax and its placement in the film — much nearer the end than in the book, and *after* the episode with the curate — reinforces the claim Beresford seems to be making for its pre-eminence.

The business with the Rev. Shepherd, the new curate, takes on a very interesting thematic significance in the novel. On most occasions, the quality of Laura's imagination leaves her exposed in the narrowly circumscribed world of the school. Just once, for a brief hour, it makes her the centre of an admiring audience as she describes her visit to the curate's house, egged on by the girls eager for details of depravities in the vestry. The novel builds to this episode by showing Laura as hopelessly gauche with the other sex, and by making clear that she wants more from life than just marriage: "it was impossible to limit your hopes to one single event, which though it saved you from derision, would put an end, for ever, to all possible, exciting contingencies" (p. 133). In the interests of conformity, though, she dreams up an adoration for Mr Shepherd, then finds herself invited to his home for a weekend when he proves to be an acquaintance of her mother's. That he also proves to be an egoistic boor and bore and the whole weekend dreary in the extreme are of no consequence: what matters in the novel is the spur the visit gives to Laura's narrative powers. She sees lying as a means of ensuring success (a typically Richardson irony on the nature of Laura's "wisdom"), and, equally important, she is astonished at her own inventive facility: "And now, by her own experience, Laura was led to the following discovery: that, if you can imagine a

Left: the Rev. Shepherd (John Waters). Right: headmaster Rev. Strachey (Barry Humphries).

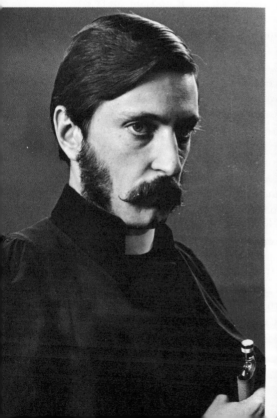

thing with sufficient force, you can induce your imagining to become reality" (p. 128). And after the visit she finds:

> . . . the plunge once taken, it was astounding how easy it became to make up things about the Shepherds; the difficulty was to know where to stop. Fictitious details crowded thick and fast upon her . . . But all the same she was not idle: she polished away at her flimflams, bringing them nearer and nearer probability, never, thanks to her sound memory, contradicting herself or making a slip, and always able to begin again from the beginning. (p. 151)

The whole episode is only mildly amusing and is drawn out beyond its intrinsic entertainment value. What stay in the mind are Laura's reflections on what you can persuade people to accept as truth and the feeling that Richardson is here offering a sort of apologia for fiction. (As Leonie Kramer has noted in her extended account of Richardson's "enslavement to facts", she was not always able to "induce [her] imagining to become reality"[6].) The value placed on a "sound memory", on "never . . . contradicting herself or making a slip", is unmistakable and has resonances that go well beyond this episode. At the heart of Laura's successful mendacity is her discovery of the relation between imaginative and factual reality. For Richardson to achieve imaginative reality required a basis in fact, as it does for Laura. The Annie Johns affair has taught Laura something about the quality of her perceptions; her fanciful account of the curate's lustful forays against her virtue teaches her something further about the nature and power of the imagination.

As I have said, the film reverses the order of these two episodes (presumably in the interests of achieving a kind of climactic effect with the Annie Johns affair), but, without the Literary Society episode to mesh the insights which the film — like the book — has given about Laura's growth as an artist, these sequences remain isolated. The film is amusing in its treatment of Laura's supposed "mash" on the Rev. Shepherd (John Waters). "They're not crams. Only stories", Laura tells Chinky, as she leads on the other girls with her fictions. The weekend with the Shepherds captures, through a skilfully deployed *mise-en-scène* of oppressive interiors and depressing people, in visual terms an admirable equivalent for Richardson's prose treatment of the scene, ironic in its contrast with the hothouse imaginings of Laura's happily deceived audience.

Unfortunately, well-done as this is in the film, it leads nowhere. The film retains enough references to Laura's talents as a fiction-maker to lead the audience to suppose these will add up to something in narrative terms. What the film has chosen to do is to present Laura in the end not as an incipient author but as a budding concert pianist — and the effect is that of crossing *What Katy Did* with **A Star is Born**. If one did not know that films are not shot sequentially, one would suspect that Beresford had lost his nerve about half-way through the film and decided instead to stress a musical motif as having more cinematic potential. To turn Laura into a

Evelyn (Hilary Ryan), for whom Laura has deep feelings, schoolfriend and Laura.

concert pianist might conceivably have worked if the film's musical references had been more coherently organized towards Laura's final success
and what it means in her development. As it is, it tends to make chunks of
the film, as well as many minor moments that seem to be pointing towards
a literary orientation, appear isolated touches at best, extraneous at worst.
What music means to Laura is never integral to the film; the fact/fiction
dichotomy that is often hinted at easily could have been.

The musical references — they are too sporadic, too unfocused, to constitute a motif — seem aimed at establishing a sturdy sense of selfhood in
Laura. When she first plays Thalberg's florid arrangement of "Home
Sweet Home" at the Stracheys' tea-party, she is expressing an exhilarating but undisciplined delight in her powers. For the other girls, having to
perform before the Principal is an ordeal but Laura throws herself into it
and the panning camera catches a stunned audience before it cuts to Mrs
Gurley (Sheila Helpman) twirling her keys in reprimand. Laura's individuality has been dealt the first of many repressive blows. Several scenes
later, Mrs Gurley tells Laura she is to have music lessons and then turns
smarmily to talk to Evelyn. The juxtaposition is important as all the film's
subsequent musical scenes and allusions are in connection with Evelyn.
The music mistress, Miss Hicks (Dorothy Bradley), is impressed with
Laura's playing of a Czerny study but, as soon as she leaves the room,
Laura turns to a "piece of Thalberg, taking out her emotions in the
playing". She is interrupted by Evelyn who talks her out of her sexual
terrors and then begins to play a Schubert Impromptu — "badly and with

difficulty".[7] Laura helps Evelyn with the difficult bits and the càmera catches them in smiling complicity. There is no further significant reference to music for nearly thirty pages in the screenplay until the following exchange takes place:

102. INT. THE MUSIC ROOM. DAY.
EVELYN is playing the piano. She makes a mistake. Silently curses, and is about to start again when she sees LAURA at the door.
    EVELYN (surprised): Hullo.
Laura is trying not to show her delight.
    LAURA (breathless): I thought you weren't coming back.
    EVELYN (smiles, pleased): I thought you weren't. How's your mother?
    LAURA: All right.
    EVELYN: My parents are still in Europe. So here I am again.
Laura smiles.
    LAURA (hesitatingly): I wanted to say I'm sorry . . . for being so awful to you.
    EVELYN: I didn't blame you . . .
A pause.
    LAURA: That Impromptu — it isn't really hard . . .
She crosses and sits at the piano beside EVELYN.
    EVELYN: Ho! Maybe not for you. Miss Hicks says that the trouble is I try to play only from the heart, and that Laura Rambotham plays only from her head.
EVELYN watches as LAURA plays the Schubert Impromptu.
    (pp. 77-8)

This scene uses the Schubert Impromptu again as a means of drawing Laura and Evelyn together, and the reference to Laura's playing "only from her head" is perhaps meant to indicate a new discipline in her efforts. It is not, however, glossed in any way, and comes at a stage in the film when Laura's musical talent has been almost forgotten. The scene of the opera performance to which Evelyn's relations take Laura contains a comment from Evelyn's aunt — "Evelyn tells me you are quite musical, my dear . . . what is it you play? . . ." — but Beresford has chosen not to use the public performance of music for the ironic effect he might have. Evelyn, several years older than Laura, comes to farewell her in the music room where Laura is practising furiously. Still smarting with jealousy over Evelyn's male admirer, glimpsed at the opera, Laura maintains her downcast gaze on the keyboard.

    It is worth noting briefly at this point that the feeling between Evelyn and Laura is realized in the film with considerable tact and warmth. Evelyn is seen at the edges of the film on several earlier occasions but her serious role in the film coincides with the development of the musical episodes. Eventually, Evelyn invites Laura to her bed to comfort her. There is sensuousness in the way the film handles this scene, with Evelyn beckoning from the lower right of the frame, the shot angled in such a way as to stress the distance Laura must traverse to accept the invitation.

However, I do not think it is a *sensual* scene and cannot share English critic Robin Wood's astonishment at the failure of reviewers, at the time of the film's release, to fall upon the film's lesbian content.[8] The truth is that the film, like the novel, in drawing on an actual and passionate friendship in Richardson's life has chosen to stress comfort and underplay sex. Neither film nor novel (the latter's reticence the result of Richardson's own tact) registers the kind of feeling Richardson described in her autobiography:

> Some may see in my infatuation merely an overflow of feelings that had been denied a more normal outlet. But there was more to it than that. The attraction this girl had for me was so strong that few others have surpassed it. Nor did it exist on my side only. The affinity was mutual; and that is harder to understand. For she was eighteen and grown up, and I but a skinny little half-grown.[9]

At Speech Day, several sequences later, Mr Strachey announces that Laura, having won the Woodfull Scholarship for Musicianship, entitling her to two years study in Leipzig, will play Beethoven's Sonata No. 21 in C Major. Laura, after looking around the Hall, as the camera pans teachers and pupils, begins to play Evelyn's Schubert Impromptu. Now, there are several things wrong with the way the film handles this scene, one wholly of its own invention. First, no one registers any surprise: the camera continues to pan, resting on several teachers but *not* on the music mistress whose reaction one might have supposed crucial. Second, there is no way in which the camera or Susannah Fowle can convey *this* piece of information from the screenplay: "There is one person, she [Laura] believes, she can thank for the Scholarship. Everyone else she silently loathes" (p. 91). The audience is meant to connect this with her playing the Impromptu as a tribute to Evelyn. (For the non-musical in the audience, the connection is elliptical indeed. They could be pardoned for believing that Laura's placing the unopened Beethoven on the top of the piano means only that she doesn't need it!) Third, I suspect the film's makers were motivated by the fact that Henry Handel Richardson was entered in the Conservatorium at Leipzig when she was 17. Perhaps, they hoped, this would round out the film with a touch of unexceptionable truth derived from the teller rather than the tale.

Well, it doesn't work that way. The scene becomes just another set-piece, like the Annie Johns expulsion. Its motivational roots have not been securely enough planted in the film for it to be acceptable as a climax to the most important things it has shown us about Laura: her effortless *verbal* inventiveness, her abrasive dealing with staff and students, the emotional turmoil of her relationship with Evelyn. It is simply an easy, romantic and dramatically flashy note to end on — or nearly end on, for there are still several gratuitous shots of staff and girls farewelling Laura in a way that feeds into her final triumph and is at odds with almost all that has gone before.

It would not be worth considering the film in this sort of detail if Bruce

Beresford and Eleanor Witcombe had not so obviously respected their source material. But they have been able neither to carry this respect through with literal-minded fidelity to the reality originally created by Richardson nor have they successfully created a new or coherent reality of their own. It becomes a film of incidental pleasures, fatally lacking an *essence* of its own. There is no sense in which the film offers a commentary on the 1910 novel's account of events 25 years earlier. It is almost as though Beresford is trying to make a 1910 film, give or take some over-anxious camera work. There is no sense of the 1970s about the film, so that at best it can offer only tasteful reconstruction without any attempt to locate in it any sort of contemporary significance. I am sorry to have to agree with Pauline Kael in her generally wrong-headed account of Australian films when she says: "When you see Bruce Beresford's **The Getting of Wisdom**, you are responding to a craftsman's view of something that is already finished."[10]

From the film, one can salvage a loving recreation of period (done with more restraint than some Australian films of the 1970s); some entertaining individual scenes, like the Strachey tea-party, and some sharply made juxtapositions; a hard-working if inevitably inadequate central performance from Susannah Fowle as Laura; and a gallery of lively supporting roles played by some of Melbourne's best theatre actresses. Lacking a firmer controlling intelligence and therefore, radically, a *centre*, the film cannot ultimately succeed either as an adaptation of a fine novel or as a new piece of art in its own right.

Notes

1. Eleanor Witcombe, *The Getting of Wisdom* (screenplay), Heinemann Education Australia, Melbourne, 1978.
2. Jane Austen, *Pride and Prejudice*, J. M. Dent & Sons, London, 1963, p. 34.
3. Reported in Nettie Palmer, *Henry Handel Richardson*, Angus & Robertson, Sydney, 1950.
4. Brian McFarlane, "The Getting of Wisdom: Not 'Merry' at All", *Australian Literary Studies*, Vol. 8, No. 1, May 1977, p. 51. Elsewhere in this chapter, I have adapted some of the material contained in this earlier essay.
5. Henry Handel Richardson, "Some Notes on My Books", reprinted in *Southerly*, Vol. 23, No. 1, 1963, p. 13.
6. Leonie Kramer, "Henry Handel Richardson", in *The Literature of Australia*, Geoffrey Dutton (ed.), Penguin Books, Harmondsworth, 1964, p. 328.
7. Witcombe, *Op cit*, p. 49.
8. The reference was made in a lecture at the State Film Centre, Melbourne, 8 December 1982.
9. Henry Handel Richardson, *Myself When Young*, Heinemann, London, 1948, p. 71.
10. "Pauline Kael and the Australian Cinema", interview by Sue Mathews, *Cinema Papers*, No. 40, October 1982, p. 24.

5. The Mango Tree

Ronald McKie's *The Mango Tree* was first published by William Collins, 1974, and reissued by Fontana Books, 1975 (page references to the latter). McKie's other novels include *Proud Echo* and *The Crushing*, which, like *The Mango Tree*, is set in a small Queensland town.

The Mango Tree was directed by Kevin Dobson, for producer Michael Pate, who also wrote the screenplay. The director of photography was Brian Probyn, the editor John Scott and the composer Marc Wilkinson. Running 102 minutes, it was released in 1977.

Ronald McKie's novel, the story of an *éducation sentimentale*, won the Miles Franklin Literary Award and the Barbara Ramsden Award in 1975. This confirms my suspicion that, in novels which win book prizes, a firm narrative is the last thing the authors have in mind. Helen Garner's award-winning *Monkey Grip* (1977) is further evidence for my no-doubt-untenable theory that the judges of literary awards find stories almost vulgar and that they will settle for Sensitivity and Experimentation any day rather than a novel which may promise a good read. By "a good read", one usually implies a strong grasp of narrative fundamentals, especially perhaps of causality and coherence. This is not to suggest that those who are interested in these qualities are indifferent to the development and revelation of character or to the evoking of a *milieu*; only that those who value narrative will tend to expect a character to be seen growing in and from action, and *milieu* not to be just a matter of setting but organically linked to narrative.

It is clear that *The Mango Tree* is, as a narrative, loose to the point of ramshackle. It is typical of the Australian fictional school of "sensitive evocation of burgeoning youth", its protagonist responding with every nerve a-quiver to the wonder of life. And in this genre, Martin Boyd (*A Difficult Young Man*), Don Charlwood (*All the Green Year*), David Malouf (*Johnno*), Kenneth McKenzie (*The Young Desire It*) and Randolph Stow (*Merry-Go-Round-in-the-Sea*), among others, have all done it with more skill and alertness and, sometimes, wit than McKie musters. Autobiographies like Graham McInnes' *The Road to Gundagai* and Hal Porter's *Watcher on the Cast-Iron Balcony*, freed from the formal constraints of fiction and merely shackled by truth, have achieved a greater richness of evocation and, at the same time, more success in a structural sense: that is, they have shown character growth as the unifying principle that binds the detailed observation of the natural and social worlds. *The Mango Tree* has a great deal of atmosphere, created in some rather lush writing, but not much sense of

Opposite: Grandma Carr (Geraldine Fitzgerald).

anything very significant happening in that atmosphere, hard as it tries to persuade otherwise.

The film, director Kevin Dobson's first and made when he was 24 and therefore close to his protagonist's age, captures the atmosphere all right. Lovingly photographed by Brian Probyn, it recreates a small Queensland town[1] and the canefields that surround it, at a time straddling the end of World War 1. But though it is often a treat to look at, the film loses the novel's, albeit tenuous, narrative link — that of Jamie's growing sensitivity — so that it seems even more than the original to be no more than a series of barely connected events. As a film it is worth noting for little more than its *mise-en-scène* — and for one performance which is as fine as any yet given in an Australian film.

McKie begins by invoking the natural setting:

> A black wind from across the mountains brought dust and grass seeds and a melancholy crying. It cuffed the long leaves of the mango tree, threw powdered cane trash against the windows. It spread dark stains on the river and the stains travelled with the tides until they were absorbed or taken to sea.

That is an apt introduction in more than one sense: it is characteristic of the novel (as of the film) in that its real strength is in establishing a place; it is also stylistically typical in that it walks a delicate line between the sensuously exact ("it *cuffed* the long leaves . . .") and the tendency to anthropomorphic over-writing ("a melancholy crying"), though there are much more extreme examples of the latter elsewhere. Further, the scene — the town on Christmas Eve — is created before Jamie appears (the film begins with Jamie's departure for the South, suggesting, quite misleadingly, that it knows where *its* centre lies). The point is that the novel almost invariably casts Jamie in the role of observer and reactor and this has a debilitating effect on its narrative grip. In this opening chapter, he watches the ritual preparations for Christmas Day from the mango tree, "though he seldom climbed it these days. He was too big and the highest perch among the topmost leaves no longer held him" (p. 10). He is, one infers, on the brink of a new set of experiences, and in this first, expository chapter it seems that McKie is laying the thematic basis for his narrative. Jamie, brought up by his formidable grandmother, has a powerful sense of continuity and community: "[he] belonged as a leaf belongs, as a stream belongs to the slopes where it is born. He was part of a whole that did not have to be explained" (p. 11). Nevertheless, he is also aware of an "alarming tumbling of his blood, a new and restless longing for something without shape or words" (pp. 11-12).

Unfortunately, McKie is not adept at working out his thematic preoccupations in terms of causally connected narrative, and there are several effects of this deficiency. The first is a somewhat numbing insistence on

Jamie's sensitivity, on his being on the verge of new awarenesses which both excite and alarm, and on his place in the human continuance he has known. McKie's failure to *dramatize* Jamie's position, poised between adolescence and manhood, leads him into a tiresome explicitness. Jamie "knew that he and the weeds and the sun and the sleeping birds and all things, the town itself, the buildings and everyone in them, were in harmony" (p. 50). And a little later, McKie writes, after his description of Saturday nights in town, that "Jamie roamed the town on many Saturday nights until weariness overcame his restlessness, his search for something he could not explain, and eased the feeling like crumpled paper in his guts" (p. 65). This recalls, and not to McKie's advantage, Stephen Dedalus' nocturnal ramblings and sexual restlessness in *A Portrait of the Artist as a Young Man*. The shifting mimetic persuasiveness of James Joyce's prose is quite outside McKie's range: McKie's prose is generally unable to enact the processes of growth and settles instead for merely telling.

The second damaging effect is that the novel quickly degenerates into a series of largely disconnected incidents. It is possible to sustain an episodic structure if the author's "voice" is compelling or distinctive enough to provide in itself a cohering factor, or if the episodes are seen to be at the service of some unifying thematic principle, or if the author can offer a central consciousness through which the reader views the episodes and which is itself largely shaped by response to those episodes. Henry Handel Richardson achieves this sort of control in *The Getting of Wisdom*: her own "voice", despite some stylistic deficiencies, maintains a controlling ironic detachment; she has a thematic interest in the growth towards self-knowledge and the sorts of obstacles thrown in its way; and, though Laura's career at the Ladies' College is a matter, largely, of discrete episodes, Richardson's interest is always fixed on Laura's developing consciousness.

In the case of *The Mango Tree*, for all the insistence on Jamie's responsiveness, the separate incidents for the most part remain obdurately that. McKie lacks a strongly individual narrative voice, and even its best effects (e.g., in sensuous evocation of place) are often vitiated by florid stylistic touches. The kind of thematic control that Richardson maintains is not matched here: Jamie's growth in awareness and self-awareness is a matter of narrative fits and starts and McKie doesn't develop the promised tension between a secure, established past and an inviting but in some ways alarming future; between, that is, the known and the unknown. Such a tension might have provided a narrative rallying point but it tends to surface in sententiae rather than in enactment. And, another point of comparison with *The Getting of Wisdom*, there is not even a consistent interest in Jamie's developing consciousness. All the material about Maudie Jones' dangerous romance with the draper's assistant, Angus McDonald, is virtually irrelevant to Jamie's growth. I am not advocating a rigid schematism whereby the relevance of each episode is clearly signposted; the point is rather that the novel has a disconcerting way of losing its centre of consciousness — and that McKie is not stylist enough to disguise this effect.

The book is constructed — to use the word loosely — on the principle of "one-damn-thing-after-another". The main events are as follows: Christmas preparations, with Jamie's grandmother, *chatelaine*-like, receiving gifts from the German and Chinese peasantry; the beating of the school dunce by a bullying headmaster; the town's Saturday night entertainments, including the "pitchers" and the "knocking shop"; the Sunday rituals; the professor's taking Jamie to the scene of the Boorool, the site of Aboriginal manhood rites; Jamie's appendectomy; Maudie's going to live with her uncle, the fanatical Preacher Jones; the dog plague; the war and the public rally it gives rise to; the preacher's ill-treatment of Maudie, his pursuit by the police, his shooting of Constable Scanlon, and his death; Scanlon's funeral, the subsequent race to the pubs, and the fire which gives rise to more drinking; the arrival of an aeroplane; the local show, circus, and Grandmother's annual ball; Jamie's private coaching by the French mistress, giving way to some very irregular verbs; love blighted; the end of the war; the cyclone; the influenza epidemic; the death of Grandmother; and — not a moment too soon — Jamie's departure for the South where, perhaps, life will be a little less crowded with incident. For this is all presented as the history of one year, with further events presented in flashbacks rather vaguely placed in time (e.g., Grandmother's rescuing Jamie from a runaway horse), and with interspersed descriptions of other aspects of the life of the town and district and of Jamie's grandmother's home. The novel's narrative procedure is essentially that of a string of beads, with a few pearls and a good deal of inferior glass, hung on the frayed and wispy thread of Jamie's growth towards manhood.

Some of these incidents are more obviously related to his growth than others. In creating a feeling for security that has governed Jamie's life to date, it is important that Mrs Carr, his grandmother, should be established as central to that "whole that did not have to be explained". When the Germans brought food "in return for help and favours" (p. 7), she is presented as a figure to be reckoned with, not just from Jamie's point of view but in the community at large. His apprehension of the inter-relatedness of small-town life derives from her egalitarian response to the needs of other people, across the class spectrum. She was "one of the rare few who knew the homes behind their [i.e., the Chinese] shops and was welcome there" (p. 7). In consequence, Jamie "had been reared with none of the prejudices of others in the town". He has also seen palpable evidence of her firm-minded, constructively generous help to others in her efforts to reclaim the professor, a drunken remittance man who describes her to Jamie in a letter left after his death as "the one and only memorable woman of my misspent life". She is a potentially interesting mixture of Presbyterian rectitude and liberal-minded pragmatism, a woman of strong principle but not easily shocked except by meanness of spirit. She dies, the reader assumes, as a result of her exertions on behalf of the victims of the 'flu epidemic.

The episode in which the professor takes Jamie to the site of the Boorool (not included in the film) seems meant to have an even more obvious significance in Jamie's growth. If observation of his grandmother has helped him to a sense of real security on many important issues and has given him a proper sense of the *past*, the visit to the scene of the Aboriginal rites of the preparations for manhood is clearly intended to reflect on his *present* situation. The professor describes to him the ceremonies related to the sacred ring of the Boorool, making claims for their unrecognized profundity and complexity of meaning. The rituals undergone by the young Aboriginals, poised as is Jamie on the brink of manhood, resonate with the notion that growing up was never easy and that it requires both a firm supportive tradition and courage in confronting the new. One cannot doubt how McKie wants this episode to be read. As the professor relates the ancient rituals, "Jamie felt the trembling. Deep inside. Like an underground stream flowing through him" (p. 77) and "shivered" as he thought of "those thousands of boys over thousands of years, who had been here and who, around these circles, had left their youth behind" (p. 81). "He felt incredibly old and incredibly young. He thought of the dark gods behind him, the dust of time . . . Of when he too would be a man" (p. 82). McKie clearly intends this episode to have a major

Grandma Carr and Jamie (Christopher Pate).

significance in relation to Jamie's own growth to manhood; his miscalculation is in not trusting to the symbolic force of the Boorool to fulfil its narrative function without recourse to portentous captions.

If the Boorool provides a correlative for Jamie's present situation, two further episodes have a more direct bearing on his *future*. In their way, each constitutes a sort of "blooding": one involves the death of Constable Scanlon by the crazed Preacher Jones, the other his sexual initiation at the gently eager hands of his French teacher Miss Pringle. Having assured himself of his grandmother's safety, he joins the search party in pursuit of the preacher and, though he faints with nausea at the decapitation of Scanlon, he refuses to go home. Though understanding the danger represented by the cornered preacher, he still "felt sorry for . . . the man up there, lost against the clouds" (p. 141), high up on the water tower. Jamie has been forced to look on violent death and has survived the nausea.

As for Miss Pringle's ministrations, it is inevitable that a sexual blooding must be a key element in the *bildungsroman* genre to which *The Mango Tree* aspires. Chapter 16 begins:

> At the end of the period, the last of the day, Miss Pringle said, 'I want to talk to you.'
> And Jamie knew. (p. 182)

The "knew" is archly equivocal: he knows his French is slipping, and he knows why. Miss Pringle's "cool hands" fix the latter, "And in a rocking pushing screaming pulsing world they submerged and drowned" (p. 185). In spite of the participial flourish here, the episode is handled with reasonable tact, and undercut by the final sentence, "And Jamie's French got worse and worse." His grandmother's reactions — she knows instinctively what has happened — are on the whole preferable to Jamie's own lush cerebrations: "If this was love he needed no other explanation, no excuse, no alchemy. It was enough. And enough that had no end and no beginning and was never started and never fulfilled" (p. 188). These do not compare favorably with Mrs Carr's matter-of-fact reply when he asks her how she knows: "It's not the first time I've seen rut . . . It's spread all over you. Thick as strawberry jam" (p. 189).

By singling out these episodes which plainly have a direct bearing on Jamie's development, and on the reader's apprehension of this, I do not mean to suggest that they are all equally well done. I think they are important to McKie's pattern but it must be said that the pattern is more a matter of intention than of successful execution. It is dangerous of course to talk of a writer's intentions; in doing so, I refer only to the kind of prominence accorded these episodes in the novel, a prominence which grows sometimes from their placement, sometimes from the author's clear insistence that the reader heeds the significance of the episode. Some other episodes seem designed chiefly to fill in the period background: for instance, the Grand Patriotic Rally at which Mrs Carr expresses some strong nationalist sentiments; the third anniversary of Gallipoli; the arrival of the aeroplane (Mrs Carr's "last adventure"); the end of the war; and the 'flu epidemic. These are, in themselves, adequately sketched but they intensify the impression of an invertebrate narrative. Nothing holds these episodes together, and they have only a tangential connection to the story of Jamie's development.

It is as though McKie is aware of the problem created by his undiscriminating narrative habits because he is pushed continually into spelling out the significance to Jamie of such episodes, when, in fact, his consciousness is not — for stretches of time — firmly at the novel's centre. As an alternative to the procedure adopted in *The Getting of Wisdom*, which builds Laura's role in, and response to, the novel's episodes into its narrative texture, a procedure which fails in *The Mango Tree*, McKie might perhaps have chosen to stress more the chief influences at work on Jamie. By these I mean his grandmother, obviously, the contrasting male influences of the professor and the preacher, the steady, solid kindness of Pearl, his grandmother's housekeeper, and Miss Pringle. However, only in the grandmother's case is there a full sense of McKie's knowing her from within, of a detailed understanding of how her character and her life work interdependently. McKie doesn't develop as richly as one might wish the interesting tension between her austere principles and generous compassion, but he does make her nationalism a convincing and palatable outcome of her long and well-lived life. The sketches of Pearl and Miss Pringle are adequate to the demands the narrative makes of them: that is, one sees easily the nature of their influence on Jamie.

The preacher and the professor are more important as representing conflicting ideological forces at work on Jamie's growth. McKie adumbrates the clash and contrast between them — "Preacher Jones and the Professor were flint and steel" (p. 106) — and allows them a rhetorical shouting match in the main street. The professor accuses the preacher: "You make God and religion hideous with your mouthings. Christ the gentle saviour. Religion the tolerant way. You make Him a monster and religion an obscenity", to which the preacher replies, "You scoff. You blaspheme. You, who spent your days and nights in debauch. A shameful example of the young" (p. 107). In his way, the professor, who "used to be" an Englishman and can never be an Australian, is a force for life: dissipated he may be, but he can still act with, and respond to, generosity. Mrs Carr clearly recognizes something worthwhile in him, and the novel acknowledges his inner value by allowing him the final rather high-toned letter to Jamie, and, more significant, by having him step into the breach as leader of the hunt for the preacher when Scanlon is killed. Again, the *intention* seems clear: the positive, life-embracing forces will overcome the dark, narrow and fanatical views urged by the preacher. As a small boy, Jamie has been afraid of the preacher; being present at his death is offered as a crucial stage in his development. However, if the pattern is there, the execution is again deficient: the professor is almost the cliché remittance man, given to addressing everyone as "Dear lady" or "Dear boy" and suggesting old world education at variance with the raw, pushful young nation in which he finds himself. Judith Wright's poem, "Remittance Man", gives a much more concise and moving account of the same phenomenon:

> The spendthrift, disinherited and graceless,
> accepted his pittance with an easy air,
> only surprised he could escape so simply
> from the pheasant-shooting and the aunts in the close;
> took to the life, dropped easily out of knowledge,
> and tramping the backtracks in the summer haze
> let everything but life slip through his fingers.[2]

As for the preacher, something genuinely dark and frightening is hinted at in his conflation of sexuality and religious fervour, but McKie is less interested in developing this in relation to the professor than in creating a marginal melodrama involving Maudie and Angus as victims of the preacher's wrath. Perhaps, too, the point about conflicting influences on Jamie would have been more strikingly made if McKie had resisted the temptation to make the preacher a madman. His life-denying brand of religion doesn't have to be allied to madness to be dangerous.

The preacher (Gerard Kennedy): "life-denying . . . religion doesn't have to be allied to madness to be dangerous."

In considering some of the novel's episodes and characters, I have been trying to make it yield up a coherence in structure and viewpoint which, finally, it will not do. As suggested, this failure derives from lack of either a distinctive authorial voice or a stronger sense of Jamie's consciousness as focus for the reader's attention. It is difficult to write about a book like *The Mango Tree* without seeming patronizing: it is essentially a kindly book, possibly a labour of love, with some attractive moments; but as a novel about growing up it doesn't begin to compare with the great works in the field. However, one doesn't need to invoke these — say, *The Mill on the Floss* or *Sons and Lovers* or *A Portrait of the Artist as a Young Man* — to feel the scrappiness of McKie's achievement. Even more modest achievements like Thea Astley's *Slow Natives* or Judith Guest's *Ordinary People*, novels which, in their tonally very different ways, offer a much more acute sense of the pain of adolescence, of the gap between perception and experience. McKie has relied too much on nostalgia and been too little rigorous in the ordering of his events to create a narrative whose hold would be more than sporadic and anecdotal.

There is some attempt in the novel to work up the eponymous mango tree into a symbol. Mentioned in the opening paragraph, it is then more fully described in Chapter 2:

> The tree was so old and freakish that as a child he feared it and even shunned its shade, but as he came to distinguish every limb and junction he was sure, with that still-bright awareness of children before explanations dull imagination, that it knew him and even liked him . . . The mango tree was a friend, a challenge, a peace, a game, a place to sulk, a place to sing impossible songs above the strings and flutes of scraping leaves. (pp. 13-14)

There is a good deal more in similar — and lusher — vein ("old wounds and fissures in the bark wept a crimson menstruation"), and one sees that the tree has, physically, offered the young Jamie a vantage point for viewing the town and a refuge. Nevertheless, though it is quite often referred to later in the novel (significantly, he is now outgrowing it), the references never really coalesce into a symbol. The tree is a presence but is never made in detail to bear the weight McKie claims for it in those early asseverations. As for the film, it retains the title, offers a few unobtrusive glimpses, but otherwise ignores it. The title reminds one of those crowded paintings that are called "Blue vase", but irrelevant synecdoche seems to matter less in relation to a painting than to a narrative art form.

Certainly the film does not open, as the novel does, with a description of place including the mango tree. It begins with a train whistle, with a young man, Jamie (Christopher Pate), waving goodbye, and, as the train pulls out and he settles back in his seat, there are soundtrack voices as he recalls figures from the past he is leaving. The older woman's voice, later to be identified as that of his grandmother (Geraldine Fitzgerald), is remembered as saying: "We're all innocent, only some are more innocent than others." Behind the ensuing credits, there is a shot of the mango tree, a pan to a large cool-looking house, a glimpse of horses and carts in silhouette and a cut to the young man cycling through cane fields. Such an opening sets up certain narrative expectations. After the first batch of shots on the train, the viewer might expect either to follow the young man's subsequent career or to find out what has led to this departure. The second batch, behind the credits, confirms the latter. In either case, to begin with the boy-man in the train suggests a focus for audience attention which the rest of the film scarcely gratifies. If the novel's centre of consciousness wobbles and dims from time to time, the film scarcely seems to consider having one.

However, as I speak of "the film", it is necessary to point out that it exists in different versions. The print shown on television re-arranges the order of incidents in a way that reduces the film's never very strong sense of coherence and cohesion. Apparently the film was cut by its producer, Michael Pate, after release. An account of its editing history was given by its director Kevin Dobson in a recent interview:

> . . . When John Scott [editor] and I were working on the film, we arrived at our cut. That was then changed a great deal, but John and I were able to change it back to some of its initial shape. The film was released like that. Then, once I had finished, I believe Michael Pate was able to get hold of more money and re-cut it again. I think he took out another five minutes, which was probably a good thing. But I wasn't involved, nor was John Scott. I spoke to Geraldine Fitzgerald in the U.S., however, and she said that she had given suggestions to Michael. Whether he was acting on them, I don't know.[3]

I quote this comment in full for a number of reasons. First, the film shown on television is the producer's re-cut version, certainly shorter (which is good) and certainly re-ordered (which is bad). Dobson, in my view, is right to have found the film too long at 105 minutes. Second, the comment stresses the collaborative nature of the film-making enterprise: when director, editor, producers and star all have a hand in determining the print the public will see, after the actual shooting has been completed, it is clearly difficult to apply the *auteurist* metaphor. Third, I should make clear that my comments will be based chiefly on what I take to be the Dobson-Scott cut which I have seen several times whereas I have seen the television version once only. In matters of continuity and dramatic coherence, the television version was in my view so seriously damaged as to be scarcely worth watching.

The film as shown in the cinema is very much worth *watching*. It is one of the most handsome-looking Australian films of the past decade, stunningly lit, full of wonderful contrasts of light and shade, heat and cool, of various times of day, and full of the most lovely compositions. Brian

Probyn, the director of photography, had previously shot the wholly idiotic **Inn of the Damned** and had contrived to make even it *look* good. Dobson has clearly responded to the re-creations of time and place which are the chief strength of the novel, and the eye is constantly ravished (even when the mind is not seduced). Bundaberg in 1917 looks an idyllic place to grow up in. There are misty morning riverscapes, marvellous shots of red paths cut through the green abundance of cane fields, sandy streets with lonely-looking verandah posts and ads for Mary Pickford and Your Country Needs YOU. As well, there are beautifully muted interiors, with stained tongue-and-groove boards, brass bedsteads hung with mosquito netting, a dinner table gracefully set beneath an elegant kerosene lamp, and weatherboard houses of unpretentious beauty or paint-flaking dilapidation. Scene after scene is unerringly composed and lit, credit no doubt due in varying degrees to director, cameraman, and art director, Les Binns. In general they have resisted, as the book does not always, the temptation to linger over the natural beauties they find in Queensland and their recreated township.

What no one — not Dobson, not producer-scriptwriter Pate — has been able to do is to conceal the fact that the gorgeousness of the film's patina covers an exceedingly rickety structure. The film never decides whether Jamie is chiefly a spectator or a participant in its action; nor is it clear how he is meant to be changed by his observation of, or his involvement in, the incidents which make up the straggling plot. For this, Michael Pate must bear the responsibility. Speaking of his working relations with the director, he claims, "I knew the book inside out, I'd written the script, and I knew the way the characters should work; and sometimes Kevin and I disagreed over an interpretation. Nothing serious though."[4] With hindsight, it is a pity that Dobson had been such a tyro at the time and thus not in a better position to challenge Pate's very fallible judgments.

There is of course no special point in apportioning blame but it must be said that the screenplay suffers markedly from a lack of structuring principle. It mirrors and exceeds the novel's faults in this respect, and only a much stronger, more varied and detailed central performance than Christopher Pate's Jamie might have papered over the cracks. The screenplay wanders disconcertingly from one episode to the next, from one point of view to the other. Almost invariably, one is more interested in what is happening to someone else than to Jamie. At the Patriotic Rally, he may be impressed by his grandmother's outspoken staunchness but it is in fact her stand that moves the viewer. When Mrs Plover, Maudie's mother, is taken off to the "loony bin", it is her blank disorientation and her daughter's angry held-in grief that move us, not what the observing Jamie is making of it. Christopher Pate may have seemed to his producer-father "the only actor who could do two things: handle the complexities of the character and be *masculine*"[5]. In the event, he cannot persuade the

Above: Jamie, who should be the film's centre, but isn't. Below: the professor (Robert Helpmann) and Pearl (Gloria Dawn), the housekeeper.

viewer — *this* viewer, at least — that anything is going on behind his conscientiously furrowed brow. Only in the obligatory but tactfully directed
scene of sexual initiation does he suggest an authentically adolescent
clumsy gentleness, and he is considerably helped by Diane Craig's
touchingly willing French teacher.

What is persistently missing is the sense of *pressure* on Jamie, the
pressure of a range of events internalized so as to lead to tension, anxiety
and growth. McKie's novel is weak in this respect too, but the very
explicitness with which I took issue in relation to it is at least an
acknowledgment that McKie knows where the centre of the novel should
be. When I reviewed the film on its release[6], I compared Jamie's departure
at the end of the film with Paul Morel's at the end of *Sons and Lovers*:

> For all the faults of his novel, Lawrence makes us feel that Paul's sensibility
> is its centre — however much we may resist the overwrought introspective-
> ness of some of the writing — and people and incidents take on a special
> importance insofar as they work on that sensibility.

Christopher Pate is too limited an actor (and too old) to fill in the screenplay's gaps or to pull its episodic narrative habits together by creating a
sense of developing consciousness.

McKie, as I have suggested, has trouble integrating the more blatantly
melodramatic aspects of the novel relating to the preacher but there is at
least a tentative move towards presenting him and the professor as conflicting influences on Jamie's growth. The film looks as if it is responding
to this hint by dressing the preacher (Gerard Kennedy) in black, making
him a physically imposing presence, and the professor (Robert Helpmann) in white, but it also fails to make the romance between the
preacher's niece, Maudie (well-played by Carol Burns), and Angus
McDonald (Barry Pierce) more than a side-track. There is at first an
interesting moral tension between the preacher's brutal life-denial ("the
devil works in all things") and the evidence of luxuriant natural life that
Brian Probyn's camera so tellingly details. The kind of climax for which
the film aims in the shoot-out in the deserted mill is at odds with the film's
gentle tenor and settles for an arbitrary narrative interest that takes little
account of Jamie's reaction to the episode.

Two other episodes call for brief comment because of the ways in which
they diverge from the novel. One has to do with Mrs Montague (Maggie
Millar), a "fallen woman", who has come to the town as a widow and
been befriended by Mrs Carr. Pearl, the housekeeper (a solidly realized
figure as played by Gloria Dawn), grudgingly admits "that woman" to
Mrs Carr's sitting-room where it transpires that she is returning fifty
pounds Mrs Carr has lent her. The point of the scene[7] is presumably to
dramatize the grandmother's egalitarianism and liberalism, the former in
receiving such a woman and the latter in her uncensorious appraisal of a
healthy woman's sexual instincts. The scene is well-written and touchingly played, Pearl's grim-lipped disapproval played off against Mrs

Montague's vulnerability and Mrs Carr's generosity. The scene is not even suggested in the novel and I assume it owes its place in the screenplay to the fact that the audience needs to see *in action* some of the grandmother's qualities which are described in the novel. It is followed by a scene, several sequences later, in which Mrs Carr virtually blackmails the headmaster (Terry McDermott) into a more charitable point of view relating to the expulsion of young Hatch. The headmaster wants to marry Laura Montague and Mrs Carr uses her position both in town ("I'm a person of some wealth and influence in this town") and in Brisbane where the teacher hopes to be transferred on marriage. Mrs Carr is quite charmingly pleased with herself, rightly believing her methods conducive to the happiness of several others. The whole thrust of these two scenes is to strengthen one's view of the grandmother's practical goodness. However, since Jamie can know nothing of them they seem curiously peripheral to the film's main action, and remain more or less incidental pleasures.

The other episode I referred to is the one in which the famous aviator, Robert Hinkler (Tony Bonner), comes to town. He is introduced as having flown with Jamie's father, killed in a plane during the war, as if perhaps at this stage of the film Jamie needs some reassurance about his father. Certainly no other man in the film offers a surrogate father figure. Mrs Carr refuses the offer of a spin in the plane[8], claiming to hate planes and having exacted a promise from Jamie that he will never fly in one. She relents and Jamie in fact has his flight, a thematic point having been made that he is poised for independence and her releasing him from his promise is a recognition of this. The novel treats the episode quite differently and for a quite other purpose. Here the aviator is not Bundaberg's celebrated flying ace, but simply a barnstormer who has come to town to make money from giving joy-rides. From this point of view, McKie is apparently adding a touch of historical progress and this notion is borne out by the complaints of the locals about how much he earns. More significant, in the novel, Mrs Carr is the first to volunteer for a ride, in spite of Jamie's being "scared for her, yet envious" (p. 166). He quickly realizes, however, "with a shock, how much this last adventure meant to her and how determined she was not to miss it . . . He understood and was happy for her." The novel wants the reader to see the episode as evidence of the courage for which Jamie admires her; the film wants the audience to view it as a step towards Jamie's manhood, following as it does his affair with Miss Pringle, whereas in the novel the aviator's visit precedes Jamie's bedding. In general, the film is less likely to keep its eye on Jamie's responses than the novel, or at least less likely to insist on their centrality, so that this alteration is worth noting.

The film's real strength is in Geraldine Fitzgerald's performance as Grandma Carr. She, not Jamie, is the heart of the film and the actress gives it a distinction that for much of the time leads one to forget the film's deficiencies. It was, in fact, a stroke of genius to cast this actress with the wonderful, lived-in face, still beautiful in its seventh decade, and with the irresistibly husky Irish voice that can crackle with authority and melt with compassion.

Geraldine Fitzgerald's career goes back to the palmy days of Hollywood in the 1930s and '40s (and earlier still in England) and, without ever being a major film *star*, she has always been one of the most interesting women in films. She had the opportunity to play great roles on the stage (e.g., Mary Tyrone in *Long Day's Journey into Night*) but in films she was too often maddeningly relegated to subsidiary roles. As Grandma Carr, she very nearly gets the chance she deserves. She makes her a great lady and a shrewd loving woman and, despite the fragmented nature of the screenplay, creates her *whole*. She makes sub-aphoristic lines sound as if she has just thought of them, and even her speech at the Patriotic Rally sounds as if it belongs to the character.

This performance fleshes out what sometimes appear in the novel as clichés of matriarchal wisdom and pioneering hardihood and takes up every suggestion for filling in the contours of the character as created first by McKie and then by Pate. Fitzgerald's physical presence and emotional resources bring together what seem scattered descriptive references in the novel (and, I should say, in the screenplay) and weld them into what is a recognizably coherent character. The controlled intelligence of her playing resists the screenplay's invitations to cliché. There is a dry wit in the voice, even when not in the lines, and a warmth and dignity in the bearing that constitute a powerful dramatic element in many scenes. Whether she is chuckling over a good story in the Bible, or blackmailing the headmaster, or reliving with dream-like clarity her encounter fifty years ago with a handsome bushranger, she appears to know quietly and exactly what the woman she is playing is like inside.

I have stressed this performance and this actress for a number of reasons. First, in the transposition from page to screen the actor — appearance (especially face), voice, movement, and gesture — is possibly the most potent single element the director has at his disposal in re-creating the illusion of reality first established by the novel. Conversely, an actor regarded as "miscast" will set up a barrier to the reader-viewer. As suggested above, Fitzgerald pulls together the collection of traits assembled first by McKie, then by Pate, and presents under Dobson's direction a fully-rounded *character*. Such detailed performances have not been common in Australian films. The way she is dressed (Pat Foster's costumes are excellent throughout) in high-collared Victorian clothes as compared with the brighter, more exposing costumes of the younger actresses makes visually an important point about her connection with a past age, and the loving care with which she chooses her jewellery, earrings in particular, makes another: dignified and austere in some respects, she also cares for beauty and has perhaps her share of harmless human vanity.

Second, she is very often placed in the screen's frame in such a way as to emphasize her physical bearing and importance. At the Patriotic Rally,

Geraldine Fitzgerald as Grandma Carr: "the wonderful, lived-in face, still beautiful in its seventh decade".

for instance, she appears at first seated at the left of the row of dignitaries in front of the crowd. Gradually, the camera pans the crowd and comes to rest on her face, now centre-screen. Severely dressed in black hat and dress, her speech by contrast is an impassioned cry (for national pride). In the beautiful dinner-table scene in which she talks of the bushranger's visit to her girlhood home, the camera and art direction reinforce Fitzgerald's virtuoso handling of the anecdote. Mrs Carr has dressed with special care for this dinner and the camera ensures that she dominates the scene by unfussily staying on her face as she calls up the memories. On a realist level, it is none too convincing that she should lean back against a beam and die having just said, "I'm utterly content"; as a way of gathering up visually a number of narrative leads it works with unobtrusive beauty.

Third, though this performance is easily the film's chief claim to distinction and its chief strength, it is also its weakness. Grandma Carr is an "achieved" woman; she has long since known what life is about and what to value in it. It is her grandson whose development should provide the film's dynamic, and, as I have said, does not. Whatever the reasons for this — inadequacies in the original novel's concept, or in the screenplay's anecdotal approach, or in Christopher Pate's playing — Fitzgerald's performance necessarily creates a shift in narrative emphasis in the film as compared with the novel. **The Mango Tree** is more memorably a film about grey power than of youth finding its wings. The film's *mise-en-scène* is able to register Mrs Carr's qualities in action in ways that it cannot reproduce the authorial comment in which McKie seeks to create Jamie's responses to his experience.

The book reads more like a reminiscence or memoir than a novel, its author suggesting a bricklayer rather than an architect. The film is never daring enough to hone in on the obvious unifying element of Jamie's growth, and settles by default for incidental pleasures. That the film offers as many of these as it does is almost entirely due to a radiant performance too strong for the structure meant to hold it. Geraldine Pascall in reviewing the film said: "In a good film this would have been a great performance."[9] There is a sad truth contained here: no matter how fine the actress playing Mrs Carr, other elements in the adaptation inevitably undermine her effectiveness. Even as one is admiring her, one is aware that in the interests of narrative coherence she ought not to be so prominently placed.[10] As it is, the reader-viewer is offered a paradox: the film's most wholly realized aspect of McKie's novel — the presentation of Mrs Carr — inadvertently works against the transposition of the novel's (presumably) central preoccupation. My interest in the film version of *The Mango Tree* derives chiefly from the power the actor has in altering the emphasis of the narrative; for those who feel strongly about "faithful" adaptations, this is a key matter to attend to. And it provides some evidence for the view that a director, even a much more experienced one than Dobson, could never be the single author of his film.

Notes

1. Largely photographed in Bundaberg, Queensland.
2. In *The Moving Image*, The Meanjin Press, Melbourne, 1946, p. 17.
3. "Kevin Dobson", interview by Scott Murray in *Cinema Papers*, No. 36, February 1982, p. 15.
4. Quoted in David Stratton, *The Last New Wave*, Angus & Robertson, Sydney, 1980, p. 258.
5. *Ibid*, p. 259.
6. Brian McFarlane, "**The Mango Tree**", *Cinema Papers*, No. 16, April-June 1978, p. 358.
7. In the television version, it appears considerably earlier than in the cinema version, to its disadvantage in my view.
8. According to those who know about such things, the aircraft is "an anachronistic biplane decades ahead of its time" (Keith Connolly, *The Herald*, Melbourne, December 1977).
9. Geraldine Pascall, "The way we were and the way we could be", *The Australian*, Sydney, 17 December 1977.
10. This is not intended to be ungenerous to Geraldine Fitzgerald; it is just that no one else in the film can match her performance.

6. The Chant of Jimmie Blacksmith

Thomas Keneally's *The Chant of Jimmie Blacksmith* was first published by Angus & Robertson, 1972, and by Penguin Books, 1973 (page references to the latter). Keneally, born in 1935, has won important literary awards for several of his novels, including *Bring Larks and Heroes*, *The Survivor*, and, most recently, *Schindler's Ark*.

The Chant of Jimmie Blacksmith was directed and produced by Fred Schepisi, who also wrote the screenplay. The director of photography was Ian Baker, the editor Brian Kavanagh and the composer Bruce Smeaton. Running 102 minutes, the film was released in 1978.

There is arguably a closer qualitative correspondence between Thomas Keneally's novel and Fred Schepisi's film version than between any other Australian novel and the film made from it. Through their sometimes strikingly different means, each provides an impressive telling of a serious, in fact important, story. Each shares a committed, passionate view of the hopelessly inhumane suppression of one race by another as it develops its narrative of Aboriginal Jimmie Blacksmith's aspirations to white culture and the subverting of these which leads to his taking a terrible revenge. Each text is impressive in its own way: the novel's spareness and irony work in essentially literary ways, though its rapid scene changes have something cinematic about them; Schepisi has opted for what the wide-screen can do better, which is to create Jimmie's solitariness against vast natural backgrounds and in the oppressiveness of antipathetic human contexts. The central narrative line has been scarcely changed in its transposition from one medium to the other.

And a very well-made narrative Keneally's source-novel offers. It falls almost symmetrically into halves: Jimmie's aspirations towards white civilization take up the first half; the second presents Jimmie on the run from the vengeful forces of that white civilization which both lured and rebuffed him. The dividing line between the sections is crossed in the massacre of the Newby women, which takes place in the novel's central chapter. None of this is intended to suggest that the novel is schematically organized, only that it is structurally cohesive and that its structure is part of its meaning. Further, the local life and particularity of the prose also work towards warding off the dangers of schematism. While the brutalization and corruption of a race is implicit throughout the novel, its power

Opposite: the half-caste Aboriginal, Jimmie Blacksmith (Tommy Lewis).

lies in its concentration on the life of Jimmie Blacksmith. Jimmie exists not as the illustration of a thesis but as an individual life whose course resonates suggestively and representatively. Keneally is readier than Schepisi to trust to this narrative resonance; he resists, where Schepisi does not always, the temptation to summarizing captions to be sure one gets his point.

The novel begins with Jimmie Blacksmith's attempt to enter the white world. His maternal uncle, Jackie Smolders, "was disturbed to get news that Jimmie had married a white girl in the Methodist Church at Wallah" and "felt distressed, a spiritual unease over Jimmie Blacksmith's wedding". Property and a white wife are, in Jimmie's eyes, the keys to that door that opens on the world he is encouraged to yearn for. With that ease of temporal movement which the novel shares with the cinema and which is denied the stage, Keneally flashes back first to Jimmie's birth and then to his tribal initiation. In the matter of Jimmie's birth, Keneally records laconically: "Half-breed Jimmie had *resulted* from a visit some white man had made to Brentwood blacks' camp in 1878." The italics are mine; Keneally trusts to his spare prose to establish Jimmie as the passive victim of historical "fact". This sort of "fact" involves blackwomen's being "rolled by white men", a result of which is "pale children" as the missionaries had warned. Keneally's irony works quietly and firmly as he relates that Jimmie's mother "believed the missionaries more or less. They took such a low view of lying in other people that they were unlikely to lie themselves."

If white veracity is obliquely appraised here, a few paragraphs later the blacks' more casual approach to truth is reflected. Jimmie has been taken from the mission station for his tribal initiation, and when "the super-intendent, Rev. H. J. Neville, B.A., kept asking where Jimmie was . . . [he] was not incommoded with any part of the truth." Already there is a suggestion that the whites' distortions of truth are in the interests of promoting their culture, forcing it on the blacks, whereas the blacks' distortions are, at most, intended merely to protect theirs. There is also a sense of their not wishing to distress, or incommode, by passing on what may be unpalatable. This somewhat laboured glossing is to indicate how much Keneally is able to suggest about Jimmie's background in the first two pages. There may be something cinematic in the fluid movement from 1900 (marriage) to 1878 (birth) to 1891 (initiation), but the ironic resonance created in words like "resulted" and "incommoded" is entirely a literary achievement. Through it Keneally gives not merely certain crucial pieces of narrative information but, concurrently, his point of view on these events and, to go further, an adumbration of the view that will create and feed the novel's over-all tonal colouring.

Rev. Neville is one of those who urges Jimmie to aspire to white goals, without any sense of what he is urging. "'If a person could be certain,' he said, a little peevishly, 'that he had imbued *one* of them with decent ambitions!'" (p. 4). The obliqueness of "a person" seems intended to clear him of mere personal moral ambition; the italicized "one" reflects his view of the general unteachability of the blacks; and for "decent ambitions", read "*white* ambitions". Neville is not a bad man; he in fact means nothing but good, as he sees it, for Jimmie. But his comment when Jimmie disappears for the initiation — "Blasted blacks! . . . The best of them are likely to vanish at any time." — sketches the limits to his understanding. Neville canes Jimmie for his truancy; he is unable, as Jimmie is not, to hold tribal and Christian ideas together. As the narrative proceeds, Jimmie will lose this capacity as he realizes the unbridgeable disparity between the two sets of ideas. It is his particular tragedy to be not a black man oppressed by the dominant white race and its ideology but to be the man in the middle. The tribal ways cease to have meaning for him and the whites with whom he comes in contact deny him access to whatever meanings shape their lives.

"If you could ever find a nice girl off a farm to marry, your children would be only quarter-caste then, and your grand-children one-eighth caste, scarcely black at all" (p. 7). In words like these the Nevilles lure Jimmie into the world of "decent ambitions", the idea enforced by a double irony. "Yer gotter better yerself, Jimmie", said Dulcie, his mother, unconsciously equating betterment with the idea of white aspiration. The other irony is that the Rev. Neville, advocating a nice white girl for Jimmie, had himself "often felt the distinctive pull of some slant-grinned black face". Jimmie, a willing pupil, yearns for a white girl, and for the other ("decent") ambitions that go with love: "landowning ambitions, ambitions for contracts, for bonding one's word and sticking to a job until it was finished" (p. 11). He is utterly willing to embrace white lore and, in doing so, "lost his black core . . . [which] had been eroded by the Nevilles' ceaseless European pride" (p. 12). After a night in gaol, he washes himself "unsparingly" in the yard, in front of the constable: "He felt elated, enough to pity the policeman. Jimmie Blacksmith was baptizing himself a white man, whereas there was nothing the constable could give himself" (p. 13). When Neville secures Jimmie's release, Jimmie assures him that he wants to be free of "that crowd. I gotta start working so I kin git property" (p. 14).

All this preliminary to his first job — for the stingy, brutal Irishman, Healy — is densely textured and evocative in Keneally's lean prose, which cuts dextrously from white hypocrisy to black messiness. "Jimmie's criteria were: home, heart, wife, land" (p. 15). In pursuit of these, he is in flight from his black origins and constantly up against white rebuffs. Cheated by Healy's skinflint treachery, Jimmie next takes a contract with an old Scot called Lewis who fears Jimmie will "turn me property into a blacks' camp" when his brother Mort arrives. Jimmie is in fact "wary" of Mort's love and his easy humour ("All the bloody time laugh, Mort, it's no good", p. 29). For Jimmie, in spite of his unpromising experiences with Healy and Lewis, is now caught between the two worlds, drawing strength from neither, cutting himself off from the black and refused serious entry to the white:

> For he was a hybrid. If he had been a tribal man, Love would have been written into the order of his day. All his acts would have been acts of solemn and ritual preference. Love would have been in their fibre.
> But having chosen to grub and build as whites do, he knew that love was a special fire that came down from God. A mere visitor. After a brief hectic season, it extended itself more soberly to your children and the boundaries of your land.
> Suspended between the loving tribal life and the European rapture from on high called falling in love (at which even Mr Neville had hinted), Jimmie Blacksmith held himself firm and soundly despised as many people as he could. (p. 27)

That is perhaps Keneally's most explicit statement of the half-caste's tragedy but it avoids didacticism through the drama of its language, through its easy mimetic rendering of the two ways. The loving rituals of the tribal life are suggested in language that contrasts in dignity with the dry irony of the prose which creates the etiolations of love in white culture.

Jimmie is educated into a world of white aspiration by the Rev. Neville (Jack Thompson) and his wife (Julie Dawson).

In order not to be lumped with those "blasted blacks . . . likely to vanish at any time", Jimmie works conscientiously to suppress his distaste for the varieties of white meanness and hypocrisy he meets, and embraces notions that make him seem "whiter". For instance, in his urge towards possession and property, he quite early loses the blacks' communal approach to ownership. In answer to questions about how much money he has, "'Christ!' Jimmie screamed and took notes and silver from his pocket and pelted them at the dust":

> It was a great loss to him. It was the measure of his experience of the world, his £2.15s. It should not have come from him so easily. Now he only had the things that swagmen have, flour, beef, tobacco. (p. 30)

The old ideas of sharing are — like Mort's laughter — a threat to Jimmie's white aspirations. These next lead him to become a policeman and to align himself with the corrupt Senior Constable Farrell in tracking down black Harry Edwards who killed a white boy. Jimmie's passion for acceptance in his new role works successfully against his awareness of its obscenity. But not for long: in the gaol Farrell sodomizes Harry who later is hanged on Farrell's belt. At this Jimmie leaves the police force, and Farrell echoes Neville's earlier comment with "Yer just git one of them into shape and they go off on bloody walkabout."

Alongside Jimmie's aspiration to property and possession is the associated, powerful need to find a white wife. After joyless sexual encounters with black and half-caste girls, Jimmie fantasizes about Mrs Healy, electing her to the

> stature of ideal landowner's-wife. It was not simply a matter of her being full and ripe: he could not have been so potently stirred by aspects so directly sexual. But combine these with her impassive air, her peculiar way of sitting still in the dray and breathing out into the morning a vapour of worship and submission for her husband — and you had something that appealed to all Jimmie's lust. In a second she had become a symbol, a state of blessedness, far more than a woman. (p. 21)

That catches astutely the thought process that moves instinctively from the physical perception to the emotional associations to the symbolic level. The note is taken up later in Jimmie's appreciation of Miss Graf, the schoolmistress who lodges with the Newbys. Compared with the "big, meaty, thick-pored" Newby girls, "although Miss Graf was a big country girl herself and could eat a pound of steak without feeling satiated, she gave off a soft musk of delicacy and knew etiquette" (p. 61). Jimmie's yearning for white women is not mindless lust; it is the result of a careful accretion of observations relating to their appearance, behaviour and demeanour, and something more, too: an effortless, perhaps even unconscious, power they exert, especially over men.

Ironically, though Jimmie Blacksmith's bride will be white, she is the antithesis of these firm-fleshed mysteriously powerful women. At the

Hayes' sheep station where Jimmie works as a sweeper on the shearing floor, Gilda is the kitchen-maid, got, it was said, "from a home for wayward girls in Sydney". But, Keneally adds, giving Jimmie's view of Gilda,

> this one did not look pretty or individual enough to justify the adjective. Her face was narrow. Most of the time she fretted about the house, her mouth gaping adenoidally to serve Mrs Hayes. (p. 47)

From the start, Jimmie feels superior to everything about Gilda but her whiteness. She has none of that subtle rich appeal, part-sensual, part-cultural that emanates from women like Mrs Healy or Miss Graf; she is unprepossessing physically and in every other way. After making "love so dismal that Jimmie, at the summer's end, could scarcely remember a single tone of its emotion or even a physical feature of it" (p. 49), Gilda is pregnant (though not by Jimmie) and Jimmie is resigned to marrying her. He is aware that she is stupid, "But a start had to be made somewhere with white women." Keneally discriminates finely among the ways in which various white women appear and appeal to Jimmie, and there is pathos for both him and Gilda as he considers "the thin, frightened girl-child he would marry".

The two motifs of property and a white wife come together when Jimmie takes work at the Newbys' property. Jimmie brings the "frightened girl-child" to the home he has built for them on the Newby land, a "little one-room house with its flue of beaten tin. The floor was earth and cold. There was a hessian bag inside the door as a doormat" (p. 59). It is not much but it is a start and, to comfort himself as much as Gilda, "Jimmie found himself making white promises about the land they would come to own." The centrally placed Newby episode, in which it appears at first that Jimmie is being more humanely treated than before, ends with the destruction of his hopes and the brutal murder of the white women whose pale flesh and mysterious authority he has craved.

The one-room house, that symbol of the property he knows to be crucial to white culture, is threatened by the arrival of Jimmie's three black relations: Tabidgi, Mort and Peter. Threatened partly because they do not share his idea of ownership, and partly because Newby uses their presence to withhold the supplies necessary to maintain this frail home, now that "the place has turned into a blacks' camp" (p. 69). Jimmie has been deceived again in money matters by white men; the birth of his son proves him to have been deceived by a white woman. A white bride has been his aim; so far from its being a shrewd move in his upward climb, it has been a source of humiliating deception.

To compound the humiliation, Miss Graf tries to persuade Gilda to leave Jimmie and come to work for her and her future husband. Miss Graf becomes the chief focus for Jimmie's revenge, the climactic working of the way racial fears and sexual tensions inflame each other. (Shortly before, Newby has exposed himself to Gilda, asserting genital superiority to any black she may have known.) It was not Newby that he wanted:

> When he put his rifle against Newby's gut, he knew that he wished to kill that honeysmooth Miss Graf. His desire for her blood, he understood, came as climax to his earlier indecencies — relinquishing Harry Edwards to Senior Constable Farrell, for example. He wished to scare the school-mistress apart with his authority, to hear her whimper. (p. 78)

This dream of blood — soon to be an actuality — is the nearest Jimmie will come to possession of Miss Graf's symbolic white smoothness. Shortly after, in prose of appalling clarity, Keneally tells us that Jimmie "then chopped Miss Graf leisurely between hip and the ribs". (This massacre, as Jimmie deals with the Newby women, is a major challenge to a film-maker and it is one that Fred Schepisi meets with both discretion and power.)

In this episode in which the blood-letting is created with a laconic detachment that intensifies its horror, Jimmie knows he has crossed a line. The world of white aspirations towards hearth and home and family has brought him this far; in the second half of the novel he is in flight from the retributive forces of that world — from the police and from the posse led by Dowie Stead, Miss Graf's conscientiously grieving fiance. Such tragic dimension as the novel achieves is in Jimmie's awareness of what he has done and what it means. He has declared war. Observing the results of the massacre:

> Though he felt buoyant enough, Jimmie Blacksmith knew that he had become an incurable. He knew in an instant that he must see into his acts the fervid illusions they were based on. He chose therefore to know and not go mad.
> At the same time he must be able to see the four hewn women as culprits, and so the mere beginnings of an agenda of mayhem. (p. 81)

In his "new era", Jimmie, having set Gilda and the baby off on the Dubbo road and leaving Tabidgi and Peter on another track, is delighted to be left alone with Mort and lives "cleanly with his brother in the forest". The proprietorial aspirations that have sustained him to this point drop suddenly away.

What he does need to sustain him in this "new era" is an awareness of his pursuers and he feeds hungrily on newspaper reports of his crimes, for "items that proved his own reality" (p. 125). He is sustained too by the sense that the punishment he had dealt out has been thorough and effec-tive, and, in a curious sense, is soothed and cheered "by the rigour of official opinion, by the absolute nature of outlawry" (p. 127) when a Government Bill is posted allowing the Blacksmiths to be shot on sight "by any citizen using any means of execution". There is a kind of purity in the official response that matches his own and contrasts with the reactions of Dowie Stead who, while feeling "elected to give chase", is also worried "that he was lightened every time he remembered that now he did not have to marry [Miss Graf]" (pp. 90-1). It contrasts too with the prurient interests of Ted Knoller, necrophiliac customer of Mr Hyberry, the Balmain butcher-hangman, whom Knoller tries to draw out on the subject of Jimmie's likely fate.

The novel loses some of its spare clarity in its latter part but it acquires an almost cinematic ease as it moves from one group of characters to another. Running through its episodes is the motif of resignation from "the white cycle" of permanence and property, and the adoption of and adaptation to the "journeying life, each camp no true point of arrival" (p. 104). This journeying life is conducted against a background of discussion about the Boer War ("I mean, all they [the Boers] wanted to do was to have their land and keep the black man in his place. Isn't that our policy, here tonight?" asks one of Dowie's men) and of the Rev. Neville's concern for Jimmie's "sickness". Keneally, aware that "The Blacksmiths had the tedium of ceaselessly outdistancing their pursuit" (p. 113), has to rely on the reactions of others to the pursuit to maintain a satisfying narrative texture.

As if aware that a story of easily outwitted pursuit will lack the drama of the novel's first half, Keneally engages in several strategies. First, the brothers do not find their comparative safety in the coastal valleys enough. Though they might have lived there undetected forever, "Yet they would not have chosen to. To deliver themselves from the ceaseless trees, they willed deliberate crises on themselves" (p. 133). This urge perhaps explains in part the episode in which they throw themselves on the hospitality of the "low Irishman", Mullett; the return to Healy's farm and the killing of Mrs Healy whom Jimmie could "sense . . . at the glowing heart of the house"; and particularly the wholly unnecessary visit to Tambourine Public School. This willing of "deliberate crises" on themselves works both as a convincing response to their situation *and* as a shrewdly placed narrative device.

Second, after the visit to Tambourine School, they acquire the teacher McCreadie, as a "hostage"[1], which they don't need, and as a distraction, which they do — a distraction from each other and from the emptiness of their successful evasion of their pursuers. From the start, "they had been treated with a sort of respect" (p. 137) by McCreadie whose educated presence enables them "to speak in their true selves". However, the "McCreadie-Blacksmith connection" doesn't work quite as Jimmie has planned. He becomes, in fact, a necessary third party between the brothers who "could not imagine speaking to each other without McCreadie about. Also, McCreadie filled and diverted their day" (p. 145). With a respiratory problem, McCreadie quickly becomes a physical burden and not long after another sort of burden because of his perceptiveness and persuasiveness as a talker. Keneally runs the risk of making McCreadie too obviously a liberal mouthpiece, the one white character free from cant and venality and viciousness, but generally avoids this cliché-trap by the unexpectedness of some of McCreadie's responses. When the brothers are fighting, for instance, McCreadie "let out his classroom roar":

> 'Be quiet!'
> The arguing brothers were jolted more than they cared to be.
> McCreadie said severely, 'If you stand there comparing evils, you won't stop till you've shot each other through the heart. You ought to know that no one does a murder unless he wants to.' (p. 140)

The sudden evocation of schoolroom discipline in the damp forest setting, followed up in the didactic implications of "severely", strikes a note both original and convincing. And so does Mort's response to this reprimand: he "put on a sulky face, as if he were hurt to be lumped together with his brother the axe-murderer, and disappointed by McCreadie's poor opinion of him".

Though McCreadie fills and diverts their day as, indeed, at this stage he helps to fill and divert the narrative of pursued and pursuers, he will eventually drive a wedge between Jimmie and Mort — Mort who used to laugh too much and has now nothing to laugh at. The use of Mort is the third and perhaps the major narrative strategy in the latter section of the novel. If there is an element of the tragic hero in Jimmie, making a beleaguered stand against the world which has mocked his ambitions,

Jimmie and Mort (Freddy Reynolds), while on the run, return to the Healy farm.

there is only pathos in Mort, and the distinction is important to our perception of Jimmie. In the passage quoted above, Mort no longer wants to be "lumped together" with Jimmie, and Keneally makes very moving the growing rift between the brothers. When the trio arrives at the sacred land, now defiled by white graffiti, the difference between the two brothers is clear:

> Mr Jimmie Blacksmith, mighty terrorizer, lost beyond repair somewhere between the Lord God of Hosts and the shrunken cosmogony of his people. Mort Blacksmith, however, still had his nearly intact black soul. Surely his brother saw it, McCreadie hoped. (p. 148)

As Mort, helped by McCreadie, tries to build up again the sacred place, Jimmie's response is altogether more ambivalent; he acts "as if from curiosity but with massive secret fear". McCreadie tries to persuade Jimmie to leave Mort, to give him a chance:

> 'The boy isn't really your brother. He's an aborigine, Jimmie. Not like you. There's too much Christian in you, and it'll only bugger him up. Like it's buggered you.' (p. 151)

Mort is essentially and wholly a victim — a loving, unaspiring nature, caught up in dreadful events — and he is shot while lying in the long grass after delivering McCreadie up to white help. Lacking Jimmie's aspirations, he also lacks his stature; not being in any crucial sense an agent, he cannot, equally, be a hero. Mort is still lapped in the mystery of black tribal love, jerked out of it by violent association with Jimmie; Jimmie has actively sought to shape his own destiny in a world which both lures and rejects him. Cut off long since from black tribal life, Jimmie is finally caught, ironically, in the bishop's bed of an Ursuline convent and, in due course, hanged by Mr Hyberry, taciturn executant of white justice.

Between Mort's death and Jimmie's capture is a curious episode, which, unsurprisingly, is not found in the film. After having half his face shot away, Jimmie drags himself to an empty school residence where he comes upon a batch of love letters from a Member of Parliament to Clarice, the teacher's wife. The MP is married to an invalid wife but writes to his "beloved Clarice" that "I could not get through my week without your letters" (p. 167). In between urging Clarice to join him in Sydney where he will "install [her] in a house", he regales her with accounts of his political opportunism. In the last letter he breaks off the correspondence in the interests of his career. The narrative point of the letters seems to me to lie in their being the novel's final, clinching example of the sterile nature of white love which, nowhere in the novel, has offered any grounds for Jimmie's ambition to attain it. In none of the white relationships — the Nevilles, the weak Rev. Treloar and his aggressive wife, Miss Graf and her lubra-loving fiancé Dowie — is there any sense of a

Opposite: Jimmie, "lost beyond repair somewhere between the Lord God of Hosts and the shrunken cosmogony of his people".

true mutuality, of a commitment to each other which transcends personal interest or which is free from debilitating weakness. The correspondence to Clarice is the final attenuation of this "European rapture from on high called falling in love". One can only guess at Clarice's lonely pain at receiving the final, venal evasiveness of "Be assured of my undying respect" (p. 167).

The novel's shape has been dictated by Jimmie's desire for a white bride and the sense of proprietorship that would accompany it. He has been willing to endure abuse and deception in moving towards his goal, untouched by the evidence of the unprepossessing white relationships he encounters. It may be claimed that Keneally offers a too-easy polarity of black/white experience; that he doesn't dramatize adequately the kinds of spiritual support of which black tribal life is said to be a repository, or that the examples of white love are chosen with a wayward particularity that unduly prejudices the case. There is no doubting the compassionate irony of Keneally's point of view, implicit as it is in the austere power of much of the prose or in the witty detachment that on occasions underlines the sheer horror of the scene. Certainly his "voice" is there in the prose, shaping reader responses, perhaps sometimes manipulating them more than necessary. This explicitness is felt in some of McCreadie's liberal tone, chastening both white experience and Jimmie's madness with a kind of judicial "fairness" that is scarcely necessary. Earlier in the novel Keneally has counted on his meaning's being made in the action of the narrative, in the taut resourcefulness of the prose. I do not, however, find this tendency to over-explicitness a major fault, even when it is attributing to Jimmie an articulate awareness one has reason to believe is beyond him. It is easier to construct a persuasive narrative around the dramatization of active pursuit of aspiration than around being pursued on a downhill trail, and Keneally has not altogether avoided the difficulty. He has nevertheless taken a terrible theme and, by exploring it through a particular life, not dishonoured its importance.

It is not always easy to be sure of a film director's point of view in relation to a particular film but the matter is likely to be clarified if he is also the author of the screenplay[2], as Fred Schepisi is in the case of **The Chant of Jimmie Blacksmith**. There is no doubt that Schepisi shares Keneally's compassionate point of view but he trusts his narrative less surely than Keneally does. Keneally's authorial comments sometimes articulate responses that would be beyond Jimmie's verbalizing capacities and one is prepared to accept these as the legitimate function of the omniscient author in dramatizing thought processes (for an example, see the early discussion on Jimmie's contemplation of Mrs Healy). Schepisi, on the other hand, has on certain crucial occasions succumbed to the temptation to spell things out, to say what the novel was prepared to leave implied. A revealing comparison is in the way Keneally and Schepisi pursue the following speech by McCready[3]:

'I can understand your being angry,' he would say in the midst of a night silence. 'Oh, I can imagine it, Jimmie. I mean, settlers still talked about *marauding blacks*. Only ten years ago they did. But how many whites really ever got killed by aborigines? No one knows. I bet it wasn't more than four or five thousand. If that. Then you might ask, how many aborigines did the whites kill? The answer is a quarter of a million. Two hundred and seventy thousand have gone. I can understand your being angry.'

The speech (p. 143 in the novel, reproduced almost verbatim in the screenplay p. 185) may in both cases be seen as a piece of liberal dice-loading but, whereas Keneally is content, and judicious enough, to follow it with "Jimmie secretly loved to hear these admissions. They were the luxuries he kept McCreadie for", Schepisi both can't be and isn't so wisely laconic: "can't be" in the sense that the film-maker has not at his command that sort of authorial comment, what Colin McCabe calls "objective metalanguage"[4]; "isn't" in the sense that he doesn't quite trust McCready's speech to have made the point and follows it with this:

The three figures hunch close to the flames to melt away the chilling reality.
JIMMIE responds.
   JIMMIE: They took away our lands, took away our pride, took away our rights.
MORT regrets.
   MORT: They jam us all togither in camps. Teach us shit. White bullshit.
   JIMMIE: In our own country, they took away our way of life. What for? What harm we done?
   MORT: Nothin' lift for a black man.
   JIMMIE: Nothin' lift but drinkin'!
   McCREADY: Yes you can't say we haven't given you anything. We've introduced you to alcohol, religion, influenza, measles, syphilis, school. A whole host of improvements.

The screenplay's descriptive comment — "The three figures . . . reality" — has an unrevealing portentousness to it that quite misses the percep-tiveness of Keneally's gloss which truly increases one's understanding of Jimmie's situation. The exchange quoted above is perhaps the film's most blatant example of using the screen for polemic rather than drama. The cadences and rhythms of Jimmie's first two speeches strike notes of rhetorical falsity because they depend on an articulate assessment of experience which the rest of the film suggests is beyond Jimmie's capacity. Further, they have a caption-making stridency which jars by comparison with the more unobtrusively dramatized evidence of cultural repression in the rest of the film and with the way crucial thematic points are often made through visual images of remarkable power. The heavy irony of

McCready's final comment so hammers the liberal anger as to deaden its impact.

Schepisi's screenplay is, for the most part, a close and careful re-working of the novel, and the version I have seen has all the marks of a labour of love. It is not a shooting script, with directions about camera movements, for instance, but a detailed, descriptive, reflective response to what has moved and excited Schepisi in the novel. It has a literariness that belongs to a writer rather than a director in the way that it goes beyond mere instruction to actor or anyone else involved in the film-making. In Sequence 96, the Newby massacre, Schepisi writes that "Miss Graf lies with the split bowl of her belly in shadow" (p. 108). "... the split bowl of her belly" (an image not drawn from the novel) is a highly literary, meta-phorical way of expressing a grisly narrative fact and points, I think, to a director who is as much an author. That is, Schepisi's screenplay, though in the main following linearly the novel's central narrative line, takes on a literary life of its own. Schepisi has responded to the passion at the core of the novel and used most of its incidents, but given it a new and distinctive life in his screenplay. The screenplay seems to have been to him more than just a blueprint and in general it is impressively humane and literate,

Jimmie and the pregnant Gilda (Angela Punch), who Jimmie believes is carrying his child.

replacing the book's ironic sharpness with a more full-throated — and more obvious — note of protest.

David Stratton writes:

> Schepisi didn't collaborate with Keneally on the script; the author didn't want to go back to the book . . ., but he always helped and gave advice when it was needed. So Schepisi wrote it alone and showed it to Keneally when he had finished. Keneally then spent a delightful afternoon going back to the book to discover if the good bits were his or Schepisi's.[5]

The answer is that the good bits tend to belong to both: that is, Schepisi has reworked some of Keneally's best writing (e.g., the Newby killing) in more specifically visual, cinematic terms, though retaining in the screenplay, as I have suggested, an unusually pronounced descriptive element.

The screenplay lets down its true and terrible story through the fault of one of its major virtues. Schepisi is passionately involved with the way the story embodies a harsh criticism of white injustice, its patronage and repression of another race, and this leads him to use the screen at certain key points as a platform. In reviewing the film at the time of its release, I wrote:

> Of course black Australians have been grossly exploited by whites, but the film makes this point better in the visually alert scene in the black camp, corrupted by white liquor and lusts, than in having Jimmie intone to McCready (Peter Carroll): 'You took away our way of life.' It is the falsest-sounding line in the film, partly because Tommy Lewis, good as he is as Jimmie, can't suggest the mature assessment of experience that would make the line resonant, and partly because it is crudely explicit about what the film does better through its visual patterning.[6]

Subsequent viewing has confirmed this opinion. For what emerges as so visually powerful a film, it is surprising that Schepisi felt such a need to underline points. The dialogue is often unsubtle. For example, young Newby's (Matthew Crosby) lament after the murder, "All dad did for 'em", is quickly echoed in Mrs Neville's (Julie Dawson) "Everything we did for them was just a waste of time." This notion — the white expectation of repayment for any show of decency to blacks — is extended a little later by Jimmie's (Tommy Lewis) saying, "They want yer to do wrong, ter bugger up. They bloody disappointed if yer don't." There is no doubt who the villains are in this story; the point does not need such underscoring. Keneally is more alive to this danger than Schepisi: of the examples just quoted, only the first comes from the novel.

Schepisi's strength as a film-maker is essentially a visual one; his ear is less true. He seems not to have heard the irony in a comment such as the following from the novel:

> It's a war, he told Mort; if he, Jimmie Blacksmith, went to those who had wronged him and asked like a gentleman to give his due to him, they'd laugh. (p. 104)

Keneally's reported speech here enables him to use a more elaborate concept and construction than would be convincing in Jimmie's direct speech. In the screenplay, the above sentence emerges in this speech given to Jimmie:

> JIMMIE: We're at war. 'n war ain't nice, but it has to be done. Can yer imagine me askin' everyone who done me wrong, like a gentleman, for me due. They'd bloody laugh. (p. 149)

That seems to me quite intricately wrong. Even the opening sentence, "We're at war", suggests an idiomatic sophistication lacking from Keneally's "It's a war", the crude irony of "'n war ain't nice" is not characteristic of Jimmie's way of speech; and the longer central sentence ("Can yer imagine . . ."), in its cumbersome rhythms, betrays Schepisi's faulty ear for what can — and cannot — be turned into direct speech. In the novel, Jimmie has picked up the phrase "declare war" on the shearing floor and later (p. 86) he says to Gilda as he leaves her on the Dubbo road, "Tell the p'lice I said I declared war. Tell 'em how bloody measly Newby was. Tell 'em all the damage done at Newbys', I did, not Tabidgi. And I declared war. Orright?" The phrase belongs naturally to Jimmie there; it has a sense of being savoured for its newness on his tongue. The film, by having it re-echo round a dangerous and dismal landscape, gives it a rhetorical flourish, a thematic italicizing, that robs it of its poignancy and naturalness.

There are unsubtleties in the screenplay, usually deriving from Schepisi's lack of humour and irony, but though these are flaws they are not serious enough to damage the central concept which has been poetically rendered or the narrative line which is preserved throughout an episodic treatment. Whereas Keneally chose to begin with a plain statement of Jimmie's attempt to enter the white world, via marriage, Schepisi announces different stylistic — and, therefore, thematic — intentions at once. He chooses to begin with the landscape ("Enveloping, swirling, clouds that melt into wisps . . . celebrating sunset") to usher in the claims of Jimmie's black world:

> Sounds rise with the landscape, haunting rhythmic and ritual earth music — the chant of Jimmie Blacksmith's initiation ceremony. Singing of Jimmie. The child to be reborn, as man, from the mouth of the lizard. (p. 1)

Schepisi wants the viewer at once to feel for the organic culture which is Jimmie's tribal birthright and in Sequence 3 the initiation rites are carried out. (Between these two sequences, the Rev. Neville is briefly glimpsed muttering about "Blasted blacks! The best of them are likely to vanish at any time.") And yet, as a half-caste or "hybrid", Jimmie's connection with this world is no more organic than with that in which the Rev. Neville (Jack Thompson, in a carefully subdued performance) canes him over the backside for missing out on the needs of the Easter choir.

Schepisi is in general more taken by the poetic possibilities of the story than Keneally, and this leads him, while retaining the same incidents, into a more obviously emotional, sometimes visually and aurally voluptuous, approach instead of the spare, ironic tone adopted by Keneally. His screenplay and his film are not — for better and worse — literal-minded translations of the novel, but a response to and re-working of the novel's original. In the film's imagistic patterns, Schepisi and his cameraman, Ian Baker, have found cinematic ways of responding to what has excited them in the novel. Rather than embark on a scene by scene comparison of how the film follows the novel's narrative line, it is more revealing to consider how some of the film's key images are made to bear aspects of the narrative's meaning.

"For he was a hybrid", Keneally says (p. 27) of Jimmie. In a film of powerful, suggestive images, those that haunt the mind longest and carry most narrative impact are those which reveal hybrid Jimmie adrift from both the worlds the film presents. Baker's camera responds magnificently to the challenge of integrating the beautiful but ominous landscape into the film without letting it dwarf the personal tragedy of Jimmie Blacksmith as it does his fleeing figure. It is perhaps the first film to capture that curiously sullen, blue-grey look of the Australian bush that offers concealment but not comfort. One is struck again and again by solitary figures overborne by a harsh and indifferent landscape. The sudden arbitrariness of great rock heaps that fill the screen with a sense of undefined terror as

Mrs Healy (Jane Harders), about whom Jimmie has fantasized, glances at Jimmie as she and her husband (Tim Robertson) drive past.

Jimmie and Mort (Freddy Reynolds) edge around them gives way to the two figures, still menaced by the physical scene, running along a blue-lit, early-morning ridge lined with dead trees. And Tommy Lewis' Jimmie appropriately never seems quite at one with this unyielding landscape, as the Aboriginal (David Gulpilil) does in Nicolas Roeg's **Walkabout**; it is part of the film's meaning that he should not. For the Aboriginal character truly belongs to the grim glare of Central Australia in a way that Jimmie does not belong to the mountain crags and forests of New South Wales. These latter, recalling some of Judith Wright's images in poems such as "South of my days' circle . . ." and "Bullocky", may provide a visual metaphor for cathedral architecture as the fugitives come upon what once was sacred ground, but Jimmie never seems organic to the scene. He is as much associated with the white desecrations of the place ("McCAFFERY SLEPT HERE", "CROKI RUGBY PREMIERS 1898") as with its original sacred rites. His alienation from the latter is enacted in his detached stance as he watches Mort flay his body "to divert the foreign spirits" (screenplay, p. 193) and in weary verbal insistence on the folly of trying to restore the place: "Yer bloody mad, both of yer. Yer'll never fix it. It'd take bloody days and yer still wouldn't fix it." The film's words and images capture powerfully here Keneally's summarizing account of "Mr Jimmie Blacksmith, mighty terrorizer, lost beyond repair somewhere between the Lord God of Hosts and the shrunken cosmogony of his people" (p. 148).

Jimmie is no more naturally at home in the muted clutter of most of the interior scenes of white settlement, whether of the missionary's abstemious dining room, the Methodist parsonage, the cricket match, Farrell's (Ray Barrett) grubby police station, or the shearing shed. Take the first of these — the Nevilles' dining-room — when Jimmie has been received back by the Rev. Neville after his absence for tribal initiations. Significantly, the camera pulls back slowly to observe Jimmie flanked by the pastor and his wife, while most of the screen on either side is filled with a dull green, confining wall. White approval has been bought at the cost of this oppressiveness and the visual image dramatizes the hybrid's awkwardness. Similarly, in the parsonage where Jimmie and the hapless Gilda (Angela Punch) are married, there is the same sense of a narrow place to suggest what adherence to white rules means to Jimmie, however much he aspires to success on their terms. In one of the few scenes devised for the film and for which no equivalent exists in the novel — the cricket match between the Newbys and their neighbours — Jimmie is made to look foolishly intense in his efforts to please. In the afternoon tea that follows, Jimmie sits on a log removed from the main group: Mrs Newby (Ruth Cracknell) leaves a plate of sandwiches on a far table for Jimmie to collect and Miss Graf (Elizabeth Alexander) makes patronizing reference to his imminent marriage. At the police station, he looks gauche in his oversize uniform, a visual indicator of the misplaced zeal which is quickly spent when Harry Edwards (Jack Charles) is hanged. His leaving here is his acknowledgment of the limits to which he will go to fit into the white world. And in the shearing shed, his brand new Wellingtons — symbol of white industry — are made the subject of ill-natured jokes.

In none of these white environments, any more than in the fear and warmth and squalor of the blacks' camp, is Jimmie presented as comfortably belonging; and against these unalluring images, none of them offering anything firm for him to hang on to, is set the vast, empty land. With the latter he has none of Mort's instinctive sense of kinship. Even in the more domesticated landscape between the Newbys' place and the nearest town, it is the desolateness that strikes us as Jimmie brings his pregnant white bride on horseback through the sprawling wheatfield to the slab hut he has built to receive her. This is followed by a long shot of the hut, isolated from the rest of the homestead and touchingly vulnerable in its isolation. Inside, the hut looks barely equal to the task of protecting its inmates from the threatening emptiness outside.

In a curious way, Jimmie looks least constrained, least obviously awkward in his environment, in the scene in which he is taking his most violent revenge upon it: that is, in the massacre in the Newby kitchen. The screenplay comments, after the first blow has been struck: "Jimmie studies the results of revenge. He is quickened by a new spirit" (p. 105). There is a new grace in his movements — he "springs", is "lightly prancing" — and a liberation of inner turmoil — he "revels" — as he goes about this monstrous business. The film handles this sequence

A wary Jimmie, and the corrupt, sodomizing Senior Constable Farrell (Ray Barrett).

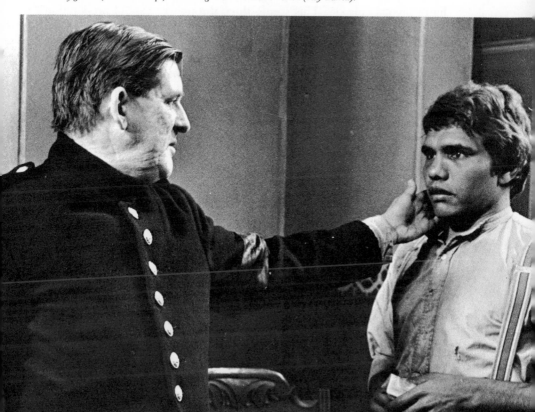

superbly and this success is due partly to its being the climax of a particular series of images, partly to the extraordinary skill with which the scene is cut. The cutting juxtaposes flailing axes with tottering delf on the kitchen dresser, the spurt of blood with the smashing of eggs or the spilling of milk, in a way that marks visually the culmination of Jimmie's frustrated rage at white complacency and injustice. The scene's sense of almost orgastic climax is created in its visual style. Its images are not decoration or even reinforcement of a theme. They are what the scene means: in his ecstasy of rage, Jimmie has lashed out at the white flesh and the domesticity he has craved.

Schepisi's account of his treatment of the violence in the film is an accurate reflection of how it appears in this scene: ". . . though I have tried to stylize it and do something different, in the end you have to front it straight on"[7]. The murder of the Newby women *is* horrific and that is how it appears. The recurring images of cutting instruments build a tension that explodes in the almost balletically conceived violence of the Newby murders. There is an element of stylization in the swinging axes which fell the women but this stylization doesn't distance the horror to the point where we can contemplate it without being appalled. Schepisi doesn't offer a gratuitous bloodbath, and he doesn't need to. The insistence on cutting edges — the sharp stone used in Jimmie's tribal initiation, the axe used in cutting off the chicken's head, the deft use of the blades in the shearing shed, kitchen knives and butcher's knives hacking their way through meat, the axe Jimmie has in hand when he hears the birth of his child — prepares us for, and provides a context of casual brutality for, the film's pivotal episode. This scene, thus, through its careful preparation and its skilful editing, carries the emotional charge appropriate to the film's climax and offers the most intense epitomization of the complex situation of rage, frustration, and paternalism that is at the heart of the film's experience. The audience, that is, cannot merely respond appalled to this scene without being forced to consider why it is so.

I have called this scene "pivotal", and claimed that its importance is created in largely visual terms. Susan Dermody describes it well when she writes that, in it, Jimmie "finally snaps from social paralysis. His moment of birth as a hero is almost instantly his moment of suicide as one."[8] Even more precisely central in the film's length than in the novel's, the scene represents the end point of all those futile efforts Jimmie makes towards acceptance in the white world. He has dined with and been oppressively advised by the Nevilles, assuring them — and meaning it — that he will heed their advice; he has built fences for stingy Healy (Tim Robertson); he has worked hard for and been underpaid by Lewis (Rob Steele); he has joined the police force and helped bring in a black whose death he fears he has all-but-connived at; he has been mocked for his interest in the federation issue and told he'll have the same rights — that is, none — after as before; he has even played cricket at the Newbys'. But in the end this is wasted effort, a "waste of love", and in the background always are those images of white women, mysterious, necessary and unattainable. Mrs Healy's upright back as she sits in the buggy beside her husband, holding his arm, acts for him as a critical rejection of the consumptive black girl he has left in the previous scene.

It is in the killing of the women that Jimmie, acting without constraint, briefly wears the look of a hero but it is, as Susan Dermody says, "his moment of suicide as one". Mort can deal with the idea of Jimmie's having declared war but not with that of killing women, and in their flight Jimmie never again looks like a hero. Schepisi persistently shows him dwarfed by the landscape, never tempted to the heroic tableau, the proud silhouette — or, if tempted, not succumbing. Throughout the second half of the film, whatever initiatives Jimmie takes, he has become irrevocably a victim. Images of his jaw half-shot away, of being caught asleep in the convent bed, and of being ignominiously bundled into the back of a police truck ensure that the audience is left with this view of Jimmie.

Perhaps the most poignant image of all — and Schepisi uses it very unobtrusively — is that of a black face among the police search party. Hybrid Jimmie is being tracked now by representatives of both of his non-worlds. In the process of trying to establish himself in the white world, he had helped Senior Constable Farrell to bring in black Harry Edwards; now, in a poignant symmetry, that same white police force has retained black help to bring in Jimmie Blacksmith, who, at the end and through-out, belongs nowhere. By their different routes, one through an austere choice of words, one through a passionate arrangement of images, novel and film make this painful fact movingly clear.

Notes

1. Bruce Moore, "A 'waste of love'? *The Chant of Jimmie Blacksmith*", *Perspectives 78*, Sorrett, Melbourne, 1977. Moore takes a more severe view of the introduction of McCreadie as hostage, claiming it as "a further sign that Keneally is finding it difficult to keep us interested in Jimmie Blacksmith's plight *when he is isolated from the white community*" (p. 149). I incline to the view that Keneally meets this difficulty and builds his answer into the narrative framework.
2. Fred Schepisi, *The Chant of Jimmie Blacksmith* (unpublished screenplay), The Film House Australia.
3. For some obscure reason, McCreadie becomes McCready in the film.
4. Colin McCabe, "Realism and the Cinema: Notes on Some Brechtian Theses", *Screen*, Summer 1974, Vol. 15, No. 2, p. 13.
5. David Stratton, *The Last New Wave*, Angus & Robertson, Sydney, 1980, p. 134.
6. Brian McFarlane, "**The Chant of Jimmie Blacksmith**", *Cinema Papers*, No. 17, August-September, 1978, p. 59.
7. "Fred Schepisi: Producer/Director/Scriptwriter", interview by David Roe and Scott Murray, *Cinema Papers*, No. 15, January 1978, p. 244.
8. Susan Dermody, "Action and Adventure", Ch. 5 in *The New Australian Cinema*, Scott Murray (ed.), Thomas Nelson Australia-Cinema Papers, Melbourne, 1980, p. 88.

7. My Brilliant Career

My Brilliant Career, by Miles Franklin (born Stella Maria Sarah Miles Lampe Franklin), is a semi-autobiographical novel first published by Blackwood's, Edinburgh, 1901, and in the Angus & Robertson Classics series, 1974 (page references to the latter). Her best-known works include *All That Swagger*, *My Career Goes Bung*, the "Brent of Bin Bin" trilogy, and *Back to the Bool Bool*.

My Brilliant Career was directed by Gillian Armstrong, for producer Margaret Fink, from a screenplay by Eleanor Witcombe. The director of photography was Don McAlpine, the editor Nick Beauman and the composer Nathan Waks. Running 102 minutes, it was released in 1979.

When Margaret Fink, producer of **My Brilliant Career**, based on Miles Franklin's novel, was asked in an interview whether she had particularly wanted a woman director, she replied:

> No, I chose Gil [Gillian Armstrong] because I believed she was the best person available for the film. I had faith in her creativity, and that faith has been vindicated.[1]

In the same journal, Gillian Armstrong, also interviewed, claimed that she and Fink "Both . . . felt **My Brilliant Career** was a film that a woman should direct, especially since Miles Franklin was such a strong feminist."[2] As Fink had said at the start of her interview, "Obviously, Miles is a proto-typical feminist, and I think I have always been one; that's probably why I responded to the book", the apparent contradiction about whether a woman director was held to be mandatory is curious. People do not always give their most considered ideas in interview, and it is now of little consequence, in appraising the film as a film or as an adaptation, how Armstrong came to direct it. She goes on to say in her interview, "Miles believed in women doing things on their own . . .", and the significant point is that that is what the film *does* show. The film at some crucial points clarifies Franklin's feminism by showing the heroine genuinely tempted by the comforts of a marriage to a rich man she finds attractive. At other points, it resists the cruder feminist thrusts of the novel which is apt to make all its men feeble, ridiculous or worse.

One can see why those of feminist sympathies might be attracted to both the book and the film, though for different reasons, the film offering a contemporary gloss on the simpler verve of the turn-of-the-century novel. The film, in establishing a much stronger sexual attraction between its hero and heroine, is in certain respects more rigorous than the novel. In

Opposite: Sybylla Melvyn (Judy Davis).

the film, Sybylla (Judy Davis) is genuinely tempted by the marriage offer from Harry Beecham (Sam Neill): Harry is not an oaf; he seems likely to respect her individuality; *but*, as she tells him in rejecting his proposal, "I can't lose myself in someone else's life when I haven't lived my own yet." And the film ends on a note of suppressed excitement as she commits herself to living her own life. Franklin's heroine makes her reasons for not marrying both explicit and confused. Early in the novel, this sometimes tiresomely exuberant Sybylla, first-person narrator, writes:

> Marriage to me appeared the most horribly tied-down and unfair-to-women existence going. It would be from fair to middling if there was love; but I laughed at the idea of love, and determined never, never, never to marry. (pp. 31-2)

At this stage of the novel, she is still contemplating the idea of marriage in the abstract, though having her parents' drab union before her daily has offered some telling evidence of the reality. Towards the end of the novel, prior to writing to Harry to turn down his offer, she reflects:

> And I believe in marriage — that is, I think it the most sensible and respectable arrangement for the replenishing of a nation which has yet been suggested. But marriage is a solemn issue of life. I was as suited for matrimony as any of the sex, but only with an exceptional helpmeet and Harold was not he. (p. 224)

Sybylla is genuinely tempted by a marriage offer from Harry Beecham (Sam Neill).

In some ways the film provides a critical commentary on the feminist thinking of eighty years earlier, offering a more restricted choice to Sybylla and as a result testing more rigorously the strength of her determination to be her own person before committing herself to anyone else. Franklin's heroine, understandably at the turn of the century, still sees marriage from a point of view no longer universally held. She opts for a bleak prospect, not in the end because marriage is "the most horribly tied-down and unfair-to-women existence going", but because Harry is not the "exceptional helpmeet" who could make marriage attractive to her. In both novel and film, Sybylla rejects a marriage offer which many women would find attractive: the different reasons for the rejection in each case derive partly no doubt from the temperamental differences between Franklin and the women who made the film (Fink, Armstrong and author of the screenplay, Eleanor Witcombe) but maybe even more importantly from the gap of eighty years that separates the two texts. **My Brilliant Career** is one of the best Australian film adaptations of novels because its makers have respected the original enough to interpret it rather than to embalm it.

It requires a certain indulgence to read Franklin's semi-autobiographical novel (she has insisted that it is not wholly so) with anything like equanimity. It is relentlessly exclamatory:

> Ah, health and wealth, happiness and youth, joy and light, life and *love*! What a warm-hearted place is the world, how full of pleasure, good, and beauty, when fortune smiles! *When fortune smiles!* (p. 98)

And the heroine's determined perkiness ("'We might have both been drowned', he said sternly. 'Mights don't fly', I returned", p. 96) sometimes taxes the reader's patience. One wants to avoid the patronage of "she-was-after-all-only-sixteen-when-she-wrote-it"; on the other hand, the book's faults, *and* its strength, seem essentially those of youth. However, Marjorie Barnard obviously believes that *My Brilliant Career* is in many ways typical of the author:

> There could be no doubt as to the authorship of this book. It is a genuine Miles Franklin. It is crude, inept, stiff, exaggerated, but it contains most of the ingredients of the later books. There is the mixture of romance and realism. Sybylla longs for love and scorns it. Her passionate feminism is recorded over and over again and Sybylla's 'Unhand me, Sir' attitude is part of Miles.[3]

Barnard is very sympathetically inclined towards the author and the woman, but she is quite aware of the difficulties the novel poses to the critical reader. Whether those faults of style belong to Franklin's youth or whether they are endemic in her work does not concern me here. Surprisingly, too, they come to matter less in re-reading the book. Barnard uses the word "passionate" about the author's feminism; and passion, not just in feminist directions, is what makes one ready not to be too distracted by stylistic excesses; it is, in fact, what accounts for the lasting charm and value of the book. There is a kind of toughness about its heroine — and, by inference, its author — that makes up for the intermittent tone-deafness of a narrator who starts a sentence with, "I was always desirous of enjoying the company of society people . . .". Out of the confusion of attitudes, and it is confusion rather than complexity, something very likable emerges: that is, a heroine who *will* be herself, however prickly and awkward a creature that may prove to be. The Fink-Armstrong film, despite shifts in narrative stress, has arrived memorably at the same result.

In some ways, the film considerably tightens the novel's plot, but it also recognizes that one of the novel's strengths is in its evocation of place. Further, both film and novel understand that place is more than a matter of setting, and that Sybylla's development is intricately connected to the changing *milieux* in which she finds herself. In the introduction to the novel[4], the author, perhaps disingenuously, describes the book as being not "a novel, but simply a yarn" (p. ix) claiming that, "There is no plot to this story, because there has been none in my life or in any other life which has come under my notice" (p. x). Though the events which make up the plot are no more architecturally planned than those in Ronald McKie's *The Mango Tree*, *My Brilliant Career* achieves a cohesion and a coherence that elude McKie. The cohesion derives chiefly from the way each new setting produces not just a change of scene but a new development in Sybylla, and the coherence is in the highly individual (if sometimes irritating) voice that interprets each new stage of experience.

Sybylla's "first recollection of life" gives rise to a vivid impression of the Australian countryside:

> . . . I can remember the majestic gum-trees surrounding us, the sun glinting on their straight white trunks, and falling on the gurgling fern-banked stream, which disappeared beneath a steep scrubby hill on our left.
> It was an hour past noon on a long clear summer day. (p. 1)

It is not just description for its own sake; it is part of Sybylla's memory because of the contrast between this apparently idyllic beauty and the lurking danger of "a big black snake which was curled at the butt of a fern tree". When Sybylla is nine, the Melvyn family moves from verdant Bruggabrong to Possum Gully, a parched, flat, monotonous place where the physical landscape provides an analogue for the inner life of the place which was "stagnant with the narrow stagnation prevalent in all country places" (p. 8). From this physically and intellectually parched place, the boys drift away in search of better things and the seeds of Sybylla's feminism are sown as she watches her father's decline into drunken shift-lessness and the effect this has on her mother, "a full-fledged aristocrat", who "grew thin and careworn, and often cross" (p. 14). The growth of her disgust with her father, once her hero, initiates her contempt for the ugliness and loneliness of poverty and the grinding weariness of hard labour, and produces in Sybylla an unslaked thirst for the arts, and a gnawing sense of how her own self is being suppressed:

> The professions at which I felt I had the latent power to excel, were I but given a chance, were in a sphere far above us, and to mention my feelings and ambitions to my matter-of-fact mother would bring upon me worse ridicule than I was forced to endure day by day. (p. 26)

Just as hatred for the life at Possum Gully is becoming unbearable, a letter comes from her grandmother, Mrs Bossier, offering her a home for as long as her mother will permit. The letter, kindly meant, is instinct with snobbery (e.g., the reference to the "danger of [Sybylla's] forming ties beneath her") and what would now be thought of as sexism ("She is young to mention in regard to marriage, but . . . it might be the makings of her if she married early . . . Sybylla, being so very plain, will need all the time she can get", p. 31). The awareness that she is "only a girl", and a plain one to boot, "came home to [her] as a great blow": "it was only men who could take the world by its ears and conquer their fate" (p. 33).

These bitter reflections subside when she arrives at her grandmother's property, Caddagat, where the marked difference in the terrain promises a new life. Nearing the place, she notes that, "A river ran on our right, occasionally a glimmer of its noisy waters visible through the shrubbery which profusely lined its banks" (p. 42). It is not only nature which wears a different face at Caddagat; inside the spacious house is a scene of gracious appointments and food for the life of the mind:

> . . . I noticed the heavy silver serviette rings . . ., and the old-fashioned dinner-plates, and the big fire roaring in the broad white fireplace; but more than all, the beautiful pictures on the walls and a table in a corner strewn with papers, magazines, and several very new-looking books . . . From the adjoining apartment, which was the drawing-room, came the sweet full tones of a beautiful piano. Here were three things for which I had been starving. (p. 43)

Putting aside the girlish raptures ("great joy!"), this is more than mere description. It is the novel's equivalent of film's *mise-en-scène* as that term is used in its fullest sense: that is, a dramatic collaboration between player and physical surroundings. Shown by her Aunt Helen to a pretty bedroom, she is struck by a portrait hanging over the mantelpiece. It is not of Aunt Helen as she supposes but of her mother when she was young, beautiful, and happy. Franklin refuses the temptation to sentimentality offered by this moment. The portrait and a photograph of her father cause Sybylla to think of her parents and the home she has left, but not in softened terms:

> I thought of a man and his wife at Possum Gully. The man was bleary-eyed, disreputable in appearance, and failed to fulfil his duties as a father

and a citizen. The woman was work-roughened and temper-soured by endless care and an unavailing struggle against poverty. Could that pair possibly be identical with this? (p. 44).

Sybylla blossoms among the pleasant comforts of Caddagat, though the blossoming does not take place without a few thornier moments that arise chiefly from her attitude to men, like the pompous English jackaroo Frank Hawden or her grandmother's sophisticated foster-son, Everard Gray from Sydney. Despite the civilized refinements of life at Caddagat, Sybylla is honest enough to acknowledge that she "was as much out of the full flood of life for which [she] craved as at Possum Gully" (p. 74). Cushioned ease cannot answer the kind of life-hunger she feels. Nor can the grandeurs of the novel's next setting, Five-Bob Downs, home of her "only *real* sweetheart", Harry Beecham. The novel's account of her arrival there economically and surely establishes its level of affluence, which is greater than that of Caddagat:

> It was sunset . . . when we drove up to the great white gates which opened into the avenue leading to the main homestead of Five-Bob Downs Station — beautiful far-reaching Five-Bob Downs! Dreamy blue hills rose behind, and wide rich flats stretched before, through which the Yarrangung river, glazed with sunset, could be seen like a silver snake winding between shrubberied banks. (p. 90)

Life at the McSwats, where hygiene is not a strong point.

There is a little more about the gardens, orchard and profusion of buildings and Sybylla responds to its luxurious beauties, the results of man and nature working in very productive harmony. Harry loses Five-Bob in the course of the novel and later it is adventitiously restored to him: the point is that Sybylla knows precisely what she is refusing when she declines to marry him. The passage quoted makes plain her admiration for the place, but she will not be lured by such beauties into marriage even with a man she likes as well as Harry Beecham. And her final rejection is made not when Harry is poor but when he is back at Five-Bob richer than before.

At the same time that Harry must leave Five-Bob, Sybylla is wrenched out of the comforts of Caddagat to go as a governess to a filthy and ignorant family named M'Swat[5] to whom her father owes money. Her life reaches its lowest ebb here:

> One wild horrified glance at the dirt, squalor, and total benightedness that met me on every side, and I trembled in every limb with suppressed emotion and the frantic longing to get back to Caddagat which possessed me. (p. 170)

It is not, however, the ignorance and filth that most brutally afflict her: "it was the dead monotony that was killing me" (p. 192). This new setting, repellent as it is in every physical aspect, makes her think more favourably of Harry's proposal, but, more important, brings her to a more tolerant understanding. Hygiene is not a strong point with the M'Swats, but Sybylla comes to realize that "Mr. M'Swat was upright and clean in his morals" and that "Mrs. M'Swat was faithful to him, contented and good-natured . . ." (p. 198). Again, response to an environment has marked an important stage in her growth towards maturity.

Escaping from the M'Swats, who fear she may be interested in their eldest son (a motivation the film rather surprisingly drops in favour of illness), Sybylla returns to Possum Gully to find life there has deteriorated considerably. Wryly she reports that her father, who "had been negotiating with beer regarding the sale of his manhood", had "completed the bargain" (p. 203); her mother wishes she had never married; and the children have complaints of their own. Sunk back in the old arduous ways of Possum Gully and with no prospect of release from them, Sybylla still refuses Harry when, in his new prosperity, he comes to renew his proposal. He has a great deal to offer her materially and will not hinder her urge to "write stories"; she has every reason to want to leave home, but these reasons will not do and she stays with "the sudden round of grinding tasks — a monotonous, purposeless, needless existence" (p. 228).

There is more to Sybylla's development than changes of scenery and there are elements other than how she interacts with each new environment and its inhabitants. I have chosen to stress them, first, because they are certainly very influential in her growth in the ways in which they toughen and modify her attitudes, and, second, because they make a useful point of comparison with the film. In reviewing the film on its first appearance, I wrote:

> As it recreates these changes of setting and their importance in Sybylla's growth, the film emerges as a triumph of *mise-en-scène*. It's not just a matter of that loving attention to detail that evokes the limited pleasures of recognition. Rather, much of the film's meaning is made in the impact of the changing scenes on Sybylla; in the tensions created between her and the places she finds herself in.[6]

Subsequent viewings have confirmed this view. It is in this respect that Gillian Armstrong's film most strikingly effects the visual transposition from the printed page. This is not merely a matter of following to the letter Miles Franklin's descriptions of the places referred to above, though production designer Luciana Arrighi's sets and the choice of locations are done with immense care and flair; it is also a matter of recognizing the crucial role they have to play in the film's narrative.

The film begins with the figure of a girl reading and moving backwards and forwards across the open doorway of a desolate corrugated iron house, then cuts to a lively face framed in a window, looking at without seeing the cow-lifting activities outside. The *mise-en-scène* at once establishes her as "belonging to the world of art and literature and music" while a more frantic life is going on outside. Reading aloud "the story of my career", she is oblivious to a sudden dust storm and shouts for help. In the

Piano as signifier of Sybylla's changing situation: here she plays a duet with Harry.

next shot, the camera pans around photographs in silver frames while Sybylla sits playing the piano with a rather florid touch. Pianos are in fact used as signifiers for her changing situation, for differentiating the genteel poverty of Possum Gully from the Collard and Collard luxury of Caddagat and from the broken wreck offered as culture at the McSwats'. Her playing in this early scene, against the background of family chores, establishes her separateness from — and, indeed, opposition to — her environment, and this is emphasized in the awkwardness of the grouping as her mother (Julia Blake), at first watching patiently with hands folded, interrupts to ask her if she can earn her living as a general servant.

Sybylla's aspiration to a higher life is made clear in a night scene with her younger sister, Gertie (Marion Shad). The contrast between the two is signified in Gertie's ringleted hair neatly tied up in disciplining rags while Sybylla's remains an unruly mop. "I want to do great things", she says. "Gertie, don't you ever dream there's more to life than this?" In those words and in the look of urgent yearning on the actress' face, slabs of the novel's early prose are condensed. Three brief scenes following offer as it were a synecdoche of "this" as it refers in the last quoted sentence: Sybylla is seen successively milking a cow, being humiliated at a pub where she goes to fetch her father, and chopping wood. She does man's work without man's privileges. The life she wants to escape from has been briskly sketched and a powerful emotional undertone created.

It is important that the strictures imposed by these early scenes be accurately captured, so that the opening-out of experience offered by Caddagat and, later, Five-Bob will be dramatically felt. She arrives at Caddagat through lush countryside, and there is a series of alert, economical scenes establishing the affluence, ease and cultivation of Caddagat. The house is all soft, tasteful interiors, beautifully furnished and decorated, and marvellously lit by cameraman Don McAlpine, here excelling himself. The camera tracks past the gracefully laden table as Sybylla is shown to her bedroom by Aunt Helen (Wendy Hughes). Dinner is presided over by Grannie (Aileen Britten), majestically framed against a glowing crimson wall, and, in registering details of the table-setting — candlesticks, fruit, blue-and-white china — and the serving of the meal, a way of life starkly contrasted with that of Possum Gully is made plain.

Luciana Arrighi has said in an interview:

> We were after two looks for **My Brilliant Career**: a documentary look, to capture the roughness and harshness of the period, which I hoped would go further than had been seen before in films, and a lush look to capture the life of the squattocracy. It was a fascinating experience to capture these two qualities in the one film.[7]

Though I do not see why a "documentary look" must be limited to the harsher settings (they are no more "real" than rich ones), it must be said that Arrighi and those carrying out her plans have succeeded admirably.

One outstanding example of how director, scriptwriter, and production designer have worked to render cinematically an important narrative link is in their transposing of the scene in Sybylla's Caddagat bedroom. As indicated earlier, the likenesses of her parents found there lead Sybylla to think of home. In the film, the camera takes in the details of her room, her mother's old one, with its pretty wallpaper, canopied bed, and luxurious white rugs. Having shared a cramped room with Gertie at Possum Gully, she seems to expand almost physically at the prospect of this room to herself. As she looks at her mother's photograph, the camera cuts to her mother working in her dingy kitchen at home. The contrast created in this juxtaposition is not just a triumph of art direction, though it *is* that too; what matters is that a point is made about what the girl has escaped from and her mother been shackled in. That is, she has escaped the debilitating poverty that has changed her mother from the beautiful young woman in the portrait to the careworn drudge she now is. It is a poverty that has no time or place for the kind of life Sybylla craves and which Caddagat, with its more formal gracious manners, can provide. It is a place where people actually listen to her as she plays their superior piano.

It has taken much longer to describe the effect of the *mise-en-scene* in depicting these physical — and other — contrasts than the film takes. Armstrong and her collaborators have not just created a pictorial version of Franklin's description: they have, through judicious framing and cutting, made the novel's narrative point more sharply and less explicitly. George Bluestone may be right when he claims that,

> . . . [Film] cannot show us thought directly. It can show us characters thinking, feeling, and speaking, but it cannot show us their thoughts and feelings.[8]

I do not doubt the difficulties involved in doing so and have adverted to this in Chapter 1. However, it seems to me that in the scene described, partly as a result of the power of *mise-en-scène*, partly of *montage* in the Eisenstein sense, Sybylla's processes of thought and feeling, and the context of that thought and feeling, have been made perfectly clear.

Just as Caddagat, and even more grandly so Five-Bob, offers interiors where the social graces and the life of the mind are more readily cultivated, so too the vistas outside contrast with the swirling dust that races through open doors and windows at home. There it seemed that an ugly landscape was forcing itself harshly on the lives of those at Possum Gully; at Caddagat and Five-Bob, the film offers verdant gardens lightly beckoning, as seen from cool interiors. In this gentler, more yielding landscape, the film understands, it is easier to be civilized and independent. This kind of natural receptiveness to man is epitomized in an exquisitely composed long-shot in which fence-rails cross the foreground and Sybylla's red sunshade dominates the dappled leafy greenness of the middle-ground through which the river runs. The shot seems not merely artistic, but *about* art and people in harmonious settings. As if to make a further point — however gratifying to the senses all this is, it is still not the answer to Sybylla's yearning — this scene has a well-judged anti-climax in which Sybylla tosses the bunch of flowers brought her by the jackaroo (Robert Grubb) into the river. This gesture is of course more than a response to the *milieu*: it is also a comment on Sybylla's attitude to male complacency: from whatever cause, it is nevertheless a telling disruption of the tableau created by the *mise-en-scène*. Sybylla, it suggests, has not been seduced by mere beauty — or flattery.

The film's visual style is more than just a style: it is the chief source of its coherence. The grandeur of the colonnade at Five-Bob recalls, and comments on, the shot of the verandah of the country pub to which Sybylla had earlier gone to find her father. Whereas the camera passes through the colonnade to the elegance within, in the earlier scene it pulls back from the verandah to subvert our notions of the pub's charm by revealing its ugly squatness. The narrative is often enriched by such visual contrasts. For example, the striking overhead shot of Sybylla dancing, somewhat wildly, at Caddagat, the angle of the shot underlining the wildness, gives way to the decorum of the breakfast scene next morning when Grannie refers to last night's "bacchanalian debauch". The wildness has perhaps been partly induced by Sybylla's reaction to Harry's presence, and the evening scene contrasts also with the soft decorum of a later scene

Sybylla with Harry and Aunt Gussie (Pat Kennedy) at Five-Bob Downs, where social graces and the life of the mind are more readily cultivated.

at Five-Bob where Sybylla, Harry and his Aunt Gussie (Patricia Kennedy) sit quietly round the fireside. These later scenes, suggesting the constraints that are at work on Sybylla, resonate with the recollection of the earlier one.

An even more striking contrast occurs when Sybylla is wrenched out of the pleasures of Caddagat to go to work for the McSwats. This unappetizing news cuts into the serene image of the girl in a blossom tree. In terse visual terms the film cuts from Grannie, comfortable in her handsome sitting-room, saying "Do her the world of good — make her think of other people", to a shot of the filthy McSwat children. The congeries of broken-down slab huts that is the McSwat farm is established in a brilliant long-shot that suggests the worst kinds of slothful incompetence. This shot, and the juxtaposed one of Grannie and Aunt Helen, in a prettily composed scene on the Caddagat terrace, makes the point about both places and their meaning for Sybylla far more economically than Miles Franklin's prose can. Compare these visual felicities with a sentence like the following and the film's effortless superiority is clear:

> Returning, she [Mrs M'Swat] invited me to enter, and following in her wake, I was followed by the children through the dirtiest passage into the dirtiest room, to sit upon the dirtiest chair, to gaze upon the other dirtiest furniture of which I have ever heard. (p. 170)

The strained rhythms and calculated repetitions produce an exaggerated and imprecise impression whereas the film's discreet cutting links shots which "say" more and mean more.

If the film is indeed a "triumph" of *mise-en-scène*, part of that triumph derives from its knowing when to stop. Too many recent Australian films — for example, **The Mango Tree**, **Storm Boy**, and even **Picnic at Hanging Rock** — have been overwhelmed by their own visual beauties to the point where the narrative appears to have ground to a halt. In **My Brilliant Career**, Armstrong is never carried away by the gratuitously photogenic aspects of the *mise-en-scène*. If the camera rests on a lush green landscape, it is to suggest a possible expansion in Sybylla's consciousness as she journeys to a new place. If it pans over elegant table appointments at Caddagat, it is in the interests of enacting a way of life in which refinements matter. If it tracks through handsome rooms at the Five-Bob ball, it is establishing the kinds of social grace that Sybylla is about to dismiss as she goes to join the workers' dance in the woolshed. Armstrong and Witcombe have known when to prune the book's sometimes rhapsodic descriptive habits. In the interview previously quoted, Armstrong said, in answer to a question about "the biggest problem" in adapting the novel, "The length", and went on to say how Witcombe and she dealt with one aspect of this:

> Eleanor was very good at pinpointing those aspects of the novel which could weaken the film's dramatic structure. For example, there is a long

central part in the book where nothing really happens, other than Sybylla having a good time . . . We realized that that would be pretty dull on the screen and decided to condense it.[9]

The power of the film's *mise-en-scène* is sufficient to create the sense of sustained pleasure and happiness Sybylla feels in her days at Caddagat and to do so with a very suggestive economy.

By concentrating on the *mise-en-scène* and how Sybylla's development is unfolded through it, I have not wanted to make the film sound schematic. What is important is the intelligent way in which one scene is enriched by contrasts or parallels with another, the ways in which one image recalls and is informed by another. Sybylla's final meeting with Harry at a dam, where she is trying to pull a calf out of the mud, recalls the idyllic punting scene at Five-Bob which ended with high spirits and a whiff of contained sexual excitement. That Judy Davis makes something so affecting out of her dam-side efforts to explain why Sybylla can't marry Harry is due partly to the film's making the viewer recall that earlier watery scene between them.

However, if much of the film's meaning is made through its visual representation of the *milieux* in which Sybylla is placed and to which she responds, there is more to it than that, just as there is more to the novel than Franklin's description of the various settings. It should be noted that the film omits all reference to the novel's earliest chapters, starting when the Melvyns are already at Possum Gully and Sybylla is about fifteen, and questioning the role of the woman: "the helpless tool of man — a creature of circumstances" as Franklin writes (p. 15). The film's sense of relationships is as firm-minded as its grasp of place. The women Sybylla has to deal with help shape her determination to be more than "the helpless tool of man" and the film takes its lead from the novel here. She is angry and appalled at her mother's decline into careworn fretfulness, and Sybylla, though recognizing her basic goodness, acknowledges at fifteen that "we do not pull together. I am a piece of machinery which, not understanding, my mother winds up the wrong way, setting all the wheels of my composition going in creaking discord" (p. 28). The film realizes this opposition in the shot in which Mrs Melvyn puts her hand on Sybylla's to stop her playing the piano and to make her listen to the plan she has for her.

Both novel and film use the character of Aunt Helen as a further strengthening of Sybylla's notion of put-upon womankind. Deserted by her husband, she is as she says "neither widow or wife". As with her sister, Sybylla's mother, marriage has brought her no happiness, though the civilized comforts of Caddagat have helped ease her situation in contrast to the way the poverty of Possum Gully has worn down her mother. As a result, Aunt Helen is not so embittered that she cannot try to help Sybylla nor see what there is to value in her. Nevertheless, her advice about aiming for "the *friendship* love of your fellows — the only real love there is" (p. 48) hardly answers the conflicting ardours of Sybylla's youth. Outstandingly well-played by Wendy Hughes, the film's Aunt Helen offers a model of grace and dignity for Sybylla, even as her situation offers a model of what to avoid: the subservience of women to passion. In rejecting Harry Beecham in the film, Sybylla, so far from being "unable to bear the touch of anyone" (as she claims in the novel), acknowledges that she is very "near" to loving him. That she does not give way to this passion and marry him is the result, not of wanting "friendship love", but of wanting something altogether different from life. She may tell Harry, "The last thing I want is to be a wife out in the bush having a baby every year", but this is not what Harry is offering. His proposal is altogether more attractive and yet she still does not accept it, and in this decision is the key to the film's feminist theme.

As for those wives "in the bush having a baby every year", she has seen in her mother and Mrs McSwat two examples that act as warnings. Not that she is ever likely to be like Mrs McSwat — "a great, fat, ignorant, pleasant-looking woman" brought to engaging film life by the excellent Carole Skinner — but the picture of a woman so sunk in slovenly domesticity is not lost on Sybylla. She concedes Mrs McSwat's uncomplaining good-nature but certainly wants never to be in a situation where uncomplaining good-nature will be required of her — a situation, that is, of poverty or intellectual deprivation or any other kind of marriage-induced oppression.

Sybylla is dressed by Aunt Helen (Wendy Hughes), a model of grace and dignity.

Of the other women of any consequence, one is Grannie whose affluent widowhood removes her from any need for subservience but whose ideas are nevertheless formed by the prevailing ideology that marriage is a woman's sphere. The other is Harry's Aunt Gussie whose spinsterhood and role as *chatelaine* of Five-Bob gives her a freedom from male oppression that is manifested in a calm, womanly authority. She is Sybylla's best grounds for wondering, "Why does it always have to come down to marriage?" Gussie seems to have managed very well without it. Perhaps Armstrong had this sort of notion in mind in including a strangely gratuitous scene in an aviary at Five-Bob. An overhead shot reveals Sybylla and Gussie in a bird-cage and the symbolism seems bluntly obvious; then, as the camera peers through the grill, Gussie says, "Birds are lucky because every day they get their food." Is this an oblique reference to Sybylla's situation of dependence? As the next scene shows Gussie with leisure to paint, is it intended to suggest that, creature comforts assured, one has time to develop the mind?

Though it is the women who dominate the film, most of the men mirroring the novel's conception of them as shiftless or pompous or ignorant, there is the notable exception of Harry as played by Sam Neill. That he is made to seem more intelligent and attractive than he is in the novel slightly distorts the latter but considerably strengthens the film's narrative. Neill and Judy Davis generate a wholly believable sexuality, a suggestion of feelings chiefly withheld but occasionally expressed in a burst of activity like the dancing at Five-Bob and in the final emotional inequality. That Sybylla rejects *this* Harry increases the sense of her determination to follow her own imperatives. In a well-argued article on the ways in which the film has modified the novel, Jack Clancy has drawn attention to "the effect of Harry and Sybylla being almost of a height with each other"[10], instead of displaying the book's disparity of a foot. He claims rightly that the effect is "to reduce Harry and to enhance Sybylla . . . The female is stronger, the male less formidable, three-quarters of a century later." In the process, though, Harry is *not* reduced as a human being or as a prospective husband and the film's narrative is made more tautly interesting as a result. Without undermining the film's feminist sympathies, the generous treatment accorded the character of Harry makes his love worth having and Sybylla's rejection of it more moving and impressive.

The film's ending is more optimistic than the novel's in that it shows a positive outcome from Sybylla's decision. She has written the story she wanted to write and in the very last scene, as sumptuously framed and shot as everything else in this lovely and touching film, the opening scene is recalled. At the film's start, as wind and dust blow round her, Sybylla, with endearing egotism, begins to read the story of her brilliant career, oblivious of her uncongenial surroundings. At the end, the early-morning freshness of long shafts of light falls between trees and behind Sybylla as

Sybylla: a determination to follow her own imperatives.

she consigns her manuscript to Blackwood's, Edinburgh. The viewer is left with a note of quiet optimism as she leans with forward-looking satisfaction on a sliprail gate. This is more than just narrative tidiness; it is the logical outcome of a dramatized argument about the possibilities of achievement for a woman who dared to take a chance of being herself. Tom Ryan may well be right in writing of the film:

> The forces that have repressed her may have receded into the background in the presentation of her drama, but, having been so forcefully depicted, they are not easily forgotten.[11]

Nevertheless, despite the vividness of those oppressive forces in the film, they cannot vitiate the effect of that complex close-up at the end: it registers painful experience past but at least equally anticipates future excitement. Nathan Waks' score, using, particularly, Schumann's "Scenes from Childhood", underlines, indeed helps to create, that tone blended of poignancy and resilience which is part of the film's meaning and which feeds into its final moment.

Gillian Armstrong believed that "Miles Franklin was an exceptional woman who was ahead of her time."[12] In some important ways the film suggests the novel she might have written if her time had caught up with her. This is not to say that the film has "merely put modern ideas into a girl dressed in period clothes"[13], but that it has made an affectionately regarded "classic" in one medium into a tougher, more affecting potential classic in another. In any case, I think Franklin would have approved.

Notes

1. "Margaret Fink: Producer", interview by Peter Beilby and Scott Murray, *Cinema Papers*, No. 20, March-April 1979, p. 289.
2. "Gillian Armstrong: Director", interview by Peter Beilby and Scott Murray, *Cinema Papers, ibid*, p. 291.
3. Marjorie Barnard, *Miles Franklin*, Hill of Content Publishing Co., Melbourne, 1967, p. 44.
4. Dated 1899. The book seems to have taken six years from the start of its writing to its publication by Blackwood's, Edinburgh, in 1901.
5. Curiously, M'Swat of the novel becomes McSwat in the film.
6. Brian McFarlane, **"My Brilliant Career"**, *Cinema Papers*, No. 23, September-October 1979, p. 564.
7. "Luciana Arrighi: Production Designer", interview by Sue Adler, *Cinema Papers*, No. 22, July-August 1979, p. 422.
8. George Bluestone, *Novels into Film*, University of California Press, Berkeley, 1957, p. 48.
9. *Cinema Papers*, No. 20, p. 293.
10. Jack Clancy, "Bringing Franklin Up to Date: The Film of *My Brilliant Career*", *Australian Literary Studies*, Vol. 9, Number 3, May 1980, p. 366.
11. Tom Ryan, "Historical Films", Ch. 7 in *The New Australian Cinema*, Scott Murray (ed.), Thomas Nelson Australia-Cinema Papers, Melbourne, 1980, p. 122.
12. *Cinema Papers*, No. 20, p. 292.
13. *Ibid*.

8. Monkey Grip

Helen Garner's *Monkey Grip* was first published by McPhee Gribble Publishers, 1977, and by Penguin Books, 1978 (page references to the latter). *Monkey Grip*, her first novel, won a National Book Council Award and her latest work is *Honour and Other People's Children*. She has worked as a teacher and a journalist.

Monkey Grip was directed by Ken Cameron, for producer Patricia Lovell, from a screenplay by Ken Cameron, in association with Helen Garner. The director of photography was David Gribble, the editor David Huggett and the composer Bruce Smeaton. Running 101 minutes, it was released in 1982.

One of the achievements of Helen Garner's novel, *Monkey Grip*, is that the heroine, Nora, does not lose hold of the reader's sympathy despite the fact that the story, as told by her, centres almost wholly on herself and her frustrations. These preoccupations — the constant pondering on what she is feeling, the analysis of what is happening in her successive sexual relationships, the sense of herself as ill-used — ought in the end to be merely wearisome to the reader. And indeed a good deal of this prize-winning novel, with its vestigial narrative, *is* tiresome, but the reasons for this lie elsewhere. In Nora, Garner has created, through the most formidably unappetizing processes, a protagonist who emerges with a credible *wholeness*. One accepts that she is sometimes boring, sometimes self-indulgent, in the way that, in life itself, one accepts that a *whole* person is likely to be so from time to time. A whole person (i.e., character) is what shuffles out of the banal and repetitive incidents that make up the plot — to use the latter term at its loosest.

In Ken Cameron's film version of the novel, the central firmness of the realization of Nora (Noni Hazlehurst) is even more striking. It is as though the scriptwriters (Cameron and Garner) and director have seen where the novel's potential unity and strength lie, and have capitalized on it. They have done so partly by keeping Nora on-screen virtually throughout, but chiefly through casting Hazlehurst, an actress of real warmth and emotional range. Her performance is an achievement not unlike Geraldine Fitzgerald's in **The Mango Tree** in the way that it works unobtrusively to pull together the narrative's suggestions about the character in question. In this case, however, Nora, unlike Grandma Carr, is clearly intended to be the centre of the action in both novel and film. The strength the film gets from Hazlehurst's performance and from its visual rendering of the novel's ambience tightens the latter's frail narrative

Opposite: Nora (Noni Hazlehurst) and Javo (Colin Friels).

grasp, but nevertheless draws intelligently on what is at least potentially there in the novel.

It is just as well that the chapters of this book do not seek to give plot synopses of the novels involved since such an enterprise would certainly founder on *Monkey Grip*. Divided almost arbitrarily into thirty-four whimsically named chapters (e.g., "Respectful of His Fragility", "Do You Wanna Dance?"), its narrative structure is, superficially, fragmented to the point of disintegration. Its bits and pieces make Ronald McKie's *The Mango Tree* look as architected as *Middlemarch*. In a sentence, the narrative explores the shifts in the relationship between Nora, a single mother of thirty-two, and Javo, her off-and-on junkie lover, a part-time actor (and a full-time bore). However often she tries to wean herself of the habit of Javo, she appears to remain essentially hooked by him as he is by smack. Part of the trouble is (as Javo says to her) "that you like me best when I'm off dope, but *I'm* always happier when I'm into it" (p. 96).

By the end of the novel, when Javo has left again, this time probably with someone called Claire, Nora feels, "A funny kind of pain, dull, not sharp, spread through my body as if by way of the bloodstream" (p. 244) and, a few lines later, "instead of that pain came the thought, 'Well . . . so be it. Let it be what it is.'" There is just a chance that Nora has by now reached the stage of accepting her life, without Javo if need be. Every rational thought has been moving her in this direction but rational thought has never proved defence enough against her need for Javo. Though the need is powerfully sexual (more so on her part than his) it is by no means exclusively so. She in fact wants a kind of stability, a more conventional set of relationships than her world is likely to offer. At one stage, envisaging a trip north, she sees them "on the road with Gracie [her daughter], looking like a ragged family. He took hold of my hand and we stood together comfortably, liking each other and feeling hopeful" (p. 90). But she qualifies this image with the knowledge that she "would have had to be a mediator: between him and Gracie, between him and the rest of the world".

The narrative surface of the novel is more crowded than the brief account above suggests. While Javo is the continuing strain of emotional engagement throughout the year of the novel's time span, Nora's life embraces many other relationships as well. Chief of these others is that with her small daughter, Gracie, who observes her mother with wry stoicism. As well there are the women friends (e.g., Eve, Rita, Cobby) from whom she receives varying degrees of support, and Lillian, whom she distrusts, mainly from Javo-based motives of jealousy; and the men who are variously friends and lovers, but mostly lovers even if that's not how they began. They include Javo's mate Martin, the latter's brother Joss, Gerald with whom Nora shares a house, and Francis. In fact, the network of shifting, drifting relationships involves a cast of characters almost bewildering in their numbers and made more so because Garner has not sought to characterize them in any detail. And yet there may be a narrative purpose in this: that sense of a loosely-knit, not-very-differentiated crowd of people, drifting past each other, sometimes touching briefly, has its point to make: these other lives are important to the narrative only as they affect Nora and none of them compares in her life with the intensity of her feeling for Javo. They have their brief moment of vividness, coinciding with their narrative function, then subside into being part of the general ambience. For instance, Angela swims into focus when she asks Nora to accompany her to a birth control clinic (she is "going to have a try at an IUD", p. 155). Angela has had love problems with Willy but they are not intrinsically important. What matters chiefly is how Nora responds to Angela: first, she is very ready to support her friend, and in this unstable circle of people there is a surprising amount of solidarity; second, she promotes the following reflection in Nora: "I silently envied the ease of her tears, the way she lived with her heart bravely on her sleeve, no levelling out of the violence of everything but full blast and shameless" (p. 156). The insight that offers into Nora and her view of her own situation is significant.

So, from the narrative's point of view, is Nora's *capacity* for such reflection. The more one reads this novel, the more one realizes that its central drama is to be found by attending to Nora's narrative voice. The most potent discourse in *Monkey Grip* is not the "subjective" utterances of characters but the surrounding (but far from "objective") narrative prose which of course belongs to Nora. And it is here, I believe, that the real drama of this novel is located. It seems to me scarcely possible to care one way or the other about most of the characters: one feels a mild revulsion against Javo, mild sympathy with, say, Angela: but one is in fact very much caught up with what Nora makes of her experience. She is not merely a recording voice, but a presence which responds, and grows through response, to a range of relationships. She is defined partly in terms of how she behaves in these relationships, partly through that voice which is sometimes reflective, sometimes summarizing, sometimes self-assessing, and always individual and working towards the reader's sense of a whole character.

This is the kind of pleasure, in reading a novel, that grows on one, perhaps making stronger claims in second or later readings. My impatience with *Monkey Grip* on first acquaintance grew largely out of dissatisfaction with its apparent shapelessness. Like many good novels, it is episodic but most of its episodes are unmemorable, particularly if measured against the crude narrative yardstick of what-happens-next. In *Monkey Grip*, what happens next is apt to be very like what happened before: that is, there may have been a visit to the local swimming baths, or a sexual encounter (invariably, monotonously and, therefore perhaps, significantly referred to as "fucking"), or a meal, or a trip to somewhere. In themselves, scarcely one of them really matters and few of them stay in the memory. That is not to say they lack all vividness: there are many sharply observed touches about people and places: but that they lack the sort of vividness one needs in order to feel that a narrative is building. Further, one remembers odd scenes but not with any exactness as to the part of the novel from which they came. The scenes, like many of the characters, become part of that hazy *milieu* in which the more things change the more they stay the same.

This impression of narrative slackness, compared say with a "well-made" novel like Kenneth Cook's *Wake in Fright*, is accentuated by the novel's structural procedures. It is as though the latter are dictated by a mimetic urge to recreate the casual, careless, messy, sometimes warmly cheerful, often dreary lives of its characters. Scene after scene — and each chapter is divided into about half a dozen, some of them no more than snippets — is introduced by sentences like the following:

> I was sitting at the kitchen table after tea when Javo came around the corner to the back door. (p. 21)
> One afternoon, when I got home from working on the paper, I found Javo asleep in my bed . . . (p. 91)
> Peg took Gracie out for the day and I went off by myself. (p. 106)
> Javo came to my house a few afternoons later. (p. 118)
> At eleven o'clock that night Chris walked in with some coke. (p. 179)
> Cobby came home from America . . . (p. 190)
> I went over to Peel Street and found Rita tidying her room. (p. 193)

And so on, endlessly. It is perhaps the most loosely strung together novel of my acquaintance. The disjointedness, the failure of anything to *build*,

Living in the 1970s, in Melbourne: Nora and house-mate Gerald (Don Miller-Robinson).

and the sense of nothing's being more important than anything else are, at least on a first reading, maddening to the reader trying to discern and hold on to some sort of narrative development. Perhaps this problem is more acute to one raised in the tradition of carefully constructed, nineteenth-century, realist fiction than to those who have spent their formative years with modernism. Certainly on re-reading, the book's apparent random-ness is less daunting. This may be the result of *knowing* that the novel offers little in the way of the usual narrative rewards (and thus not expecting them) but is, I believe, really due to recognition and acceptance of different moves towards narrative coherence — and to accepting monotony as part of its meaning.

There is no point in looking for an A→B→C pattern of causality but there are other elements in the narrative that work to give shape and flavour to the book. The major one, as I have suggested, is in the drama enacted in Nora's linking voice. In a two-paces-forward-one-pace-back fashion, she is gradually revealed as a protagonist trying to pull herself and her life into some sort of manageable shape. One's chief interest is concen-trated in this rambling but oddly compelling and endearing inner action. When she finds Javo's "fit" left lying around in Rita's house, she realizes that one of the chief pressures of her life is that she "was guarding them all from each other" (p. 72). Sometimes her voice registers the pressures as unbearably demanding, but there are also occasions such as the one when

> I was flooded with the possibilities, the theatre was full of people I liked and loved and whose work was joyful to me. Child beside me, friend to sleep with, body loose from dancing and laughter. Coasting! for a while. (p. 118)

It is a voice which establishes itself as honest so that it is worth listening to for its own sake and for the light it sheds on others.

There is, too, a thematic concern, enunciated on two occasions in connection with Angela but which goes well beyond her in its resonance. Her problem has to do with "Willy's determined constancy in loving both Angela and Paddy, while living with neither" and with finding this situa-tion "no less painful to her for being ideologically impeccable" (p. 156). Later, when Willy has started an affair with Rita, there is talk about "breaking out of monogamy" but Angela is "too miserable to care about theory" (p. 192). These two remarks (about a character of no special consequence) point to a crucial and pervasive source of tension in the novel. Nora and her friends are all living what in 1975, the time of the novel, would have been called an alternative life-style. It is located mainly in Melbourne's inner suburbs and involves an approach free to the point of permissive in matters like where one lives and sleeps, and with whom, in experimentation with drugs, and in drifting from cafes to bars to fringe theatrical and film-making activities. Negatively, it implies a rejection of monogamous, orderly households, of women performing traditional sex roles, of steady, gainful employment, of the careful ordering of one's life. However, while much of the freedom, the indulging of instinct as opposed to behaving conventionally, is undeniably attractive to people like Nora, it brings with it its own kinds of pressures and hurts. The gap between the ideology and importunate reality often lets the draughts in. Nora has never tried to get Javo off the smack — "I didn't want to hold him, or stop him hitting up, or be with him twenty-four hours a day" (p. 66) — but this apparent easy tolerance of the junkie habit is no protection against the pain she feels each time he leaves her to look for a "score".

Beneath the surface disjointedness of their lives, she cannot help looking for a pattern that would help her to make sense of them. There is certainly no longer any hope or help for her in the suburban ordinariness of her Kew-based family whom she visits on Christmas Day, nor in the prospect of marriage. In trying to work things out in her own mind she contemplates herself and her women friends in these terms:

> . . . we all thrashed about swapping and changing partners — like a very complicated dance to which the steps had not yet been choreographed, all of us trying to move gracefully in spite of our ignorance . . . (p. 192).

The image of the dance is in itself a sign that she wants to find, in the constantly shifting aspects of her life, a pattern, a sense of order, to which a key *does* exist but the finding of which the very nature of their ideological convictions makes improbable. The above reflection comes shortly after the Christmas inspection of her relations and it is completed by her resigned acceptance of the fact that "though the men we know often left plenty to be desired, at least in their company we had a little respite from the grosser indignities." Nora, that is, cuts her losses in a way that engages one's respect: for "plenty to be desired" one may read "reliability", or "supportiveness"; for "the grosser indignities", the sort of superiority her "big boss" uncle exudes in his treatment of his plump blonde wife. He is, she recognizes, implacably "the enemy".

"What's love? Being a sucker, I suppose" (p. 63), Nora asks and, wryly, replies. Quoted out of context the remark may look portentously theme-stating, but in the pattern of her life, with and, more often, without Javo, and of the lives of the loosely knit group of friends, it is a constant preoccupation. It is also a question-and-answer that points to one of the ways in which the narrative is held together. The women in the novel are looking for a tenderness and kindness in their relationships with men, and Garner, through Nora, expresses a need for a mutuality of affection that precludes contracts but requires commitment, that insists on independence but yearns for steadiness. In writing about *Monkey Grip* and Glen Tomasetti's *Thoroughly Decent People*, Susan Higgins and Jill Matthews have claimed that:

> Both novels are unobtrusively shaped by a critical examination of the way such cultural norms as the entrapment of women in domesticity and the attraction of romantic love are deeply internalized, and this makes it legitimate, even necessary to describe them as feminist.[1]

As far as Nora is concerned, she is aware of the possibilities of "entrapment" and is, indeed, firmly entrapped by her role as mother and lover. Despite the casual junketing around (e.g., to Tasmania, to Sydney, as well as on lesser expeditions), she is always aware of Gracie's needs as a pressure upon her. And while ostensibly resisting the notions of "romantic love" and what it implies for the woman involved, she also longs for *some* of its concomitants: for male tenderness, support, and answer to her sensual needs.

Her apparently casual, relaxed attitude to embarking on her relationship with Javo will be harder to sustain than she imagines. When Eve says, "You're not — you know — doin' it again, are you?", Nora "knew what she meant and could not control a grin of guilt. She meant *falling in love*" and replies "Yeah, I suppose I've done it again" (p. 6). Already, on the next page, she shows an awareness of what it means:

> People like Javo need people like me, steadier, to circle around for a while; and from my centre, held there by children's needs, I stare longingly outwards at his rootlessness.

She is genuinely attracted to the drifting life but is equally aware of her "entrapment". Much later, having arrived in Sydney at 6 a.m. with "Javo foul-tempered again, Gracie tired and frightened", she reflects, "I have to keep us together somehow" (p. 98). Whatever love is, it is not easy for Nora; as Barbara Giles, reviewing the novel, claims, Nora "is caught, as fast as Javo, her blue-eyed junkie, only her addiction is love"[2]. In its grip, despite the feminist ideology which elsewhere offers her a good deal of comfort and practical support, she is, as Giles goes on to say, "caught in the usual feminine bind, of responsibility for bringing up a child, of love which makes demands on her". The men she knows, including the ones she sleeps with, do not make the demeaning demands on her that conventional monogamy may, but the monkey grip of passionate need is no less inescapable for that. Her love for Javo may be generous and unpossessive but that is no guarantee that she will not sometimes be "used" by him.

None of the other women, despite the warmth of sisterhood, is any better placed than she is. The book seems to me honest about the gains and losses in the feminist approach to love and sex. The way they persevere with their lives, trying to square their ideology with the often chilling facts of "love habit", is done with enough humour and perception to make one bear with some of Garner's sloppier narrative habits. Certainly there is enough of both to make one feel the unfairness of Ronald Conway's characterization of "all this sweltering narcissism dolled up as group fellow-feeling"[3], and to make the present writer mildly ashamed of having once described it as an "almost ostentatiously tedious novel"[4]. If I cannot, even on re-reading, find it "a tremendous book" as Barbara Giles does, or "overpoweringly real" and "overwhelmingly filled

Above and below: the bad and the good of Nora and Javo's relationship. "What's love? Being a sucker, I suppose."

with love and understanding" as Veronica Schwarz does[5], I think there are now more things holding it together than I at first supposed. And the way the women grapple with the ideas of love and friendship and sex (the grappling is not limited to Nora) is one of these elements which help to provide a narrative cohesion not offered by a firmly made plot.

So, too, is Garner's meticulous re-creation of the *milieu* in which the novel's lives are lived. The physical scene of the inner suburbs of Carlton and Fitzroy, with a variety of overcrowded, sometimes lonely houses, the swimming baths, cafes and bars, is not there in the sense in which landscape is in a Thomas Hardy novel: that is, a presence having something like a life of its own. It is a cliché to speak of Egdon Heath in *Return of the Native* as being almost a character in the novel. That is not the way Garner uses the setting. It is there all right, in casual, exact noting of streets and shops (like Myer or Readings Book Shop), and in brief but telling references to doing "four loads of washing at the laundromat", to walking

> dully past the kid's adventure playground, across the car park, and up the broken stairs to the series of empty rooms over the Italian grocery, where [Javo] had a mattress in a corner and a heap of things he called his. (p. 44)

The references both specify a real place and indicate bits of personal landscape. Garner has said in an interview: "Another thing I like is what you find in nineteenth century Russian writers, a certain use of detail and description"[6], and she goes on to suggest how this certain use renders the detail organic rather than merely scene-setting. In *Monkey Grip*, the firmly established sense of place, and the cultural life that goes with it, provides a network that catches up the semi-nomadic tribe that peoples the book, and both shapes them and gives them something to respond to.

It could not have been done by someone who did not know the life at first-hand; it is not a matter of research, but of living and understanding what holds these people tenuously but tenaciously together. The acutely rendered ambience is of course as much a matter of time as of place, and time is felt in several ways. The changing seasons, too glib a metaphor for what is going on in the human lives, are therefore not used as a metaphor but as an agent for coherence: lives drift by haphazardly and their unpredictability is felt the more strongly against the sharp, sensuous noting of the year's moving from summer to summer. But time isn't just nature: the novel's period is placed in references to singers like Stevie Wonder and Skyhooks, to films like **Dog Day Afternoon** and **The Discreet Charm of the Bourgeoisie**, to the Australian Labor Party's being "done like a dinner" in 1975, in "push[ing] our way through Friday night crowds . . . back to Peel Street to watch **Shoulder to Shoulder** on TV" (p. 174). The cultural climate of Nora's world embraces fringe theatre and film-making (Nora works all night on a "junk movie"), the Melbourne Film Festival, *Rolling Stone*, and endless novel-reading. The titles of her reading include Jean Rhys' *After Leaving Mr McKenzie*, Agatha Christie's *Murder on the Orient Express* (coinciding with the film version released in 1975), Tolstoy's *War* *and Peace*, Virginia Woolf's *To the Lighthouse*, and, at the end, significantly perhaps, *Washington Square* which finishes with Henry James' heroine accepting the loss of her suitor and resigning herself with dignity, "as it were, for life". It is a nice touch to allude to this novel at this stage of Nora's life; it is even nicer *not* to make it (or Nina Bawden's *A Woman of My Age*) the novel's last reference but to whip Nora into *To the Lighthouse* instead. If there is, however, a thematic pattern in this reading it is well-concealed: there is a certain tendency towards novels about women in situations of entrapment, but Christie and Tolstoy remove the element of potential schematism. There used to be an old examination question asking students to consider the proposition that "In a good novel, setting is never merely a matter of background." On this criterion, *Monkey Grip* is a "good novel". If it is not good enough to avoid some *longueurs*, it is extremely sharp in evoking a time and a place, so sharp and sustained that ambience becomes an important narrative element.

Ambience is of course one of the areas in which a film ought to have least trouble in the enterprise of adaptation from a novel. Ken Cameron, whose first feature **Monkey Grip** is, has certainly succeeded to a remarkable extent in making his *mise-en-scène* replace Nora's narrative voice in the novel. Further, by retaining a good deal of the novel's "metalanguage" in Nora's voice-over, he achieves an often startling replication of the feel and tone of the novel.

The film's opening few minutes show both strategies in action. In a series of deft strokes, Cameron sketches in an impression of the real pre-Javo happiness in Nora's life, in an audio-visual equivalent of the novel's

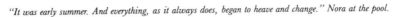

"It was early summer. And everything, as it always does, began to heave and change." Nora at the pool.

opening paragraph which presents a warm breakfast ("noise, and clashing of plates, and people chewing with their mouths open, and talking, and laughing. Oh, I was happy then"). The film arrives at the breakfast table only after several other significant images: a blue screen gradually shimmers into life with an underwater shot of legs swimming in a chlorinated pool; these — or other — legs are then seen cycling through suburban streets; there is a cut back to the pool; and then the camera moves in the breakfast scene with people snatching at bacon and eggs. But if these images suggest cheerful casualness, the voice-over is suggesting something else: "Looking back, you see you've already plunged in when you thought you were only testing the water with your toe." The tension established between aural and visual means here is an example of the cinema working very economically. The pool, the cycling, the breakfast table are part of the shifting communal life of inner suburban Melbourne; the voice-over anticipates what is going on in it for Nora and Javo. It is a tighter, subtler start than the novel's which follows its opening paragraph with two short, explicit sentences: "It was early summer", "And everything, as it always does, began to heave and change." The film makes its meaning more unobtrusively, the *mise-en-scène* and the voice-over working contrapuntally as it were.

Even during my dissatisfied first reading of the novel, it seemed to me that *Monkey Grip* had distinct cinematic possibilities: that is, that a director sensitive to its social-cultural-political setting might make an attractive *milieu* study from it. And that is what Cameron, abetted by David Gribble's splendid camerawork, has done. Unclamorously but surely they have put on film the novel's small world of inner suburban streets and shops, recording studios, scungy lanes, and grotty-to-comfortable houses and backyards. He has caught accurately those aspects of Carlton that the National Trust isn't interested in preserving or that the developers haven't developed. No other Australian film has caught so well this faintly seedy aspect of Melbourne — of *city* — life, nor in placing it in the lives lived there. The film's direction and screenplay offer a wry, sympathetically divided view of the characters' emotional lives, offering a parallel to the novel's sometimes painful apprehension of the gap between the ideology and the reality. The film balances a clear sense of rootless, itinerant camaraderie (less strongly feminist than in the novel), stressing the supportive aspect of its drifting, non-nuclear households against the emotionally draining, unfulfilling relationships of people who feel able to come and go at will. Sandra Hall, in a perceptive review of the film, has said:

> [Cameron's] characters are continually testing one another in love affairs and friendships, every relationship is a new challenge, yet the mood is understated. People move in and out of one another's lives without ceremony and with as little explanation as possible.[7]

The film catches authentically the committed casualness and the longing
the women feel for something more and does so with a greater succinct-
ness than the novel can. One suspects that Garner, co-author of the
screenplay, must approve of the tightening up (without needless spelling
out) of this shaping thematic interest.

Nora's apparently cheerful "I'll see you when I see you" approach is
touching as it becomes increasingly clear that she'd like something more
dependable. Her voice-over may say "All the splinters of my life fitted
together again" when Javo (Colin Friels) comes back from Asia, but,
resilient as she is, she knows that it is likely to shatter apart again when he
next succumbs to his addiction. She and her friends talk so much about
their emotional lives and needs that it becomes clear how inadequate to
them are the uncommitted relationships in which they mostly find themselves. The endless talk along the lines of "I love you, but I can't handle
it", or "It seems I only get to see you when you want something" strikes
again and again authentic notes of unhappiness and banality. Despite my
phrase "endless talk", the film really works very selectively in creating this
impression: it reduces the number of shadowy characters from the novel
and, inevitably, those that are left are fleshed out by the mere presence of
actors. Whereas in the novel the discussions about love and sex are
between Nora and any one of many (deliberately?) undefined women,
and some men, the film by putting faces to these names forces the
audience to identify them. In my view, the emotional content of the film is

Nora and daughter Gracie (Alice Garner): friends and family.

sharpened by the selectiveness and by the use of actresses as distinct from each other as Lisa Peers (Rita) and Christina Amphlett (Angela). What can begin to seem like a monotonously long-playing record in the novel gets a spike of individuality from the acting in the film.

If Cameron has been lucky with his cameraman, his production designer (Clark Munro) and his musical director (Bruce Smeaton) in creating the *mise-en-scène* for these cheerful, painful, uncertain lives, he has been even more so in the casting of Noni Hazlehurst. Through her performance, Nora's attachment to Javo (intelligently played by a too-healthy-looking Colin Friels) is not just the source of a series of episodes but the shaping force of the film. She has, to start with, just the face for Nora: mobile, intelligent, embattled, vulnerable, with accesses of warmth and humour, and a mouth that can also turn down moodily. She clearly *belongs* to the scenes in which she is presented: in the office of the women's paper, all flagons, posters, and tank-tops; in the house she shares with Rita until the strain of guarding her from Javo proves too great; in a beautifully composed and lit scene in which she works at her desk in a pool of light, while Javo sprawls on the bed. Hazlehurst and Cameron have worked successfully to make Nora's emotional progress the motivating factor for everything else in the film.

It motivates, for instance, some of the film's most kindly and good-natured scenes: those between Nora and her daughter Gracie (age raised several years from the novel, to about ten or eleven). Gracie (Helen Garner's daughter, Alice, in a very engaging performance) is clear-eyed about her mother's somewhat feckless emotional life: without ever becoming a knowing tot, she *does* know what's what. When Nora asks her, out of little more than idle curiosity, "What do you feel about Javo?", she says "You should just be nicer to him and leave him alone." It is not censorious or wise-childish; just a plain answer, given because it was asked, to a difficult question. This is a very compressed version of a fine short scene in the novel (p. 102) and it works with beautiful directness. Gracie's clarity of vision contrasts with Nora's emotional messiness at this point. The film underlines how unlikely Nora is to be guided by advice, however sound, by having her rail at Javo in the next scene when he comes back stoned, having forgotten that he was due to take Gracie out. The film, by this juxtaposition, sharpens one's sense of the emotional dis-orderliness of Nora's life. And one of the sweetest moments in the film shows Nora and Gracie, companionable and relaxed with each other on the Manly ferry at night, after Javo has left. The feeling between mother and daughter has been established with so much affectionate detail that Nora's final comment on it — about the pleasure and pain of seeing one's child "taking off" — resonates affectingly with what has gone before. There is sometimes an amusing sense of Gracie's being calmer and older than Nora, but the director does not let this develop into a cliché because Nora's proper, maternal love for her daughter has also been made plain.

Nora and Javo, as it sometimes can be.

It must be said that the film's greater sharpness and tightness do not always work in its favour. It is one thing for Nora's voice-over to reflect, "I couldn't live for long with his restlessness, his violent changes of mood" as she cycles past suburban fences. A comment like this cannot, however, dramatize — even if it does encapsulate — the *experience* of a long-drawn-out, difficult relationship in which the restlessness and violent changes of mood are enacted in a succession of incidents. The hundred minutes the film lasts as opposed to the much greater time it takes to read the book removes a lot of the tedium of the original; but the inevitable pruning necessarily dissipates some of the monotony that is also part of the book's meaning. An affair like Nora's with Javo produces long periods of disappointment, loneliness and aching need between the spells of well-being and happiness. The film, by tidying up the novel's narrative procedures, runs less risk of boring its audience but, in doing so, cannot help losing some of the specific kinds of pain that the more discursive form of the novel allows the reader to register. I am not making a point about "faithfulness" to the original; merely adverting to what has happened in the transposition. One has to accept, in statement in the film, what the novel in its more leisurely way can impress upon one through repetition. Clearly, there are gains and losses for each. The cinema, the medium less susceptible to the reflective mode, is no doubt wise to engage in the subtle modification of a narrative which even its original form, the novel, perhaps allows its central character, let alone its readers, more overt reflection than is wise.

When reviewing **Monkey Grip** at the time of its release, I finished by saying that "it has understood that a film can dramatize monotony and repetitiveness without succumbing to either." Now I am less sure of this. It seems to me that comments like the one quoted above, or Nora's voice-over saying, "Naturally I remembered the good and lovable things about him [Javo], not the drugs and resentment", have more of a summarizing than a dramatizing function. In spite of their often retaining Garner's original words, the very selectivity with which they are chosen for the screenplay is an admission that film cannot cope as a novel can with the sustained inner play of thought. The feeling one has in reading the book of listening to a dramatic monologue, in which, as in a Browning poem like "The Bishop Orders His Tomb . . ." or "My Last Duchess", everything is filtered through the consciousness of the protagonist-speaker, is missing. What Javo and Gracie, Angela, Martin and the others are like, or what the city itself feels like, are no longer a matter of an individual's subjective impression. They inevitably take on an objective life of their own[8]. One can no longer be sure of seeing them just as they appeared to Nora because there they are, with their own physical presences, the latter making as much claim on attention as Nora's perception of them. What has happened in the transposition of Garner's novel to the screen is that, while the original tone is largely maintained through the use of the voice-over (and aspects of the *mise-en-scène*), the *process* of thought remains elusive. In Chapter 1 it was suggested that rendering this process might well be one of the adaptor's chief difficulties. Cameron's film, careful and intelligent as it is and based on a screenplay collaboration with the novel's author, has not really found an answer to this. If Sandra Hall is right in saying that "The challenge is to transport the novelist's tone intact", then Cameron must be said to have gone a good way to achieving success, but it is in certain important matters a qualitatively different achievement from that of the novel.

Notes

1. Susan Higgins and Jill Matthews, "For the Record: Feminist Publications in Australia Since 1975", *Meanjin*, 3/1979, p. 329.
2. Barbara Giles, *Luna*, 3/1978, p. 42.
3. Ronald Conway, "Lost Generation", *Quadrant*, May 1978, p. 77.
4. Brian McFarlane, "**Monkey Grip**", *Cinema Papers*, No. 39, August 1982, p. 366.
5. Veronica Schwarz, "Multiplying and Dividing", *Australian Book Review*, June 1978, p. 18.
6. Anne Chisholm, "A love of language", *The National Times*, 4-10 January 1981, p. 31.
7. Sandra Hall, "Drifting along with a monkey on your back", *The Bulletin*, 6 July 1982, p. 95.
8. This will, of course, be true of any first-person novel transferred to the screen; true, that is, in varying degrees according to how far the "I" character is a participant in or observer of the narrative, how far (s)he can be relied on. Nora seems to me very differently placed in these respects from, say, Pip in *Great Expectations* or Nick Carroway in F. Scott Fitzgerald's *The Great Gatsby*. In spite of the first-person narration, the characters of these two novels have an objective reality not to be felt in the shadowy lives of Garner's characters.

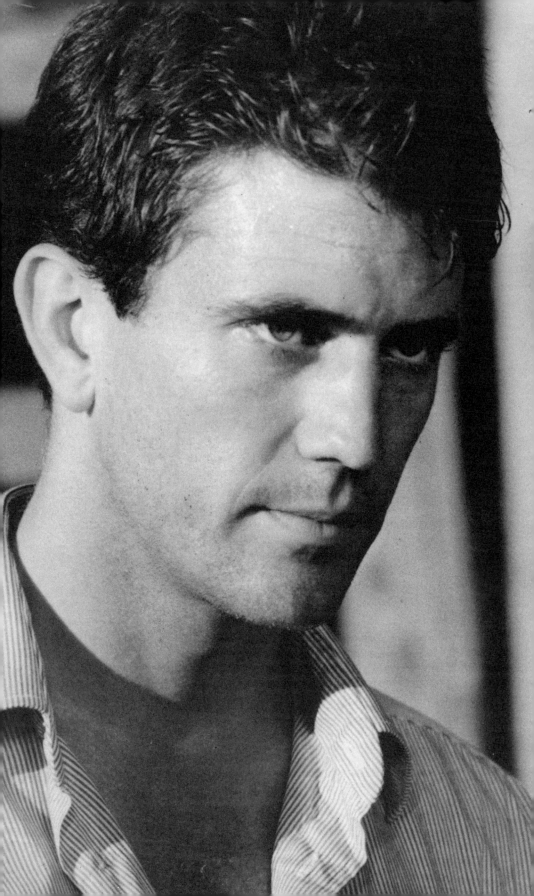

9. The Year of Living Dangerously

C. J. Koch's *The Year of Living Dangerously* was published by Thomas Nelson Australia, 1978, and reprinted as a Sphere paperback, 1979 (page references to the latter). Koch is the author of several other books with Asian settings, including *Across the Sea Wall*, and of *The Boys in the Island*, set in Tasmania.

The Year of Living Dangerously was directed by Peter Weir, for producer Jim McElroy, from a screenplay by David Williamson, Peter Weir, and C. J. Koch. The director of photography was Russell Boyd, the editor William Anderson and the composer Maurice Jarre. Running 105 minutes, it was released in 1983.

In C. J. Koch's *The Year of Living Dangerously*, "Great Wally", one of the Australian journalists in Jakarta in 1965, explains to Guy Hamilton, an Anglo-Australian journalist newly arrived in Indonesia:

> Do you know what the President called this year in his Independence Day speech last August? He gives each year a title, Guy, and I take the Sukarno year to run from one Merdeka Day to the next. The one we're in now is called the Year of Living Dangerously. Hm? (pp. 11-12)

1965 does, of course, prove to be a year of living dangerously for Sukarno, marking as it does the end of his all-but-godlike reign in Indonesia and the end of his manipulation of the forces of the Left and Right, within Indonesia and beyond. By the end of 1965, there will have been an aborted left-wing coup, followed in turn by the installation of a new right-wing hero, Suharto.

Against the background of seething political unrest, a background that keeps threatening to change its status by virtue of the persistent sharpness of its evocation, one is made aware that this is also a year of living dangerously for several of the novel's invented characters. It is especially so for Guy Hamilton; he is not just in political danger from a possible communist coup, but more seriously in danger of an emotional commitment he has sedulously avoided since an unhappy affair some years before. The narrator claims:

> A foreign correspondent has a life without continuity, without a centre; he has few real relationships . . . There isn't the time, there isn't the trust, nor, to be truthful, the inclination. (p. 59)

In the course of 1965, Guy finds himself drawn into two relationships,

Opposite: Australian journalist Guy Hamilton (Mel Gibson).

drawn further than he has customarily allowed himself: one is with the Australian-Chinese dwarf cameraman, Billy Kwan, and the other with Jill Bryant, attached to the British Embassy. Billy loves Jill and asks Guy to intercede with her on his behalf; he also hero-worships Guy and, when he accepts that Jill cannot love him, Billy does all he can to push Guy and Jill together. By the end of the first of the novel's three parts, Guy and Jill, both bruised by past relationships, have acknowledged love for each other. Guy has, that is, committed himself to Billy and Jill, and later he will feel that he has betrayed his commitment to both.

For Jill, such emotional involvement is to live more dangerously than she intends. Her relationship with the much older Colonel Ralph Henderson at the Embassy is "satisfactory" to her. "He's an old friend of my family's; we've got a lot in common; and he's so terribly kind. He's just a marvellous man, under that *pukka* manner. I never think about his age" (p. 119), she explains to Guy as to why she has thought of marrying Ralph. Just a little before, she has been very dismissive about the idea of marrying Billy: "Marriage! Are you joking? . . . I'm very fond of Billy; he's a marvellous little guy — but one marriage has been enough for me" (p. 106). She is clearly not looking for the disruptions of passion, for a relationship any more than "satisfactory"; before the end of Part Two she is imploring Guy: "*I'm so cold. Can't you love me at all?*" and "He drew her against him, with empty pity" (p. 195). Koch is not particularly good at filling in the details of this affair, despite gestures such as their shared nostalgia for England, but the contours are clear enough: in this year, each has been pushed out of the safety of the emotional shallows into uneasy depths which are paralleled in the growing turbulence of the country.

Guy's dilemma in relation to Jill is intensified in two ways. First, from what he has read in the "files" Billy keeps on everyone he knows, he believes her to be pregnant though the matter has not been mentioned between them. Knowing this, and despite her plea, "*Can't you love me at all?*", he leaves her to make a potentially dangerous expedition into Central Java to cover the Chinese-inspired "Long March". His departure also causes a rift with Billy who accuses him of betraying Jill and of "car[ing] for nobody *enough*". Embarked on the journey, Guy realizes that Jill's

> . . . repeated question, sounding in his head, had assumed great importance for him. It had broken down his resistance, not just to her, but to that faceless baby he so much feared, which might imprison him in a suburb; and he realized, as he drove, that Jill was at the core of a remarkable new happiness. (p. 199)

On this journey, the two aspects of Guy's living dangerously converge.

Second, his moral dilemma is tightened by his knowledge, given him by Jill, that the Indonesian Communist Party (PKI) is poised for a take-over, and is awaiting a Chinese arms shipment before launching a coup. It is exactly the kind of news he needs to persuade the Sydney office not to transfer him away from Jakarta, but having promised Jill not to reveal the source of his information he must find independent evidence of the PKI plans. Jill is both his reason for wanting to stay *and* the inadmissible source of the information that would ensure his staying.

This relationship ends on a note of muted promise as Guy and Jill fly out of Jakarta bound for Europe. Koch's oblique narrative method ensures that the reader is kept at a distance from these characters. The narrator from time to time describes their feelings without there ever being a very convincing sense of inner lives, of the emotional complexities, the hesitancies and doubts, which would have fleshed out the promising but still essentially bare bones of the relationship. What is offered is a recording, not an enactment. As Guy observes the sleeping Jill on the flight to Athens, he saw that "her character . . . would always sway between the sweetness and unreliability of the weak" (p. 294). "Sweetness", "unreliability", "weak": not one of these characterizations is substantiated in the narrative; one is asked to accept them merely as *données*. The same is true of a good deal of the emotional information about Guy. The following claim from the narrator suggests more interesting resonances about Guy than the novel actually knows what to do with:

> But I came to believe it was more than some ultimate news event Hamilton waited for. He was one of those people who are secretly waiting for something more: that vast and glorious happening, delicious as speed, bathing everything in gold, which perhaps never comes at all. (p. 66)

The relationship between Guy and Billy Kwan — Sir Guy and his loyal squire — is more interesting than that between Guy and Jill. This is partly because, through Billy's files, often quoted by the narrator, one is given a fuller sense of how at least half the journalist-cameraman team is thinking, and partly because it is more intricately connected to the "covert violence" of Indonesia's political history in 1965. Billy senses in Guy a "hybrid" like himself, a man of divided cultural heritages:

> It shows in our physical appearance. Scots ancestry makes you a mixture of Anglo-Saxon and Celt. I'm a mixture of Anglo-Saxon and Chinese. But I think it runs a little deeper than that. I'm unable to be Australian because of my Chineseness. You're unable to be Australian because of your Englishness. Or is it the other way round? (p. 83)

Guy initially rejects the comparison ("I'd like to share your problem, but I don't", claiming that he *is* English), but they do become, in Billy's term, a "team". There is an element of symbiosis here. Billy can alert Guy to aspects of the Jakarta political climate; he can arrange an interview with Aidit, head of the PKI, which will make Guy's name; as an expert cameraman, "I can be your eyes", he tells Guy. What he gets from Guy is the companionship of one who seems genuinely indifferent to his physical freakishness, who treats him entirely without patronage, and who offers an object for hero-worship. The novel is not especially convincing about why Billy should feel such devotion to Guy. The explanations are there as data: the notion of their being "hybrids", Guy's freedom from the kinds of boorishness and cynicism exhibited by the other journalists, and so on, but these scarcely add up to a *sufficient* image to account for hero-worship by one who seems Guy's superior in most ways.

There is, for instance, in Billy a degree of active commitment — political and social — which is not found in anyone else in the novel. He defines himself as a Christian radical and as such he has to be concerned for the poor of Jakarta: "'they're my brothers'. It was the sort of thing he seemed able to say without self-consciousness" (p. 96). His concern has taken the specific form of trying to help Ibu, a deserted Javanese woman with two small children. He writes in his dossier on her: *"In another country she would be a decent woman. Here, she begs, and perhaps sells herself . . . Her tragedy is repeated a million times in this city."* The narrator follows this with the gloss that:

> No other dossier provides such a clear graph as Ibu's does of the obsessions that would come to dominate Kwan's mind as the Year of Living Dangerously drew on. And it is possible to see, at this point of the year, that his prowlings are not caused just by the heat or insomnia. (p. 131)

Australian-Chinese cameraman Billy Kwan (Linda Hunt) gives money to Ibu (Norma Uatuhan) to help save her sick child.

For Billy has been moved by that question put to Christ by St Luke, "What shall we do then?", a question later taken up by Tolstoy, in regard to the poor. Billy, early in his acquaintance with Guy, asks this question, and it is clear that Guy, moved as he is by the "opposite intensities" (p. 20) set up by entering the slums of Asia, is far from Billy's state of concern.

Further, whereas Guy, like most of his colleagues, sees shifts in political power as matter for news, political figures as good for a possible scoop, Billy has hitched his wagon to the Sukarno star. He genuinely believes in Sukarno's love for his people, worships him with a single-minded devotion that mocks and is mocked *by* the press corps in the Wayang Bar. The cynicism of the latter, of course, proves to be well-founded, but it is one of the achievements of the novel to make Sukarno's magnetism convincing and thus, similarly, Billy's idolizing of him. Koch creates him as "a baffling mixture of menace and playboy appeal" (p. 9) and, in the end, having promised and failed to deliver "a Paris, a city of light to inspire struggling humanity" (p. 27), he is let off lightly by Koch's narrator. Of his "great years", of the years of Billy Kwan's idolizing, the narrator writes: ". . . you were all things to your people: they lived through you in the great years. But you ceased to go to Pasar Baru" (p. 263). It was said that Sukarno had gone to Pasar Baru at night, disguised in shabby civilian clothes, "to 'bathe in the crowds', to rub against the masses who intoxicated him" (p. 133). It is this Sukarno, champion of the Marhaen, the poor landowning peasants of Indonesia, who is Billy's hero, "the *Bung*, the daring elder brother, who carried out every outrageous scheme they had ever longed for" (p. 9).

His disillusionment with Sukarno coincides with his sense of betrayal by Guy. Udin, Ibu's little boy, has died and this becomes Billy's focus for blaming Sukarno's failure to help his people. In his file on Sukarno, the entry for 29 August reads:

Ibu wept now, riding in her betjak. Did her wails reach your ears, Bung Karno, in the Merdeka Palace? Udin died of a simple complaint, from which no child in the city need die, were it not for your folly: gastro-enteritis. (p. 240)

Billy's anti-Sukarno feeling is intensified by his solitariness after his expulsion from the Wayang Club and by his break with Guy. At the Wayang he "had launched without warning into a diatribe against his former hero" (p. 215), drawing on himself a sarcastic defence of Sukarno from the journalists who have previously been sceptical of his reverence for the Bung. Now, he claims, Sukarno has forgotten the people, except as extensions of himself, and while they starve he has said, "Let them eat rats." The narrator glosses the Wayang Club's response with "No idealist can publicly change his mind without being mocked, I suppose"; Billy has turned as fiercely against Sukarno as he was once whole-heartedly for him. In anger he turns against the journalists, specifically against Wally, for using people as objects of pleasure — in Wally's case, Indonesian boys.

In Part Three, "Patet Manjura: Amok", it is Billy as well as Indonesia that is amok. Much earlier, at the end of Chapter 10, the narrator sees in hindsight Billy's "two parallel obsessions": his doubt over Sukarno's policies for Indonesia (linked with his concern for the well-being of Ibu and her children), and his "strange, proprietary interest" in the affair between Guy and Jill. "Step by step, these preoccupations begin to lead him to a wild disappointment" (p. 134). It is one of the narrative's major achievements to keep these two preoccupations clearly before the reader and to show them as inextricably linked in Billy's mind by an outgoing concern for others that no one else in the book can match. Of all those whose fates are settled in the Year of Living Dangerously, his is the most complex; it is the only one, in fact, in which the author offers a real sense of inwardness. It is crucial that this should be so if one is to feel for Billy's death. He is murdered by Sukarno's BPI (security) men who push him from the hotel window from which he has hung a banner bearing the legend, SUKARNO, FEED YOUR PEOPLE. His death, passed off officially as suicide, has the effect of temporarily reuniting Guy and Jill.

The last fifty pages of the novel miss Billy: he has been the focus for its chief thematic interests and for its most intense emotion. Koch is left, on the political side, with the overthrow of Sukarno, speculation on his juggling of the forces of Left and Right, the victory of the Wayang of the Right over that of the Left as Suharto emerges as the new hero, and, on the personal side, with Guy's fears of losing Jill, the injury to his eye when he tries to seek entrance to the Palace, and the last-page reunion with Jill. What Guy as journalist has wanted has always been a good story; his time in Jakarta has pushed him, through association with Jill and Billy particularly, into more demanding and dangerous emotional territories. The novel's central narrative line works through the inroads made on Guy's professional neutrality, gradually giving way to reluctant involvement. If this is not a strikingly original premise, it is given a satisfying texture by the meshing of personal and political dramas, and notably by Billy Kwan's catalytic function in both.

Between Peter Weir's film, **The Year of Living Dangerously**, and its source in Koch's novel, two major changes have taken place. One, the loss of the novel's narrative voice, works very much in favour of the film; the other, a change in emphasis from the political to the romantic, leaves the film open to a charge of over-simplification of important issues.

The novel's narrator is Cookie, one of the elder statesmen of the foreign press corps in Jakarta 1965, and for the most part Koch seems content to leave him uncharacterized, a neutral voice as it were. The following passage suggests Koch has had some qualms about this:

> I don't quite know why I became a father confessor to my friends in the Wayang Bar; but I did. I suppose a Catholic, even a lapsed one, is good at

this, after years of observing the role in that coffin-shaped booth where all solutions to anguish seem possible — at least for a time. At thirty-seven, I was not quite ready to see myself as a father figure, but this is what I had become — even, ludicrously, to Great Wally, who was two years my senior. I was separated from my wife, which also probably fitted me for my part. A separated or divorced man either becomes a bitter bard reciting his wrongs, or he becomes a good listener. I became a good listener. (p. 58)

This is almost as much as the reader ever knows about Cookie, and this somewhat detached *persona* would matter less if Koch had either given him a more compelling or distinctive voice, or if he had managed the narrative difficulties inherent in the first-person narrator with more skill.

For the first-person narrator must always be a constraint upon an author. Martin Boyd in his "Langton" novels[1] generally avoids the pit-falls. The voice of the ageing, avuncular Guy Langton, wittily recounting and judging events of fifty years earlier, is one of the real pleasures of the sequence, offering the reader a point of view but warning him not to rely absolutely on it. Even Boyd though, in *Outbreak of Love*, does not altogether escape the awkwardness of describing incidents at which Guy cannot possibly have been present and of which no one could possibly have given him an account. This is a minor blemish in *Outbreak of Love* because there are other kinds of interest to be found in Guy. In general, it seems that authors favouring a first-person narrator should be rigorous in limiting themselves to what the narrator can reasonably know, as, say, Dickens does with Pip in *Great Expectations*. By the time the reader reaches the passage quoted above from Koch's book, he is likely to have been struck several times by the clumsiness of the device.

It seems, in fact, an unnecessarily distancing and complicating strategy which strains credulity at a number of points. Cookie, the narrator, is constantly being forced into remarks such as:

'I learnt, when we came to know each other, that . . .' (p. 37)
'It's not hard for me to picture how he felt . . .' (p. 39)
'. . . Billy's part in getting him started was a secret I was to discover only months later.' p. 43)
'What happened then was something Hamilton was later to discuss with me in the Wayang Bar. He knew he had won, it seems . . .' (p. 52)
'Hamilton was surprised at the strength of his own reaction. He was later to describe to me the extraordinary outrage he felt . . .' (p. 76)
'With all the goodwill in the world (as he put it to me later), Hamilton was not sure that . . .' (p. 83)

In spite of the previously quoted paragraph characterizing him as "father confessor", Cookie remains an uninteresting voice, best forgotten and working best *when* forgotten. It is not just the awkwardness of his filtering through to the reader information which he is unlikely to be privy to; as a *persona*, he remains too nebulous, too irrelevant to the action of the novel, to be able to offer the reader any valuable *commentary* on the events he

reports. One feels, in fact, that he merely serves to remove one from the sharp immediacy of the events themselves by reminding one of his presence: the "strength of [Guy's] own reaction" and "the extraordinary outrage he felt" suffer a considerable loss in intensity as a result of being presented so obviously as second-hand responses.

One of the chief sources of Cookie's information is Billy's files which he rescues from his bungalow after Billy's death. The film virtually begins with these, the credits having been accompanied visually by the strange, shadowy shapes of the *Wayang* puppets and aurally by a pounding musical score. These give way to Billy sitting at his desk, working on Guy's file, 25 June 1965, and the film subsequently settles firmly for Billy's point of view. It is better to be wrong, as he later believes himself to have been about Sukarno, than not to have committed oneself with the sort of fervour Billy displays for him — or Guy. Guy, as played by Mel Gibson, is presented as less mature, less life-battered, more boyishly vulnerable to experience in Weir's film than in the novel.[2] He is consequently more open to Billy's (Linda Hunt) influence than is the novel's protagonist. After his first meeting with Guy in the Wayang Club, when it is clear that Guy's predecessor, Potter, has left him in the lurch without providing the necessary introductions, Billy feels sorry for Guy and takes him under his wing. As they leave the club and move out into the crowded, poverty-stricken streets, full of noise and sleepless life, Billy warns Guy, "Most of us become children again when we enter the slums of Asia." That is, one's previous misconceptions will need to be refurbished in the light of this experience. This line in the novel comes as part of the narrator's detached commentary; the film gives it considerably more dramatic relevance by attributing it to the character who has the clearest first-hand knowledge of those slums. Further, Billy's subsequent quoting from St Luke and Tolstoy, "What then must we do?", also takes on an added emotional weight through juxtaposition with the previously quoted line.

Billy's, then, becomes a much more satisfactory "voice" than Cookie's. Billy is observer and participant, both detached and passionately involved. His files, which lead Guy to wonder for whom he is working, come to the audience direct, not merely as source material discovered some time later by Cookie and fed to the reader in small portions as the narrative demands. "Here on the quiet page I am master," he claims, "just as I am in the developing room." Billy's is the position of one who knows Indonesia from the inside, not just as a scoop-hungry journalist might, but as one who shares its suffering. His physical oddity has given him ease of access across the social and political range, so that he is the most knowledgeable guide to the country a newcomer like Guy could have. Though the film's point of view comprehends more than that of any individual character, it is with Billy's consciousness the audience is chiefly

Opposite: Billy and part of his "files".

asked to align itself. When he writes in his file on Guy, "You have changed, you are capable of betrayal", one's interest is, notwithstanding Mel Gibson's star charisma, with Billy. It is not that one has to accept him as being objectively *right*; rather that this informing voice has made more insistent emotional demands on the audience than either Guy or Jill (Sigourney Weaver) can do. They are less interesting intrinsically than in Billy's view of them. There is no reason, in the novel, to care what Cookie makes of them; there is every reason, in the film, to care how Billy sees them. Cookie's cool assessing tone is too much a matter of being wise after the event whereas Billy's assessment is made under the pressure of immediate and personal involvement.

In the opening paragraph of this section I have proposed that the film suffers a loss of complexity in political matters, favouring instead a romantic emphasis. Its precedent is, I suspect, **Casablanca** in which, for all the sense of turmoil in "this crazy world", it is the Great Love between Humphrey Bogart and Ingrid Bergman which has made it one of the world's most popular films. Up to a point, **The Year of Living Dangerously** sustains the comparison. There is a genuinely exciting sense of a country teetering on the brink of violence, of its being so divided within that its President's puppeteering control of the Left and the Right begins to look precarious, of individual lives' being dwarfed by the political problem. However, Sukarno is never, apart from a wonderful low-angled shot of him on his palace balcony, the dynamic presence that he is in

Billy surveys the couple he has placed together: Guy and Jill (Sigourney Weaver). Ralph Henderson (Bill Kerr), Jill's boss and past lover, surveys his rival.

Koch's book. The book is much more interested in trying to understand Sukarno than is the film, whose makers have, perhaps rightly, assessed how far the desired mass audience is likely to be interested in the details of *Konfrontasi* (Sukarno's policy of confrontation with Western influences) or in an analysis of why Sukarno's star shone so brightly for a time. Koch is lively and knowledgeable on these matters and one of the chief interests of the novel is the way he has responded to the charm, deceit and folly of Sukarno.

On the political level, the film inevitably settles for a few bold slogans: for example, "You're an enemy here Hamilton — like all Westerners"; "Sukarno is the voice of the third world"; "At least they [i.e., the Communists] will give us discipline." None of its somewhat skimpy political talk is as striking or eloquent as the overhead shot of Billy, in grief at the death of Ibu's small son, looking up at a vast poster of Sukarno which dwarfs the squalid dwellings and the people scrabbling for rice spilt in the street. That is, the film's political content is largely a matter of tableaux, of set-pieces like the anti-American demonstration by the PKI, and, of course, the Bulgarian Independence Day celebrations at which Billy makes his brief, futile stand against Sukarno.

Whereas in the novel Guy Hamilton's career as a journalist and the ascendancy he acquires with the help of Billy's contacts and pictures are subsumed into the larger context of the country's political restiveness, they are foregrounded in Weir's film. Like **Casablanca**, and unlike Costa-Gavras' **Missing** which kept Chilean politics and the rapprochement of its characters on an equal footing, **The Year of Living Dangerously** opts for being a romantic melodrama in an unusually exotic and well-realized setting. But "setting" is what the politics essentially are, and the film's considerable holding power is in the movement of Guy and Jill towards mutual commitment and in Billy Kwan's view of this. In this respect, the film is well served by the attractive performances of Mel Gibson and Sigourney Weaver (an American actress who has convincingly mastered a British accent, as Jill), if less well served by the screenplay which makes claims for them which it fails to substantiate. For instance, Billy Kwan, sensing a potential in Guy, asks in his files, *"Can you be the unmet friend?"* and later claims that he and Guy are "divided men . . . not quite at home in the world". Simply, the script does not make Guy interesting enough to justify these promising expectations, and Gibson's *persona* is not complex enough to fill in the lacunae with reserves of his own. Similarly, Billy's file on Jill discerns that she has "little real feeling, yet has a reverence for life. Could lapse into the promiscuity and bitterness of the failed romantic." The Jill of the film cannot bear the weight of such characterizations.

Within these limits, the love story grows more or less satisfactorily. It begins lightly, with a mutual wish for non-involvement; gains a certain texture from the attitudes taken towards it by Ralph Henderson (Bill Kerr) and Billy; and, reinforced by a somewhat lushly romantic score (by

Maurice Jarre), generates a persuasive aura of sexual hunger in the kissing sequence outside Guy's office. If the political aspects of the narrative have been simplified in their adaptation from Koch's novel, so too have the romantic elements. The issue of pregnancy and the subsequent possibility of abortion have been eliminated, and there is a playing down of Guy's dilemma over the Chinese arms shipment ("war in South East Asia versus a relationship" is an overwrought statement of how it appears to Guy). As Guy slides past the airport guards, while security men wreck his tape-recorder, he and the film are heading towards a very old-fashioned ending: the last-minute romantic reunion and clinch. One can be pardoned for believing that this has been mainly a love story after all.

I hope I have made clear the chief shift in emphasis and the chief change in narrative strategy that occurred in transposing Koch's novel into a film. I do not believe it is a matter of Peter Weir's seeking to achieve the novel's equilibrium by his own — cinematic — means; rather, the film bears the marks of looking for a different centre of interest. Little purpose would be served by doggedly tracing the film's chief incidents to arrive at statements about parallels and divergences. The time given to the love story, the use of physically attractive players, their careful placement against a range of picturesque backgrounds ("Oasis" poolside; Priok Harbour) and in a variety of social settings (Wally's bungalow-warming, the Embassy party), and the calculatedly romantic music that is associated with them:

Guy at the Wayang Club with the Canadian journalist, Pete Curtis (Michael Murphy).

the screen version "privileges" the lovers in these and other ways, so that there is no doubting their pre-eminence. The fact that they are so carefully watched by Billy also works to ensure that they command the viewer's attention.

There are two other aspects of the narrative that should be considered briefly in relation to each text: first, the function of the journalist in a volatile society, and, second, the use made of the symbolic *Wayang*. The novel connects the two by naming the press corps' meeting place in the Hotel Indonesia the Wayang Bar. It is in this bar that Guy is introduced, and in both film and novel it is important as the scene of one sort of running commentary on the narrative action, political and sexual, offering some justification for Billy's describing all journalists as *voyeurs*.

The group that gathers there centres on Great Wally, Wally O'Sullivan (Noel Ferrier) in the film, and he, along with the two other chief *habitués* of the bar, the Canadian Curtis (Michael Murphy) and the Australian Kevin Condon (Paul Sonkkilla), are each characterized in terms of their sexual preferences. Wally's preference is for Indonesian boys and in 1965 the threat of scandal in this matter is enough to lead him to leave Jakarta; Curtis patronizes "the cemetery in affluent Kebayoran, where the teeming prostitutes of the city patrolled the walls at night, waiting to be picked up in prowling cars" (p. 62); Condon, "a humourless, finicky man, essentially conformist in every way" has an insatiable passion for bare Javanese breasts, but strictly as an observer. In one way or other, then, all three, as Billy says of Wally, are guilty like Sukarno who "uses the people as objects for his pleasure" (p. 217). Given the peculiar isolation of journalists in a strange and imminently hostile country, the Wayang Bar becomes a necessary club for them. Sukarno's policy of *Konfrontasi* has meant for them:

> . . . life under a regime whose hatred for all Westerners had reached the dimension of insanity. We carried our white faces through the streets like ridiculous badges, ignoring insults and jeers and malevolent brown-eyed stares that had the intensity of religious fervour . . . we retreated gratefully to the Wayang, a foreigner's bar in a foreigner's hotel, out of reach of all but the most wealthy and powerful Indonesians. Off-stage, in these cool hours, we could be ourselves, no longer men in white masks. (p. 9)

If tempers become frayed in the Wayang Bar, it is not surprising as it is the one place where these men whose lives are "without continuity" can be themselves. Not that Great Wally, in 1965, can afford to be wholly himself, and there is, as Cookie reflects, "an artificially heightened good fellowship" at the time of Guy's arrival; because most British and American journalists have been barred, there is an increasing camaraderie among those who remain.

Koch makes the Wayang Club an important centre for the sifting of news, a place patronized by men whose job it is to catch and report events, to be always alert for a promise of news in the whiff of rumour or gossip. It is a solidly realized presence in the novel — relaxed, cynical, venal. The film picks up the novel's suggestion that "the Wayang Bar followed the American practice and sealed itself against all natural light" (p. 3) and distinguishes it clearly from those other centres where the West gathers its superiority about it, such as the Oasis swimming-pool behind the Hotel or the British Embassy. The film's decor for the Wayang Bar is mostly a subdued red and, for decoration, it has illustrations of the puppets which give the bar its name and which have a symbolic centrality, in the novel at least, if a little more perfunctorily deployed in the film.

Weir has rightly understood the importance of the *Wayang* puppets in the Javanese way of looking at experience, in a general sense, and in relation specifically to Sukarno's situation, and this insight is registered in the *Wayang* shadows appearing behind the credits. Nevertheless, though used in this way as a motif to open the film, there is even here a touch of the merely decorative. The film's use of the *Wayang* is not wholly free from a suggestion of gratuitous exotica.

Koch, on the other hand, has located them more centrally in his narrative. He waits longer than Weir to introduce them but when he does he ensures that we cannot miss their importance. In Billy's bungalow, he asks Guy:

> 'Did you see my *Wayang* puppets? Beauties, aren't they? If you want to understand Java, Ham, you'll have to understand the *wayang*'. (p. 81)

He identifies several (including Semar, the patron of all dwarfs); representing conflicting aspects of human nature as perceived in Hindu doctrine. During the dry monsoon, by the end of June,

> the screens of the *wayang kulit*, the shadow-shows, light up all through the countryside. Whole villages stay awake until dawn, watching the capering, beloved silhouettes, lost in the ancient dreams of the Ramayana and the Mahabharata. (p. 123)

A striking contrast with men without continuity. And, a little later, "In that hottest month of the year, when Hamilton went out to Central Java alone, the *Wayang* of the Left were everywhere triumphant" (p. 196). On this journey, Guy watches a performance of the *Wayang*, "its lit screen hanging in the dark like that of a drive-in cinema" (p. 202).

The word "*wayang*" pervades the novel as it undergoes a series of transmutations. From its specifically religious (i.e., Hindu) connotations, Koch makes clear that its ideas of see-sawing, conflicting morality moved out to a broader cultural significance: for the Javanese, the *Wayang* is both religion and theatre, mysterious and yet part of everyday life. In a special modern context, it has come to stand for the forces at the opposite ends of the political spectrum. Sukarno, arch-puppeteer, has finally been caught in the middle. Reflecting on his fall, the narrator suggests:

> The West asks for clear conclusions, final judgements. A philosophy must be correct or incorrect, a man good or bad. But in the *wayang* no such final

conclusions are ever drawn. The struggle of the Right and the Left never ends, because neither side is wholly good or bad. (p. 265)

In trying to account for Sukarno's disappearance from the dais of a large stadium, the narrator inclines "to the theory that Sukarno had finally decided to back the *Wayang* of the Left against the *Wayang* of the Right, and had been called from the dais to be given a last-minute briefing on what would take place after midnight" (p. 268): that is, the murder of his generals. Sukarno has been safe, even victorious, as long as he has kept the *Wayang* of the Left and the Right in play, but maintaining this kind of equilibrium proves as difficult in politics as in personal relationships.

The binarism of the West makes the Westerner subtly unadaptable to Indonesia, wanting not a constant sense of struggle but definitive propositions instead. The film gives Billy a scene in which he explains to Guy the importance of understanding the *Wayang*, and in almost the same words as those quoted above (p. 81), but there is no sense of its being allowed to permeate the film in the shifting symbolic way it winds through the novel. Perhaps, if politics is regarded as the kiss of death at the box-office, there was also a fear that the mystique of the *Wayang* would be too esoteric for mass tastes. If so, this is surprising since Peter Weir has never been a director to espouse literal-minded realism. In **The Last Wave** particularly, he showed himself sympathetically aligned with attempts to reach beyond rational explanations. His hero in that film, the lawyer David Burton (Richard Chamberlain), has more in common with Guy Hamilton than has any other of Weir's protagonists. Like Burton, Guy is a man up against a situation beyond his European understanding; unlike Burton, Guy is not pushed by director or screenplay into acknowledging the validity of a radically different set of beliefs from those he is used to. I think the film suffers somewhat as a result, not just because it is therefore a thinner experience than the novel on which it is based, but as well because it has not been moved to pursue its own insights as far as it might.

Notes

1. *The Cardboard Crown* (1952), *A Difficult Young Man* (1955) and *Outbreak of Love* (1957), the first three "Langton" novels, are told through Guy's first-person narration.
2. Koch has claimed in a radio interview with Terry Lane, 3LO, Melbourne, 26 January 1983, that the screenplay is mostly his work, though the credit is shared with David Williamson and Peter Weir. See also "Letter to the Editor" by Koch, *Cinema Papers*, No. 42, March 1983, p. 10.

10. The Night the Prowler

Patrick White's *The Night the Prowler* was first published by Jonathan Cape, 1974, as one of the short story collection, *The Cockatoos*. It was subsequently reprinted singly, along with White's screenplay adapted from it, by Penguin Books and Jonathan Cape, 1978 (page references to this edition). White, who was awarded the Nobel Prize for Literature in 1973, has published eleven novels, including *The Tree of Man*, *Riders in the Chariot* and *The Twyborn Affair*.

The Night the Prowler was directed by Jim Sharman, for producer Anthony Buckley, from a screenplay by Patrick White. The director of photography was David Sanderson, the editor Sara Bennett and the composer Cameron Allan. Running 90 minutes, it was released in 1978.

Throughout the 1970s, one kept hearing reports that Patrick White's *Voss* was to be filmed by Joseph Losey, from a screenplay by David Mercer. Harry M. Miller had bought the rights and various names were suggested for the lead. Nothing, though, ever came of it, and White himself seems never to have had anything to do with the adaptation. One would not suppose White easy to adapt to the screen: despite the often powerful visual effects his work achieves, his prose style is so idiosyncratic — allusive, elliptical — as almost to resist transfer. Without the distinctive Whitean voice, *The Tree of Man* for instance might have reached the screen as no more than another family saga, running the gamut from pioneering hardihood to modern-day etiolations (not necessarily a bad thing, of course).

White finally reached the screen in 1978 when Jim Sharman's film, **The Night the Prowler**, based on a White short story, opened the 25th Sydney Film Festival. Unlike in the abortive *Voss* enterprise, he was very much involved in **The Night the Prowler** for which he wrote the screenplay[1]. Though Sharman had "the normal director collaboration", which he described in an interview in *Cinema Papers*[2], a comparative study of the short story and the screenplay shows a very close correspondence. Both exhibit — for better and worse — characteristics to be found throughout White's work. Though of course developed in more detail in the novels, the preoccupation with a selfish, insensitive middle-class, its antennae quivering with distaste at any sign of individuality, is rendered in the story with sharp, witty perception *and* a predictable nastiness which makes one suspect the author's tolerance. As elsewhere in White's work, the sensitive — usually maimed in some way — are sifted from the insensitive rest of us with a thoroughness that borders on élitism. In *Riders in the Chariot*, his sixth novel, only four arbitrarily chosen characters, each notably scarred

Opposite: Felicity Bannister (Kerry Walker).

or underprivileged, are admitted to the mysterious status of riderhood. Virtually everyone else is crude or vicious or complacent or venal. The heroine of *The Night the Prowler* achieves by the end of the story, in a derelict house with a naked, dead old man, her place in the chariot, which is not yet, in the canon of White's work, bursting at the seams.

David Stratton makes considerable claims for the film version of the story:

> **The Night the Prowler** is a remarkable film which miraculously fuses the talents of two of Australia's most formidable creators, Patrick White and Jim Sharman. While remaining very faithful to White's original story, the film also emerges as a close cousin to **Shirley Thompson versus the Aliens**.[3]

Not having seen the last-named example of Sharman's work (it was released in 1972), I cannot say how close in spirit it is to **The Night the Prowler**; the latter hasn't, apart from some rather flashy effects, much in common with the only other Sharman film I have seen, **Summer of Secrets** (1976). Stratton's phrase "two of Australia's most formidable creators" seems premature applied to Sharman, whereas, like his work or not, White has undeniably produced a major *oeuvre*. **The Night the Prowler** is essentially a Patrick White film in its themes, its limning of character, its distaste for the Australian bourgeoisie. Sharman apparently was enthusiastic about the cinematic possibilities of the story and has

The night the prowler: Felicity and would-be rapist (Terry Camilleri).

certainly kept "faithful" to it, even down to details of *mise-en-scène* and dialogue. In fact, he appears to have largely effaced himself in ensuring that White's intentions are preserved.

In the *Cinema Papers* interview Sharman spoke of some of the problems in adapting *The Night the Prowler*:

> They were lesser than if I had adapted a novel. Usually it is the style of writing in a novel that makes it unique. So if you decide to film it, you have to be confident you can generate a visual style that will equal the prose style. Secondly, of course, you have to allow for the natural impulse of people to say, 'It's not as good as the book.'
>
> With short stories, however, you don't have that problem, because people don't feel so protective about them. They are slighter works in scale and it is not so much a holy writ situation.[4]

Apart from sharing the common belief that style is somehow separable from content, the comments on problems in adapting the novel seem true enough, and Sharman is probably right that "people don't feel so protective about" short stories. However, the problem of style, or, more accurately, of tone is as germane to the short story as to the novel. As it is, in **The Night the Prowler** the tone remains unmistakably White's, the middle-class animus intensified by the camera's insistence on yapping mouths or mouths stuffing themselves with food or on wobbling flesh. More significant in the adaptation of a short story is the idea contained in his next remark:

> There are, of course, things in the film that aren't in the story. With a novel you have to decide what details you should dismiss; with a short story the situation is reversed — you have to expand this.

In fact, *The Night the Prowler*, at fifty-seven pages, offers slight enough material for a feature-length film, but White has invented only one new major episode in its transposition to the screen. Elsewhere, some scenes suggested by the original are stretched with additional dialogue or with visual expansion of points more briskly made in the original.

The short story tends to focus on a single point of crisis, its development being in sketching the associations of the crucial moment and/or working towards a resolution of the crisis. Perhaps the very form militates against frequency of adaptation, at least at feature-film length. Exhibitors are apt to require the latter to be, roughly, between ninety minutes and two hours in length. Given the short story's habit of focusing on a single narrative event, film adaptation would be likely to enjoin a diluting or dissipating effect on the original concept. There have been goodish film versions of D. H. Lawrence stories, **The Rocking Horse Winner**[5] (1949) and **The Fox** (1967), both feature-length; and in the late 1940s and early '50s, three successful English films — **Quartet**, **Trio**, and **Encore** — were made by adapting batches of Somerset Maugham stories. However, the portmanteau idea of these latter was rarely repeated and never with such success, even when the great John Ford filmed three Irish stories as **The Rising of the Moon** (1957). The short story proved more adaptable to television's characteristic fifty-minute time slot, and there were attractive seasons of stories by Thomas Hardy, "Saki", and, again, Maugham, among others. The really remarkable short story requires an uninterrupted narrative burst from its teller and a holding of the breath by the reader. *The Night the Prowler* is not a tale of this order though its narrative pivot is striking enough.

White's story begins in crisis: "Mrs Bannister reached the bathroom in time to vomit into the wash basin" and, a few sentences later: "At last Felicity had consented to take Dr Herborn's sedative. They had all, even Humphrey, accepted pills." Something "ghastly" has happened. In order to bring the reader up to date, Doris Bannister telephones her friend Madge with an account of the prowler who broke into Felicity's bedroom and raped her. A major issue for Doris is: who will tell John, Felicity's rising young diplomat fiancé? But Felicity has already written to John breaking off their engagement, almost as if glad of a reason for doing so. Felicity is emerging as a girl of some character, with a certain dignity and strength. She has refused to allow the doctor to examine her and she refuses the banal comforts of "a nice-looking kidney" for breakfast or a visit to the hairdresser's which, Doris claims, would do her a world of good.

This uncomfortable little family, its members perhaps predictably failing to communicate with each other, is then the subject of a brief flashback. White concisely establishes the Bannisters' early married life on the edge of Centennial Park, Sydney, which proved "such a blessing" when their only child, Felicity, was born. During the war Humphrey is posted to New Guinea: Doris sends him a fortnightly snap of Felicity and (in a revealing sentence) "Humphrey described in return a formal nostalgia for home which failed to persuade her he wasn't a fairly fulfilled adjutant" (p. 20). In this exchange of tokens, Doris and Humphrey's relationship is lethally sketched. There are suggestions that the child, on Humphrey's return, has not been able to establish an easy rapport with her father, not helped by Mummy's remarks like: "I'm sure Daddy's too tired and hot to enjoy a heavy girl on his chest" (p. 21), and Felicity becomes a quiet girl "because we've always been so close as a family", Mummy tries to believe. The importance of this brief section is in its intimation that Felicity's capacity for affection is suffocated by her parents' various inadequacies. She is awkward at the carefully arranged dance for her sixteenth birthday, full of guests from "good addresses"; and she is more awkward still when Humphrey delivered his "first lecture on 'keeping clean and pure for the man who will eventually put all his faith in a girl'" (p. 22).

The man who eventually does so, Felicity having become "a radiant young woman" and the flower of the neighbourhood, is John, of External Affairs, with whom she enters into an engagement, "so drawn-out you sometimes wondered whether it was on" (p. 25). It is not, White appears to suggest, a relationship that draws out the passion in Felicity. After the night of the prowler, the engagement ring disappears and the neighbourhood perceives a change in Felicity, first at the level of dress and hairdo, then of starting to "talk clever". Having revealed the neighbours as being nastily nosy, White then diminishes John whose

> mouth had been formed by tactful conversation, foreign languages, and the strategic smile, though he enjoyed doing his duty by a kiss.
> 'I mean — you don't imagine I can love you less?' He was now doing his duty by words.
> 'Yes', she said. 'I know.' She didn't believe him passionate enough ever to be unfaithful to her. (p. 30)

No one, that is, really wants to know the inner, passionate Felicity, and John is satirized for mere dutifulness. There is a Whitean meanness in the way he characterizes *everyone* but Felicity as obtuse, limited or malicious.

She embarks on a strange new life, herself becoming a prowler of the night. She takes to the streets, becoming "more purposeful, her mind less blurred by memory and the instincts. Her body grew muscular inside the protective skin of slithery leather . . ." (p. 35). Whatever has happened to her on the night the prowler (as the title cryptically puts it), the effect has been to arrive at acceptance of "that frightening, still partly dormant, cone of her own will" (p. 36). Considering the form it takes when it becomes active, one can only feel there was much to be said for dormancy. For part of Felicity's new sense of power in her own resources, of liberation from the stifling world of familial complacencies, is to break into and slash about in "a house not unlike their own in its ugly splendour and convinced inviolacy" (p. 36). While Felicity is thus enjoying some sort of revenge here, slitting leather chairs and the like, it is hard to resist the idea that White is also relishing the vicious expression of his own animus against the prosperous middle-classes.

As she lies back among the wreckage of "Harve" and "Darl's" house, she recalls, in a flashback episode, what actually happened on the night the prowler. Which is to say, nothing, except that she quickly turned the tables on the night intruder with the "little jagged decalcified teeth" (p. 41). She would have been "ready to grapple with him in the glorious but exacting game in which she had never taken part" (p. 40), but he is unequal to the occasion and after frightening him witless she lets him out. She conceals, for later use, the knife she has taken from him and also, in a pretentious zeugma, "the heart of a moral predicament they [parents and others] couldn't possibly understand" (p. 44). It is the use of the knife on Harve and Darl's property that recalls the night, and the ironic awareness that, though "nothing" had happened, in some curious way it has released her into a new — real? — self.

White has always been an author for underlining his themes, for explicit attention to ensuring that his reader has got the point; and "the point" in *The Night the Prowler*'s last ten pages is hammered home. In entering and wrecking houses, "she continued in her efforts to expend, by acts of violence, the passive self others had created for her; though this behaviour too, she suspected, was ending in conformity" (p. 47). Never caught, "Over and over, she demonstrated the stupidity of those who were out to catch her; men, of course." Her father, John, the prowler, the doctor she refused to allow to examine her: all in their various ways have been "out to catch her". Wandering in the park at night, she comes upon an assortment of derelicts (including a drunken old woman), furtive copulaters, and a bunch of singing Greek youths ("milk-bar kids getting a kick out of false pathos", p. 52). In a curious sense too, she feels a camaraderie with these after-dark visitors to the park: "All of us in here at night are on the wrong side of the railings" (p. 50).

Final wisdom comes from an encounter with a naked old man in a decaying house. Having failed to persuade him to dress or let her wash him, she suggests that he still has his memories. He does.

> I was thinking of the days when I could still enjoy an easy piss. And stools came easy. That's the two most important things, you find out. (p. 55)

He tells her, "I believe in nothing. And nothing's a noble faith. Nobody can hurt nothing. So you've no reason for being afraid." Having delivered this inspiriting credo and accepted her offer to stay by him ("No rats . . . And an easy pee"), he dies, leaving her to report the death of one she "knew as intimately as herself, in solitariness, in desolation, as well as in what would seem to be the dizzy course of perpetual becoming" (p. 57).

Like very many short stories, then, *The Night the Prowler* begins in the middle of a crisis; unlike many, the true nature of the crisis is not revealed until the story is about two-thirds finished. It thus has an unusual structure whereby the reader is aware of reactions to and developments from the crucial event before knowing the exact nature of the event itself. The story's structural irony is that the changes which take place in the heroine and her way of life, held perhaps to be the result of rape, prove to derive from the fact that she was not raped. In a curious way, the prowler is both one of those "who were out to catch her" *and* yet another of those who fail to meet her needs. The prowler is unready to deal with her surprisingly matter-of-fact, even inviting response.

> Then he was getting down beside her. It was so natural. As it was what she had always been expecting, she now realized, she turned her face towards that side of the dark from which his eyes must be looking at her. (p. 40)

There is, for Felicity, a "naturalness" and inevitability about this encounter that has been missing from her life with her parents and fiancé.

Opposite: Doris Bannister (Ruth Cracknell) agonizes with her daughter over the "rape".

It is as though the truth about the prowler is only revealed when Felicity is able to face fully the implications of her supposed "assault". That is why the episode is inserted into the house-wrecking scene: as she puts paid to Harve and Darl's *parvenu* aspirations, she "lay there only half-credulous of what was after its fashion a consummation" (p. 40). I take this to mean a consummation of inarticulate but passionate longings for a form of self-expression which has only begun to find release since the night of the prowler.

Such a premise — release through non-rape — might have been the basis for black comedy and there are indeed elements of this genre in the story. White, however, appears to have loftier things in mind as some of the quoted passages indicated. Felicity's brush with "the glorious but exacting game" the prowler seems to offer founders on his ordinariness and she is aware of "her failed intention: to destroy perhaps in one violent burst the nothing she was, to live, to be, to know" (p. 44). There is White being quite explicit about his heroine's hitherto passive acceptance of life, never questioning, never engaging with it, very far from "the dizzy course of perpetual becoming" (p. 57) which she apprehends by the story's end.

My difficulty with the story is that, though the pivotal event is inventive, there is a marked disparity between White's depiction of the forces that have acted as constraints on Felicity's growth and that of the course of action that marks her liberation from these forces. White is, characteristically I would claim, more persuasive in denunciation than in affirmation. The suburban satire of the Bannisters' lives, created in their language (the night has been "ghastly" for Doris; Humphrey talks to Felicity of "the right man") and in malicious observation of their rituals ("garbage day", Doris reminds Humphrey on the morning after the night the prowler . . .), is sharp and funny, often quite lethally perceptive about middle-class obsessions and ambitions. John Galbraith, the budding diplomat, is presented as an answer to one of the latter:

> Doris Bannister's own sensibility was charmed by the erect young man in charcoal flannel; his wristwatch made her feel quite drunk; his receding hair saddened her as she realized how history repeats itself. (p. 24)

To Doris he is an "intolerably desirable young man", but it is John as well as Doris who is nailed in the description quoted. The pervasive malevolence of White's view of middle-class Australia (cf. also Thelma in *The Tree of Man*, various predatory/frail social ladies in *Riders in the Chariot*) is always in danger of overkill. The comparative brevity of *The Night the Prowler* protects him from his own worst excesses (though he has a characteristic moment of self-indulgent satisfaction with Felicity's adolescent acne). The thrusts are sharper and more discriminatingly made than is sometimes the case in the longer works, but there is still an unrelenting vindictiveness in White's view of suburban Australia. The best one can hope to be in this soul-destroying ambience is dim; the other end of the spectrum is crowded with possibilities like "vicious", "complacent", "vulgar", "smug", "cruel" and so on. It is acutely done but White has done it so often that one begins to wonder whether he is not marshalling sledge-hammers for egg-shells.

However, the denunciatory elements of the story are clearly realized by White; what is less clear, and less convincing, is the series of events which seem designed to constitute an affirmation of Felicity's growing realization of herself and her place in the world. For one thing, White devotes very much less space to these "liberating" incidents: the wrecking of houses of the rich, the night-prowling through the park, the final meeting with the old man. For another, their narrative thinness leads White into the kinds of declamatory statement which often look like replacement for unrealized intention. About the drunks in the park, for instance, one reads that Felicity would

> . . . lie beside them, uncritical of the stench from rotten teeth, alcohol, and feet; she would put up with anything, provided it did not offend against her sense of scale, and promised some kind of revelation. (p. 49)

It is not just that the affirmative aspect of White's vision is jejune — revelation growing from decay — but that it is spelt out with the subtlety of desk-calendar wisdom. As a result, one is less moved by Felicity's situation (and especially by the final illumination) than one should be. Faced with positive, life-enhancing experience, White falls back on statement and gesture, failing to dramatize it with anything like the vigour displayed in the flaying of restrictive suburbia.

Kerry Walker's fine performance as Felicity in the film goes some distance towards righting this balance in spite of the screenplay's efforts to relish the nastiness. Sharman has claimed that he "needed someone who could sustain the entire film with her performance". Walker cannot quite do that, but comes near to satisfying his next requirement: the film "needed someone with a hidden passion who would be able to convey certain emotions without words"[6]. Rightly deciding that the close-up is the cinema's best means for suggesting thought processes, Sharman makes full use of her expressive face, mask-like in her encounters with the non-comprehending, sullen, obsessive, relaxed (with the old drunk woman), and finally entranced, and of her somewhat awkward figure which responds to the script's demands for suburban *couture* and, later, for zipped-up black leather. Walker copes very well indeed with those scenes which give her something to *do*. She helps the viewer to understand how the "rape" has stirred her as nothing else in her life has. She is responsible for some sharply effective moments, such as when she tries to explain to her fiancé what the assault has meant to her. A trifle obviously, perhaps, in a nearby park a dog is kept at its owner's heel in an obedience trial. And there is a striking image in which Felicity imagines herself, blank-faced and *soignée*, arriving in a Rolls-Royce at Parliament House. The image is dramatic in the way it enacts her premonition of what the future life may be and her sense of its being the product of an obedient past. Later, as she strides around in black leather, wielding the shark knife she has taken from the prowler, she is a commanding presence, a new grace and purposefulness in her movements. She compels interest, through her physical presence, in a way that White's rather meagrely imagined episodes fail to dramatize convincingly one's sense of the new Felicity.

In this respect, the film gains in relation to the story; in general, though, its strengths are those of the novel. The first half of the film deals knowingly with the suffocating rituals of suburban life. The film's title dissolves into a shot of a very ordinary, pleasant weatherboard house against a deep blue sky and the focus remains on the house throughout the credits as the camera pulls slowly back to reveal the substantial whole of it. The film announces the time as summer in the late 1960s, then cuts in turn to close-ups of a sepia photograph of a baby, of a glass clock chiming, of a girl's face on a pillow in an ultra-feminine bedroom. All this deceptive normality is sharply undermined as the camera reveals Mrs Bannister (Ruth Cracknell) peering through the keyhole, then looking distastefully in a mirror, before going to the bathroom to vomit. In a close-up of her hand, she is revealed as "almost dabb[ing] herself with Humphrey's mouthwash before the shape of the bottle suggested it wasn't her eau de cologne" (p. 7). In most of these details, White's script and the film follow almost

Doris, compulsively cleaning up "a cup the moment it is used".

exactly the information given in the story, and to the same end: that is, to establish the fact that, in the apparent normality of the scene, something extraordinary has happened. In fact, the opening shots of the house's exterior, by contrast with its aim of sleeping stillness, intensify the sense of the crisis within.

Then, instead of Mrs Bannister's telephone conversation with her gossipy friend Madge (Maggie Kirkpatrick) as a means of filling in the narrative information for the reader, the film offers a dissolve in blackness and a scream, and there is a flashback to the scene of several hours before. Mrs Bannister and husband Humphrey (John Frawley) hurtle down the stairs to find Felicity sobbing at the table, for Felicity is still behaving as she believes others will expect her to. The interrogation that follows is conducted in the dining-room and the camera establishes the solid affluence of the Bannisters by shooting across the elegant table, set with silver candlesticks, and establishes Doris and Humphrey's wish not to face the truth about Felicity by having them turn away from her in unison. There is an obviousness in this piece of direction that matches the overt thematic statements of the novel, but generally in this early part of the film direction and camera work to stress the rituals of the Bannisters' lives. Doris compulsively washes a cup the moment it is used; Humphrey, despite, or even because of, the alarms of the night, is in the garden pruning little bits off his roses; this sight is revealed by Doris' aggressive, curtain-opening performance; and the earlier talk about "Daddy's good Napoleon!" suggests a household in which categories are preserved.

All this early study of the family — sympathetic in the case of the clamped-down, lumpish Felicity, satirical in that of the parents — is well-paced and well-observed. There are excellent performances from John Frawley as the conventional, inhibited Humphrey and, despite some rather stagey movements, from Ruth Cracknell as Doris. At the centre of their hovering behaviour, and that of the police and doctor, is the girl's enigmatic behaviour, and Kerry Walker's acting has here an alert stillness that is arresting and that works more intensely through contrast with the others. The family situation offers promising drama: the mother's concern for her daughter is secondary to that for herself ("You don't know what I've been through", she intones to Madge) and the father, having tried to buy police silence on the matter, takes refuge in the garden. However, the film, like the story, is determined to flay the parents. It falls into overstatement of the mother's prurience, possessiveness, obsessive tidiness, and social prattle ("one of the detectives was such a charming little man . . . grows staghorns", she tells Madge), and only a little less so in presenting Humphrey as obtuse, conventional and deficient in understanding. White's vision is never comprehensive or humane enough to recognize that their limitations might demand pity.

Adrian Martin has described **The Night the Prowler** as "the most ambitious film involving family relationships yet produced in Australia"[7].

It is ambitious and, in its first half, successful, even allowing for certain miscalculations of emphasis (e.g., the over-insistent use of mirrors and telephone to signal Doris' prattling self-absorption). The issue of sexuality within the family is intelligently raised by presenting Felicity as a victim of her parents' repressive reticence and their oppressive attempts at articulateness on sexual matters. The nice young man, promising diplomat John Galbraith (John Derum), is essentially an extension of the ethos of Felicity's parents. In fact, it is clear that Doris' infatuation with the idea of John is a stronger feeling than any Felicity shows for him, and this is dramatized in her hovering about them with a watering can as they sit talking on the verandah. Certainly John's "understanding" later on is no more profound than Doris' "advanced" talk (to Madge) of "all this sleeping around nowadays".

Neither film nor novel chooses to pursue the theme of family, a fruitful source of drama as film-makers such as Douglas Sirk or novelists such as Ivy Compton-Burnett have shown. White, like them, seems at first inspired by Samuel Butler's words about the family: "I believe that more unhappiness comes from this source than any other."[8] However, as Adrian Martin points out, "the film changes direction abruptly, so that Felicity's dilemma is presented as being purely individual ('I know myself') and no longer related to the family."[9] This is disappointing because the motif of sexual repression is capable of fuller delineation. It is established early in relation to the family: in the child's wanting more

Doris bursts enthusiastically in on Felicity and her diplomat fiance John (John Derum).

affection than the father can offer; in the bath sequence when the mother takes over briskly from him for the more intimate drying processes; in the teenage Felicity's compulsive eating and furtive reading of *Peyton Place* in the lavatory; in the cutting of her sixteenth-birthday cake, shot in such a way as to suggest a public release of private repression. The sex lecture Humphrey offers to Felicity is given largely in a two-shot which emphasizes the metaphorical significance of the space between them. The only post-prowler scene in which Felicity's sexual tension is worked out in terms of her relationship with her parents is that in Harve and Darl's house where she slashes at a vapid blonde family portrait (of Darl when younger), and she sprawls at Harve's desk and has a sudden vision of her father opposite her.

Elsewhere her "liberation", as in the short story, is an enigmatically private affair, as Felicity emerges from the cocoon of her middle-class life and plunges into the murky byways of Sydney night-life. The film fills out these nocturnal prowlings at somewhat greater length than the original does. With her black leather, her shark knife and her lump of lava, Felicity is presented as strange even among the strange ("Jesus 'Liss . . . what do you add up to?") as she zips up purposefully or roars off on the back of someone's motor bike. There is a new look of relaxed pleasure and affection on her face as she is seen talking to the drunken old woman (Dorothy Hewett) in the park; she laughs cheerily when a repulsive old drunk offers to show her "a real surprise", his hand straying towards his fly; she runs after a bunch of hoods, whirling a bicycle chain at them; and some young Greeks, singing about a heartless woman, are, unsurprisingly, embarrassed at her outburst to them. "The heart", she announces vehemently, "is in anybody — only waiting to be torn into — by somebody big enough — to perform the bloody act" (screenplay, p. 151).

In these incidents the film faithfully mirrors the story's simplistic notions that only among outcasts of rotten bourgeois society is one likely to find not merely one's true self but the true meaning of life itself. These encounters reach their climax, as story and film near their ends, when Felicity comes upon the naked old man in the derelict house. In contrast to upholstered suburbia (given a final twist of the knife in the Bannisters' party, invented for the film), he has reduced life to its bare essentials and, repeating the words of the original, he has found that he believes in nothing and that "nothing is a noble faith." The film picks up this description from the story:

> In fact the masses of hitherto colourless, or at most dust-coloured wall, were illuminated: the tributaries of decay had begun to flow with rose; the barren continents were heaped with gold. (p. 56)

This offers a visual invitation scarcely to be resisted, and a glimmer of light comes through the slats nailed to the window, giving Felicity a suggestive aureole in her moment of revelation. At this point, the film

Felicity, alienated from family in her very bourgeois bedroom.

breaks with the story to show Felicity walking home in the morning with new confidence. There are signs of ordinary life on the move: a young wife kisses her husband goodbye; a boy polishes a surfboard; Humphrey is shaving; and the camera pans up over the series of apartment balconies, each with its domestic tableau, then rests on a wide city-scape, before cutting back to the old man. Once there, the camera pulls away to reveal Felicity, lit from side and rear, in a state of mystic illumination, having told the police, "I knew him . . . as I know . . . myself." The interleaved shots are perhaps meant to indicate the unthinking nature of normality or to suggest that Felicity now sees them with new eyes.

This insertion is one of the few invented for the film and its effect, in disrupting the scene with the old man, is faintly gratuitous. The one main sequence which has no counterpart in the story is that of the Bannisters' cocktail party which gives White, abetted by Sharman's direction, a last opportunity for a kick in the groin of suburban society. The guests (pitched at a social level somewhat higher than one would have expected) are stuffing in canapés, guzzling drinks, and talking fatuously of communists, cars, and "the old days on the Orient Line". Into this scene of decadence and superficiality wanders Felicity, shoeless and blank-faced, the symbol no doubt of an honesty which criticizes their shrill vulgarity and affectation. A glance at the screenplay reveals White making a meal of this scene. The direction for Scene 149 (p. 142) is: "Shots of mouths, pleated, or smooth, or downy, false teeth or precariously real biting into savouries, a mouthing of glasses, in one case a mopping at spilt liquor." A little later there is a "Shot of Patti Stevens' arched eyebrows, rounded mouth like a pullet's arse about to drop its egg" (p. 145). Who knows what arcane researches feed White's passion for the repellent simile. He is obviously much taken with the "pullet's arse" comparison since he had used it previously in *The Vivisector* in which Mrs Courtney "was looking at herself in the mirror, making a mouth like a pullet's arse the moment before dropping its egg".[10] In conjuring up images of disgust at suburban society, he has a willing accomplice in Sharman. The camera has a cruelly ecstatic time with Darl's fat, wobbling hysteria when she and Harve return to their violated mansion; the overhead shot of Darl lurching fatly upstairs is a perfect visual analogue for the vicious prose White uses to hack at bourgeois *arrivisme*.

Rod Bishop and Fiona Mackie have claimed that "**The Night the Prowler** highlights the process of alienation by caricature, more symbolic than realistic."[11] There is some truth in this statement as it applies to the heightening of family repressions and to Felicity's attempts to cut herself off from her family. But the approach is not consistent: the episodes symbolizing the values of upper-middle-class respectability are firmly rooted in the realist observation of detail, whereas those encapsulating Felicity's move towards illumination are almost surrealist in their explicit concern with her mental state. The disparity it draws attention to is one that is endemic in White's work. The best of his writing is concrete, visually powerful, rooted in the real; the worst is in the declamatory spelling out of themes that resist dramatization. In the transposition from page to screen, Sharman has been too much in awe of White, too little ready to provide any commentary on the original. As a result, the latter's faults as well as its strengths tend to be preserved intact.

Notes

1. Patrick White, *The Night the Prowler*, Penguin, Melbourne, 1976. The short story was republished with the screenplay.
2. "Jim Sharman", interview by Robyn Anderson and Sue Adler, *Cinema Papers*, No. 20, March-April 1979, p. 270.
3. David Stratton, *The Last New Wave*, Angus & Robertson, Sydney, 1980, p. 168.
4. *Cinema Papers*, *op cit*, p. 270.
5. Leslie Halliwell, however, considered it "a very short story . . . fatally over-extended", *Halliwell's Film Guide*, Granada, 1977, p. 639.
6. *Cinema Papers*, *op cit*, p. 271.
7. Adrian Martin, "Fantasy", Ch. 6 in *The New Australian Cinema*, Scott Murray (ed.), Thomas Nelson Australia-Cinema Papers, Melbourne, 1980, p. 111.
8. T. A. Bartholomew (ed.), *Further Extracts from the Notebooks of Samuel Butler*, Jonathan Cape, London, 1934, p. 31.
9. Martin, *op cit*, p. 111.
10. Patrick White, *The Vivisector*, Jonathan Cape, London, 1970, p. 81.
11. Rod Bishop and Fiona Mackie, "Loneliness and Alienation", Ch. 9 in *The New Australian Cinema*, *op cit*, p. 157.

11. Martin Boyd on Television: *Lucinda Brayford* and *Outbreak of Love*

Martin Boyd's *Lucinda Brayford* was first published by Cresset Press, London, 1946, and reprinted by Lansdowne Press, 1969 (page references to the latter). Like many of his novels, it reflects the Anglo-Australian background of his distinguished family. *Outbreak of Love* was first published by John Murray, London, 1957 (page references to this edition), and reprinted by Lansdowne Press, 1971. It is the third volume in the tetralogy based on the lives of members of the Anglo-Australian family, the Langtons. The others are: *The Cardboard Crown*, *A Difficult Young Man*, and *When Blackbirds Sing*.

Outbreak of Love was directed and produced by Oscar Whitbread, from a screenplay by Howard Griffiths. The lighting supervisor was Peter Simondson, the senior cameramen Roger McAlpine and John Tuttle, the videotape editor Marianne Prodmore and the composer George Dreyfus. Running as four 50-minute episodes, it was televised in 1981. **Lucinda Brayford** was directed by John Gauci for executive producer Oscar Whitbread, from a screenplay by Cliff Green. The lighting supervisor was Clive Fell, the senior cameramen Roger McAlpine and John Tuttle, and the videotape editors Ken Tyler (episodes one to four) and Kevin Sheeran (episode four). Running as four 50-minute episodes, it was televised in 1980.

Given the way the rejuvenated Australian film industry has ransacked Australian literature for source material, it is surprising that Martin Boyd has so far been avoided as a subject for the big screen. It is perhaps less surprising that larger-scale works such as Henry Handel Richardson's *The Fortunes of Richard Mahony* and Xavier Herbert's *Capricornia* have been neglected: to do anything like justice to the sweep of those two would clearly be a very expensive enterprise. They have other aspects — like *Richard Mahony*'s extreme pessimism — that perhaps make them daunting, but one would suppose Martin Boyd's novels, on a markedly smaller scale, were right up the alley of recent Australian film-makers. One thinks especially of *Lucinda Brayford* (1946), and the four "Langton" novels: *The Cardboard Crown* (1952), *A Difficult Young Man* (1955), *Outbreak of Love* (1957), and *When Blackbirds Sing* (1962). All are set securely in the past: *Lucinda Brayford* finishes in World War 2, the Langton sequence, apart from a sort of prologue to *The Cardboard Crown* set in "present-day" 1950s, stops at the end of World War 1. They offer, therefore, that opportunity for nostalgic indulgence which recent Australian films have seized on (cf. **The Mango Tree**, **The Picture Show Man**, etc.) and for exposing

Opposite: Lucinda Brayford (Wendy Hughes).

the past to critical scrutiny, in which films have, generally, been less interested. As well as the charms of period sets and costumes, the strengths of these novels include: a range of attractive/amusing/interesting characters, none of them too reliant on the dramatizing of complex thought processes for transfer to screen; a variety of incidents providing opportunity for display of character; and more verbal wit than any other Australian novelist provides.

Having made those claims for the novels, it is necessary to add that there is one major distinction between *Lucinda Brayford* and the Langton novels (except the last) and that it bears on their adaptability to the screen. Whereas *Lucinda Brayford* and, disastrously, *When Blackbirds Sing* are straightforwardly presented as third-person novels, the first three Langton novels depend for a great deal of their charm and cohesion on the narrative voice of Guy Langton. It is perhaps the major narrative achievement of the sequence to maintain the reader's sense of at least two levels of reality: that is, the way Guy perceives people, places, and events, and the way the reader, allowing for Guy's particular sensibility and prejudices, subconsciously teases out his own view of that reality. In the light of this strength, it becomes less surprising that these novels have not been filmed, though there were rumours in the 1970s of a screen version of *A Difficult Young Man*. As suggested in the first chapter of this book, an author's *tone* is perhaps the most distinctive and the most unfilmable element of any novel

Arthur Langton (Frank Thring). **Outbreak of Love**.

one values: to try to film Boyd's novels without establishing in the transposition an equivalent for that tone, a film-maker is likely to be left with the bare bones of character and event. That these are often engaging in Boyd is due less to their intrinsic qualities than to the wry, witty, avuncular tone in which Guy observes them, giving, in recording his observations, a further crucial dimension to the reader's understanding and satisfaction.

Howard Griffiths' adaptation of *Outbreak of Love* for ABC television (1980) sought to overcome this problem by using a good deal of "voice-over" technique. As in the film of Helen Garner's *Monkey Grip*, this has the twin effect of reminding the viewer of the tone of voice of the original *and* doing something different, and less dramatically central, in the film. The "voice-over" acts usefully in **Outbreak of Love** to link episodes but it doesn't catch the drama between the ageing Guy who narrates and his young self who participates in the events narrated. In fact, Boyd's use of Guy is less graceful and assured, sometimes downright clumsy in *Outbreak of Love*. Nevertheless, the discontinuity of the older Guy's voice removes some of the viewer's interest in the young Guy, so that he becomes little more than a cardboard figure of "Nice Young Man", little short indeed of "a guy". The film loses the sense of the young man's being, like all the other characters, the product of the older Guy's perception; it also loses entirely, for a variety of reasons, the sense of this anxiously correct young man's ever being able to grow into the owner of the narrative voice.

This is running ahead a little but the point is that, though the Langton novels may seem to offer a good deal of readily filmable material, it is at least arguable that their chief attraction is likely to resist transposition. (To drop Guy's narrative voice in the last book of the tetralogy, *When Blackbirds Sing*, was an almost unmitigated disaster: by that stage of his career, Boyd "straight" had become irascible, simplistic and monotonous.) *Lucinda Brayford* seems on the surface a more expansive prospect than any one of the Langton novels: it is a multi-generation family story which moves from Cambridge to Australia and back to England. It is more straightforward in technique than the tetralogy but what it gains in straightforwardness it loses, in my view, in the richness of the perception of the tetralogy. *Lucinda Brayford*, may appear to be a substantial "good read", not very different in its appeal from such popular family-chronicle films as Tay Garnett's **Mrs. Parkington** (1945) or Vincent Sherman's **Mr. Skeffington** (1945) or George Stevens' **Giant** (1956) — all three based on novels — but this is not really the case. Although it is told in the third person, it is still the narrative voice which chiefly accounts for such coherence as the book has. Certain thematic concerns — for example, relating to class structure or to pacifism, the Mediterranean versus the Teutonic impulses in European life — exist as much in the novel's authorial comment as in the people and events created to dramatize those concerns. In spite of this, it is hard to resist the idea that *Lucinda Brayford* might have made a splendid vehicle for a star performance which could have given the story a different but perhaps viable centre for consciousness. It may appear, then, that *mise-en-scène* could do more for *Lucinda Brayford* than for the Langton novels which more overtly rely on their narrator's voice; I am suggesting the third-person voice in *Lucinda Brayford* also presents a major challenge to the film-maker.

Despite difficulties of tone, especially in finding a film equivalent for the narrative strategy of the Langton novels, Boyd still seems like an interesting prospect for filming. He holds a special place in Australian fiction, partly as its wittiest and most graceful stylist, and partly because of his skill and sympathy as a "recorder of and commentator on a vanished time and class, its habits, behaviour and ways of thinking".[1] In the monograph from which this quotation comes, I went on to praise Boyd for his "attractive and original narrative technique", for his ability to "create a sure sense of time passing and of people ageing and changing", and for the "real sensuous beauty in his evocation of place" (p. 56). These virtues are variously accessible to the film-maker. The last-named, relating to evocation of place, enjoins an expensive attention to *mise-en-scène* which may be beyond the budget of most Australian feature film-making and certainly proved to be so in the television serials of *Lucinda Brayford* and *Outbreak of Love*. Some of those other virtues may be difficult to achieve for reasons less external than that of finance. Nevertheless, Boyd's vivid account of life in pre-war Melbourne among a once-influential class; his response to the divided sensibility which derives from what he calls "geographical schizophrenia"[2]; and his continuing concern for civilized values, for cultivated habits of mind: these are some of the claims that insist on Boyd's importance in the history of the Australian novel.

Lucinda Brayford is, despite its length, really a less substantial achievement than the Langton tetralogy or even than any one of the first three of the sequence. It begins in Cambridge and ends there: in the opening sequence an enmity is developed at Clare College between two students, Vane and Chapman, both of whom migrate to Australia, and who are the maternal great-grandfathers of Stephen Brayford, whose ashes are scattered from Clare Bridge on the last page of the novel. Chapman's daughter, Julie, marries Vane's son, Fred, and after a harrowing period of drought on a Riverina property, Noorilla, they strike it rich. In some of Boyd's most sure-footed writing, Julie throws herself into the process of social advancement while Fred, half-contemptuous, is also half-pleased to have his riches displayed in a Toorak mansion and all that goes with it. Though Boyd takes satirical pleasure in Julie's upward rise, she is kept free of imputation of the more sordid aspects of *arrivisme* because, as Paul Brayford says, "She has the necessary foundation of culture . . . She lives for pleasure." Paul is not consistently Boyd's mouthpiece: he is too extreme and too inconsistent for that: but on this occasion, and in this respect, he is fairly clearly speaking for the author. Much of the vitality of the novel's first third, which is set in Australia, derives from Julie's pleasure principle in operation.

It also derives from Boyd's acute observation of changing social *milieux*. As the novel moves from Clare College in its opening chapter to drought-stricken Noorilla where the graces are minimal, from the Vanes' family home in Kew where Fred's sisters in genteel poverty have run a school to the boarding house in Flinders where the family spends Christmas, to the culminating triumph of Tourella, the Toorak house Fred buys, Boyd gives an utterly convincing picture, on a social level, of the fluctuations in a family's fortunes. There is something irresistible about a narrative which creates so vivid a sense of life as a harsh struggle and then shows how the chief strugglers respond to a sudden change in circumstances.

Fred, hardened and coarsened by the years of struggle, is never again quite able to value anything but money. He collects stations, and is prepared to dole out large amounts for appropriate projects. He is, for instance, willing to buy his sisters' way out of running a school or to buy Tourella because these acts will reflect on his position as a man of substance. As well, he is prepared to "buy" Hugo Brayford, aide-de-camp to the Governor, as a husband for his older daughter, Lucinda. One of the novel's chief ironies is that, given Lucinda's beauty and charm, she should have married someone who needed the added inducement of several thousand pounds a year. It is also ironic that Fred, whose attitude is strongly anti-English, should be ready to see Lucinda's marrying Hugo as a *coup*. While Fred is willing to lay out vast sums on enterprises that he feels increase his standing, he retains too a streak of parsimony about small expenses for which he can see no return; his irritation with Tony Duff, Julie's "poodle-fakir" friend and Lucinda's tentative admirer, leads to stingy outbursts from Fred about how much of his wine Tony has drunk or about the prospect of including him in a Tasmanian holiday.

Julie applies herself assiduously to learning to be a Toorak hostess. Hers is not exactly a Cinderella story: her father has been a canon of the church: but the hard days at Noorilla with the sauce bottle on the table have left her with a hatred of poverty and an appetite for pleasure. In her upward climb, she relies on Tony Duff's artistic advice (he is one of the epicene young men who recur through Boyd's novels) and doesn't care to be reminded of Noorilla days. Her sheer delight in social life and her essential good-nature help to counter her *parvenu* urges — and to make her the most fully realized character in the novel. Not given to cerebration and living as far as possible on a social level, she is a character who can be presented to the reader almost entirely in terms of how she responds to, and conducts herself in, social situations. And as she does so, one feels that her "emerging from the middle classes into grandeur" (p. 88) is a more or less harmless snobbery.

The first part of the novel finishes with the triumph, felt equally in their different ways by Fred and Julie, of Lucinda's marriage to Hugo

Brayford. Julie has had the highest expectations for Lucinda and a powerful element of the book's essential sadness is that these will not be gratified. Concerned at the romantic feeling between Lucinda and Tony, Julie is prepared to throw her to Hugo whose family home, Crittenden, she has visited on a trip to England. Hugo is presented by Boyd as having a strongly sensual appeal that quite effaces Tony and, for Lucinda, places in perspective her adolescent feeling for Tony. She is awakened sexually by Hugo and, in a summer picnic scene, Boyd suggests the passion of their love-making with a sharp, physical intensity uncommon in his novels. And, characteristically, he does so with a tact that is far removed from the obligatory scene of heavy-breathing gymnastics in the average best-seller.

If this tact is one of Boyd's major virtues, it can also have a debilitating effect on the narrative when the absence of a credible sense of physical, sexual passion obscures motivation. This is true, in my view, of the main relationship of *Outbreak of Love*, and it is cripplingly true of the central section of *Lucinda Brayford*. Early in her married life, which is passed wholly in England, Lucinda discovers Hugo's continuing infidelity with his former mistress, Mrs Fabian Parker. Hugo's brisk unsentimentality in his love-making with Lucinda is dramatically feasible: his real feeling lies elsewhere. However, when Lucinda contemplates taking Pat Lanfranc, Hugo's friend, as a lover, Boyd is not able to make one feel her sexual need or even, in any piercing sense, her humiliation at Hugo's treatment of her. Lucinda grows from luminously lovely girlhood into faintly uninteresting womanhood. At least as far as her emotional life is concerned, Boyd cannot make the conflict she feels over leaving Hugo for Pat seem crucial to her. Boyd writes, as Lucinda contemplates cutting herself off from Hugo's relatives to whom she has become attached:

> She hated the idea of losing such good friends for whom she had so strong an affection. The sense of a disintegration of her life, which, though primarily caused by the crisis of her marriage, had also been helped by worrying trivialities such as the luncheon with Mrs. Galway and Julie's cables, had become over-powering. (p. 20)

There is something too measured about that, too much a weighing of one thing against another, to suggest the kind of emotional conflict that the novel needs at this stage. Fate in the form of Hugo's dreadful injuries in France saves her from decision here and when she and Pat finally become lovers there is something too stiffly conventional about his approach and too externally described about hers for the reader to be able to care much about it.

The strength of *Lucinda Brayford* is ultimately not centred in its epony-mous heroine, and this is also characteristic of Boyd. That is to say, he never quite confronts head-on the emotional lives of his protagonists. Alice Langton in *The Cardboard Crown* and Diana von Flugel in *Outbreak of Love* are both, like Lucinda, grossly deceived by their husbands, but the indirect approach through Guy-as-narrator keeps the reader at a remove from what one may assume to be their profoundest emotions. This matters less in the tetralogy where Guy's *perception* of what is happening is as much part of the drama as the events themselves. It may, of course, be a very wise strategy of Boyd's to choose a *persona* who works within the limits of his creator's emotional and imaginative range. In *Lucinda Brayford*, the third-person narrative skirmishes around her most painful moments, not quite offering a sharp enough insight into Lucinda and not offering a compensating dramatic interest in the narrative voice. The latter is, as suggested, very important in *Lucinda Brayford* but its importance is reflective and discursive rather than dramatic.

In the passage quoted above, perhaps the key word is "disintegration", for this names the process at the heart of *Lucinda Brayford* and the Langton novels. *Lucinda Brayford* reaches a high point with the heroine's marriage. Boyd makes the first 150 pages, chiefly concerned with the growing prosperity of the Vanes, extremely lively, maintaining a tight grip on reader expectations and fulfilling these with the shrewd social insights in which he renders the Vanes' progress. Very sharply, too, he makes clear why Lucinda would have been throwing herself away in marrying Tony, though as it turns out she could scarcely have suffered more than in marrying Hugo. However, at the time of her marriage, in the full bloom of her youth and beauty, she responds sexually to Hugo in ways that displace Tony, who belongs to her adolescence, from serious consideration as a husband. There is a robust smell of success about this early part of the novel, venal enough in many ways, but not wholly to be despised if it has produced Lucinda.

Very little goes well for Lucinda in England and the novel itself never recovers its narrative verve either. She may well experience at Crittenden ". . . the excitement of finding yourself in the living stream of culture" (p. 154), but, though she begins "the long process in which she forgot that she was Australian" (p. 152), she never truly becomes a part of that "living stream". And what, for her, does it consist of? The notion of English culture is most tellingly embodied in Crittenden, country seat of the Brayfords for several centuries, and in some of Boyd's best writing, sensuously exact and evocative of a dignified way of life:

> Out in the park the long shadows were spreading till the last touch of sunset vanished from the grass, and the long English twilight began. In the saloon, with the fading twilight, the yellow shaded lamps grew steadily brighter. In their gentle glow the room appeared even more beautiful than in the afternoon. The old English gilt, the paintings, the ceiling and the damasks, blended in softer and richer harmonies than by day, and the fine proportions of the room were evident. The atmosphere of the place was more powerful than ever. Lucinda felt it almost like a drug. She felt that she could stay here for ever, where, against a background of such dignity, life was lived with a natural simplicity . . . (p. 158)

". . . a natural simplicity" deriving from life in a country house, unobtrusively instinct with the accumulated culture of centuries, is one aspect of that "living stream". However, though Boyd, in passages like this one, shows a fine eye for a harmonious setting, for Lucinda Crittenden is unable to provide enough sustenance. It is there that the first cracks in her marriage appear (Hugo's gambling debts, mention of Mrs Parker); it turns into a lonely prison for her when she must stay there to look after the hideously disfigured Hugo; and if Arthur (Lord Crittenden and Hugo's eldest brother) and his organizing, middle-class wife Marian are kind and friendly they do not offer much stimulation for the mind. The other main aspect of English life which Lucinda samples is that of London smart society. In its higher reaches this is represented by Lady Susannah, Hugo's mother, with her retinue of ephebes and elderly millionaires; in its nastier manifestations, it runs to the malice-ridden luncheons of Mrs Galway, like Lucinda an expatriate Australian. Between these two, Lucinda establishes herself in a discreet flat where she entertains Pat Lanfranc to discreet dinners. Julie's social whirl in Melbourne seems vigorous, expansive, and openly competitive, by comparison with the trim, tasteful little world that Lucinda creates to shore herself up against loneliness.

Lucinda and her epicene admirer, Tony Duff (Sam Neill). **Lucinda Brayford**.

For this, increasingly, becomes a story of failures. Lucinda's relationship with Pat founders on his conventionality which she has misjudged; her son Stephen, whose marriage to his socially ambitious cousin Heather founders on her adultery, comes to believe that "Lucinda had never behaved like a normal mother to him" (p. 523) as he sweats it out in a military prison; Lucinda, who never returns to Australia, finds herself more and more estranged from those of her family who visit England; and she comes to believe that the Vane influence has helped to undermine Crittenden and what it stands for, and that she has been the "carrier" of this influence. "Geographical schizophrenia" is a condition that encourages the processes of disintegration: it would take a much more active, vigorous personality than Lucinda's to make something new and valuable out of her Australian heritage and her English experience. In the event, Kathleen Fitzpatrick seems to me right in writing of Lucinda that "she becomes a brittle London society woman, in whose career it is difficult to feel much interest."[3] Lucinda's life in England does not blossom: her promise and her "brilliant" marriage are both blighted.

Fortunately, for the interest of the book, there are several other peripheral characters who from time to time move towards the centre of attention. These include Paul Brayford, Hugo's elder brother, who is at once a free spirit (he goes to live in the south of France with a footman from Crittenden) and the most relentlessly conservative of the Brayfords; Lucinda's brother Bill (really her half-brother, product of a shipboard liaison of Julie's) who marries Muriel, "one of nature's Mayoresses" as Paul describes her; and their daughter Heather who helps to wreck Stephen's life. But despite the entertaining range of characters, vivified by Boyd's gift for dialogue, the sense of disintegration is pervasive.

The narrative scheme of the novel becomes one of frustrated hopes, of patterns glimpsed but not realized. There is an irresistible downward movement in the novel's latter two-thirds which cannot be deflected by incidental wit and graces. Reluctantly one comes to feel that Boyd's talent is more vividly felt in the service of a dark vision of life than in rendering the beauty and joy of which he claims life is capable. There is no reason why such a view should not make for a powerful novel, but the fact is that, after the splendid opening section in Australia, *Lucinda Brayford* suffers a loss of unity, a loss of narrative control over its long family chronicle. As a result, the novel seems infected with the debilitating procedures that characterize the decline in the fortunes of the Vanes and the Brayfords. What one takes to be Boyd's "voice" is sometimes put in Paul Brayford's mouth, sometimes in Stephen's, and, of course, most often in the novel's metalanguage. But, vivid though this voice often is in its love of certain kinds of beauty, its hatred of war, middle-class vulgarities and upper-class brutalities, it is in the end too dispersed to hold this very long novel together. It remains, therefore, no more than the sum of its parts, some of them undeniably attractive. Fitzpatrick is right again when she claims that:

> The chronicle form . . . does not suit him [Boyd]; he has never been able to build on the grand scale; had he practised as an architect he would have been better at private houses than public buildings.[4]

The Langton novels, collectively Boyd's finest work, are distinctly private houses rather than public buildings. In them, he finally found a mode that suited him; one that enabled him to draw extensively on his family's history without the sense of clutter that disfigured his first chronicle, *The Montforts* (1928), or the unwieldiness and disunity that threaten the seams of *Lucinda Brayford*. *Outbreak of Love* is the third of the Langton novels and it stands a little to one side of the sequence. Its genre is that of comedy of manners, set in pre-World War 1 Melbourne, and acted out in a series of social occasions. Boyd understands very well that people may reveal as much of themselves and learn as much about others at a dance or a tea-party as in more portentous circumstances.

The motif of the book — the outbreaks of love suggested in the title — is worked out through a series of such social occasions. The central relationship of the novel — that of Diana von Flugel and Russell Lockwood who meet again after twenty years, during which time Russell has been in Europe — is based on mutual cultural interests, especially a shared sense of Boyd's geographical schizophrenia. Their many discussions of life and art, and the different manifestations of these in Australia and Europe, constitute Boyd's most explicit statement of the condition. Too explicit, perhaps, for the novel's good, for the theme of the divided heritage is elsewhere dramatized in terms livelier and more amusing than it emerges from the rather soulful talk of these middle-aged, would-be lovers. Diana has been trapped for twenty years in messy domesticity with Wolfie, the composer-husband she loves but who is in many ways a maddening, self-indulgent child, and with three children of whom only the youngest, Josie, shows promise of living the sort of pleasant, cultivated life for which Diana yearns. Russell, whom she has known as a child, returns to Melbourne at a stage in Diana's life when she feels the need for a new stimulus, for a widening of intellectual horizons, and for a sense of being appreciated. Russell, pleased to be back in the freer social modes of Australia, comes trailing clouds of European culture, and seems like an answer to her needs.

Their relationship begins again on a Melbourne street. Before recognizing her, Russell on seeing Diana again thought:

> 'That woman is somebody', by which he did not mean someone who had money and went to the right houses, but someone who from childhood had been accustomed to certain ways of thinking and who knew the different modes of life, and above all, whose awareness was similar to his own. (p. 7)

Expecting this common "awareness" to develop, Diana is disappointed at Russell's failure to pursue the relationship. They meet again at a party given by Diana's rich and socially irreproachable friend Elsie Radcliffe to launch Wolfie's preludes. Russell, though attracted to Diana, has been feeling his way cautiously back into Melbourne society and it is only when he sees her at Elsie's, looking superb and drawing from Miss Rockingham, who knows European royalty by Christian names, the accolade, "That woman's a lady" (p. 52), that he feels confident of his own judgment. Russell invites Diana and Wolfie to a luncheon party at Menzies which is dominated by a pair of cultural bores, and after it he and Diana stroll through the Fitzroy Gardens pursuing their favourite Anglo-Australian theme.

Russell admires in Diana the fusion of complementary influences. She has the grace and elegance of the older, European culture and the unpretentious, more casual charm of one who has lived most of her life in Australia, much of it in somewhat straitened circumstances. From this point of view — of fused heritages — the central scene of the novel is that of the impromptu meal Diana prepares for Russell in her shabby Brighton home. In this episode, a triumph of tone and structure, Australian casualness and European elegance are very attractively blended, and this is exactly the combination in Diana that draws Russell's appreciation. One of the motifs of this scene is found in his discovery of a picture which may or may not be a Parmigiano, hung in the von Flugels' drawingroom. He sees in this an analogy with Diana herself: "You're like that yourself. You're full of all kinds of qualities but you just put them away in a dark corner" (p. 96). It is the unaffectedness with which Diana wears these qualities at this stage of her life, when she no longer expects much, that makes her attractive, and Boyd sketches them with sureness of touch. As she prepared a table for their omelettes, fruit and wine, doing so with instinctive grace and taste, Russell says, "You take elemental things and make them elegant", adding somewhat prosily, "That is civilization" (pp.96-7). The last remark to one side, the scene has made its point about Diana's unpretentious simplicities and the openness of her affections. The rest of the scene discriminates with quiet exactness between her easy receptiveness to ideas and Russell's acute but somewhat jaded, too "finished" responses to a larger world.

Their growing feeling for each other, which the reader must take mainly on trust since Boyd's strength does not lie in rendering the growth of sexual love, receives its next impetus at the Government House ball. Here Diana realizes that the drunken woman who has insulted her (Mrs Montaubyn, nee Gladys Cumfit) is Wolfie's mistress. Long tolerant of his flirtations with young girls whose inspiration he claims to need, she is justly aggrieved that he should have dealings with this vulgar creature. The ties of loyalty seem to snap and she agrees to go away with Russell. That they do not finally elope after her daughter Josie is safely married is

Above: the von Flugel family: Josie (Jackie Woodburne), Wolfie (Larry Held) and Diana (Rowena Wallace).
Below: Guy Langton (John Higginson), John Wyckham (Lewis Fitz-Gerald), and Cynthia (Susannah Fowle)
and Anthea Langton (Sigrid Thornton). **Outbreak of Love**.

partly because war has broken out and she feels she owes it to Wolfie, a German, not to abandon him, but "The real reason is that I am married to him, whatever he does" (p. 252). Russell sails to England and marries Miss Rockingham; Diana is last glimpsed sitting with Wolfie

> . . . at lunch on the verandah, while the winter sunlight gleamed on the hock bottle, and tinged with pale gold the far purple forests of Gippsland. (p. 254)

In this final sentence of the novel, Boyd draws together the threads of Diana's life that have worked to hold her here: it recalls the elegance of the impromptu meal Russell has admired and the peculiarly Australian beauty of Walter Withers' painting, "Winter Sunlight", which she and Russell have discussed as epitomizing a truly indigenous culture. The sentence also incidentally recalls Wolfie's sensuous response to Mrs Montaubyn's ripe charms which suggested to him "the vineyards of the Rhine" (p. 21). Diana is tied by long associations, good and bad, to this scene; without realizing it in such terms, she has rejected Russell's rootless aestheticism in favour of the limited rewards of family ties and old affections.

If there were nothing more to *Outbreak of Love* than this central relationship, readers, finding it, in Brenda Niall's phrase, a "tepid affair"[5], might well feel the novel's charm is somewhat thin. As Niall goes on to say, "it is likely that Boyd intended the relationship to be superficial." That may well be so, but it would not be enough to sustain the narrative impulse of the novel. To do so it would have been necessary for Diana to share Boyd's awareness of Russell's emotional limitation. As it is, there is something touching in her eager belief that she has found a kindred spirit in him whereas the reader, through Guy, realizes that his graceful, cultivated surface is the truest thing about Russell. The scene that most nearly approaches an enactment of the feeling that may be supposed to motivate two middle-aged lovers on the verge of elopement founders on language of a triteness rarely met in serious fiction: ". . . I would like this afternoon to go on forever." "So would I. I don't want to leave you now", "I don't want to leave you", etc. (p. 238). After this stimulating exchange, Russell "took her in his arms and kissed her tenderly." This is some of Boyd's worst writing. It does more than simply recall the confined bird of Russell's emotions; it suggests an author who has led his characters into a place where, as a writer, he is not equipped to follow them. Diana has earlier suggested an amplitude to which the banalities above fail wholly to do justice.

The novel does not, however, rely on Diana and Russell for its appeal; nor, fortunately, does it rely on the outbreak of love experienced between Josie and the Governor's aide-de-camp, John Wyckham. This pair of pretty sticks elicits Boyd's lyrical mood which is his response to — and evasion of — the springs of mutual sexual feeling. Josie and John's love buds, appropriately enough, at the party for Wolfie's music, one of the preludes being distinctly erotic in flavour and all of them redolent of romantic yearnings. It flowers at the Government House ball, where it is interrupted by John's having to remove Mrs Montaubyn, and it blossoms into engagement among "the sad saplings" of Warrandyte where it gives rise to prose of quite remarkable banality. My strained floral metaphor is brought on by Boyd's describing how Josie's

> eyes were full of light, and she was like the flower opening in the sun. He [John] kissed her quickly, several times on both sides of the face. Then they stood back and looked at each other. They laughed and she went into his arms. (p. 165)

Boyd cannot make uncomplicated innocence interesting. He is much sharper and wittier in presenting Wolfie's fleshy trysts with Mrs Montaubyn or, more peripheral, Anthea Langton's thwarted romance with Freddie Thorpe, numbskull nephew to the Governor and aspirant to a profitable colonial marriage.

Perhaps the most interesting of all, however, is the young Guy's more generalized "outbreak of love". Sometimes he imagines he loves Anthea, sometimes her twin sister Cynthia, both of them socially and intellectually formidable, and neither of them taking Guy seriously for a moment. But for Guy, at twenty, they glitter with an erudition and glamour that obscures their snobbery. Guy's responsiveness to his world is amusing and, in the novel's pattern, important; and the best-done relationship in the book is that between him and his spinster Aunt Mildy. Only in presenting this relationship does Boyd cut through the comic surfaces to touch veins of real frustration beneath. Guy and Mildy are two typically Boydean figures. He is one of Boyd's epicene, unfulfilled "appreciators", in many ways a youthful version of waspish old Arthur Langton and indeed of Russell Lockwood, but here made comically self-aware and given an engaging enthusiasm for life at large. Mildy is a spinster whose natural sexuality and commonsense have been paralyzed into simpering affectation and a life-inhibiting gentility. It is not of course a sexual relationship in any overt sense: his feeling for her is just gratitude for the physical comforts with which she surrounds him; hers is a smothering possessiveness which leads her to self-pity and ungenerous depreciation of others. Their relationship is consistently well-judged, and for most of its length very funny. Its tone deepens satisfyingly at the end when Guy realizes that Mildy's love for him "had no moral basis of any kind" (p. 247). The older Guy, the novel's narrator, realizes that Mildy has made his younger self the focus for all her frustrated desires, and in this comically unequal relationship he achieves his most perceptive treatment of sexual motivation in the novel.

Entwined with the "outbreak of love" motif is Boyd's recurring preoccupation with the Anglo-Australian malaise. Set wholly in Australia, unlike the other novels in the tetralogy, *Outbreak of Love* is much concerned with the effects of trying to transplant intact in harsher Australian soil the tender plants of European cultivation. The half-serious conversation between Diana and Russell as they walk through the Fitzroy Gardens pinpoints the yearnings of many upper-middle-class Australians of the time of the Europeanization of Australian social life:

> 'Australians should have been colonized by French or Italians, or some people who know how to live in this climate.'
> 'Then we shouldn't be here.'
> 'No, that would be dreadful', he said. 'All the same there ought to be a restaurant here with a French chef. It ought to be the thing to come here — like dining in the Bois.'
> 'D'you think you will stay long in Australia?' she asked.
> 'Why? I intend to live here.'
> 'But your mind is in Europe. You like Australia now because you are thinking of all the European things that could be done to it. There will never be a French chef in the Fitzroy Gardens. When you realize that, will you want to stay?' (p. 78)

One of this novel's sharpest insights is that it is not possible to transplant a culture, holus-bolus as it were, from one continent to another. The efforts to do so are frequently made to look pretentious and absurd. In the society Boyd is writing of, it is still flattering to be considered English in manner, taste or habits. The behaviour of the Old World often looks odd in the freer social modes of Australia but it is still the behaviour by which others

Freddie Thorpe (Brendon Lunney) and Anthea. **Outbreak of Love.**

are judged. Often though, Boyd makes it clear that among those who most pride themselves on their Englishness, like the Langton twins, Anthea and Cynthia, their real vitality and value owe as much to Australia as to England. Guy reflects that,

> the twins themselves, though brought up so carefully to be English gentle-women, had caught a slight savagery from the hot sun, which combined with their erudition, made them I think a good deal more entertaining than the girls on whom Cousin Sophie had intended to model them. (p. 92)

Josie, he tells us, "had more the air of being used to English lawns".

Two amusing caricatures embody Boyd's criticism of English intellectual mediocrity passing itself off as the flower of Old World learning abloom in the cultural sands of Melbourne. The first is Lady Pringle, wife of a professor at the university, who ponderously introduces Wolfie's prelude at the Radcliffe party, and the second is Mr Hemstock who has come to Melbourne to lecture at the university. In these two, cultivation has run to pretension and pomposity and they see themselves as bestowing the fruits of their learning on unlettered natives.

Lady Pringle asks the audience's attention for the first prelude in these words:

> . . . imagine that you are in some woodland on a spring morning, perhaps in a forest in my beloved Bavaria, or even in one of those strange sad glades of saplings above the river at Warrandyte. (p. 55)

Of the third prelude, she intones:

> This prelude reminds me, with its glowing colour, its rich and yet idyllic interpretation of the natural world, of the *Thalysia* or *Harvest Home* of Theocritus. (pp. 57-8)

In this scene, Boyd satirizes the name-dropping gush which the Australians are meant to mistake for true learning. (The twins are also alarming, cultural name-droppers, believing this is the way to impress English visitors.) Lady Pringle says elsewhere that she is "certain that Australiah has a great cultural future" (p. 75), but Boyd makes it clear that she will not be one of its pioneers. In relation to the source of Wolfie's inspiration, the fun derives from our knowing the much earthier circumstances that gave rise to it.

Mr Hemstock's contribution to colonial culture is demolished with single-minded wit and malice by Boyd. At one of Arthur Langton's very English tea-parties he tells the following anecdote:

> 'I met my Lord Bishop of Yackandandah in Collins Street yesterday,' he boomed. 'I said to him, "My Lord Bishop, you are reported as having, on the second Sunday after Epiphany, split an infinitive in your pro-cathedral." To which my Lord replied, "Mr. Hemstock sir, it's preferable to splitting hairs," which I thought considerably prompt. In fact I laughed at my own discomfiture.' As no-one followed his example, Mildy, wishing to be kind, said: 'How very amusing.' (p. 94)

The incident ends with the bubble of his intellectual conceit pricked by a small colonial barb. If a culture is to make itself felt in another setting, it can't afford merely to "show off" as Hemstock and Lady Pringle do. Boyd recognizes humbug, pedantry, and gush, and sees that they have no place in the growth of a real culture.

The English are more critically exposed in this novel than in any other of the Langton sequence. This is partly because we never see them in their own backyard and this means that their culture always looks a little out of place — whether it is a matter of wanting a French chef in the Fitzroy Gardens or of the Government House set generally condescending to the locals. However, Boyd's fairness in this matter is seen, equally, in presenting, first, Miss Rockingham (a friend of the Governor-General's wife) as truly accomplished in a way that no Australian is seen to be, and, second, Harry, Diana and Wolfie's pompous jackaroo son, who despises the way Australians kowtow to the English, as one of the most unlikeable characters in the book.

The novel accepts the Anglo-Australian ambivalence as an inevitable element in the fate of many Australians of the time but does not make the mistake of simply equating civilization with Europe. Though Russell makes pronouncements about civilization, one feels that it is Diana who has the surer grasp of what it is. It is not a matter of knowing things, not even knowing about great works of art as Russell does, but of an instinctive response to what is valuable or beautiful in life. And unlike Russell, her understanding of life comes from living it rather than observing it. Civilization, as she understands it, is as likely to be found in messy Australian family life as in the galleries of Europe. To capture an understanding like this on film, as distinct from rendering events and characters, is a large order.

To make a television serial from a novel is clearly, in certain crucial ways, a very different enterprise from making a feature film. Some of the same problems must be met: finding a visual equivalent for the author's narrative voice; choosing actors whose physical presence and emotional range will enable them to replace — or *dis*place — the reality created by the novel's characters; producing a *mise-en-scène* that does the work of the novel's descriptive element; and so on. The differences, however, are at least as striking. Whereas a feature film will normally be viewed in a single sitting of one-and-a-half to two hours' length, the television serial's running time is likely to be at least twice as long, and to be broken into a number of episodes of equal length. These two, perhaps most obvious, differences have immediate implications for how the transition from the page to the (small) screen is made.

In the matter of length, the serial can much more nearly imitate the novel's tendencies to leisurely development and is under less demanding pressure in the matter of selection of incidents and characters. It can simply include *more* of the original; that is not to say it will necessarily retain more of its essence but it certainly has the opportunity to reproduce more of its surface realities. The BBC version of Evelyn Waugh's *Brides-head Revisited* ran through twelve episodes of fifty minutes each, and one of ninety minutes, visually representing almost every incident from the novel, and where the adaptors stumbled on something not readily film-able it was simply read on the soundtrack. *David Copperfield*, more than twice as long as *Brideshead*, was served up with relative briskness in six episodes. There is not necessarily any reliable connection between the length of the original novel and that of the serial version. Of the two Boyd novels under discussion, *Lucinda Brayford*'s 540 pages were serialized in four fifty-minute episodes while *Outbreak of Love*, a mere 250 pages, ran to three of the same length. All one can say, in general terms, about the effect of the greater length of the television serial's total running time is that it offers its makers a greater opportunity for expansiveness, and a greater temptation, to which not a few succumb, to mere stateliness. In either case, the greater length is plainly a matter for serious consideration.

As to the breaking into episodes, this characteristic of the serial enjoins on its makers a need to shape material so as to produce some sense of self-containment in each episode. Not that the episodes of a serial will be really self-contained, as they may be in a series which merely uses the same set of characters and basic mode and setting (as, for instance, **Minder** or **To the Manor Born** do). Rather, the viewer will — subconsciously at least — expect some sort of shape and rounding out, some sense of moving towards a climax, in each episode; and this can sometimes produce a distorting influence for the viewer who is looking for a faithful version of the novel. The notion of an intervening week before the viewing audience takes up again with the lives of the serialized characters must have implications for the adaptor. Unable to count on the continuity of experi-ence offered by a film in the cinema, he will need each time to re-establish audience familiarity with the *mise-en-scène* and characters, perhaps in the process sacrificing some of the subtlety of character-drawing or sustained psychological action one might expect of either the feature film or the tele-vision play, let alone of the original novel.

There seems not to have been very much serious work done on the adaptation of well-known/classic novels to television and this chapter is not the place for it. I am interested in how certain aspects of Martin Boyd's two televised novels have fared in transition to the visual medium, chiefly from the point of view of the changes in emphasis this distinguished author's work has undergone in the process. The most useful discussion of the literary adaptation on television that I have found is Paul Kerr's essay, "Classic Serials — To be Continued"[6]. Whether or not one is prepared to allow the Boyd novels "classic" status, Kerr's claim that "serialization itself" is "of all television's institutional imperatives the most important", and his distinctions between long-running serials and those adapted from novels offer a valuable starting point for the study of this particular kind of transposition. I have done no more than advert to one or two very obvious — and obviously important — ways in which adaptation of the novel to television serial makes very different demands on its creators and viewers from those made in the process from novel to cinema.

Each of the three episodes of **Outbreak of Love**, adapted by Howard Griffiths and directed by Oscar Whitbread for the ABC, focuses on a major social occasion: in the first episode, it is the party given by Elsie Radcliffe (Anne Charleston) to launch the latest composition by Wolfie von Flugel (Laurence Held); in the second, the action reaches a climax at the Government House ball at which Diana (Rowena Wallace) learns that Wolfie has a mistress, the vulgar Mrs Montaubyn (Val Lehman), and this brings to a head her growing feeling for Russell Lockwood (Tony Bonner); in the third, Diana's daughter Josie (Jackie Woodburne) marries the Governor's aide John Wyckham (Lewis Fitz-Gerald). In the events following the latter, Diana decides against elopement with Russell and settles for remaining in Australia with Wolfie.

Howard Griffiths' adaptation builds skilfully to each of these occasions and contrives to include a good deal of the periphery of character and incident. In fact, the periphery tends to fare better than the big set pieces, not because of faults in the writing or direction but because the budget for the series has not been equal to the demands of the *mise-en-scène* on these occasions. There is simply not enough sense of physical opulence about the Radcliffes' show-place (scene of the wedding reception as well as the musical *soirée*) or the Government House set, and all three suffer from a somewhat underpopulated look. If one compares any one of these events with, say, the dance at Five-Bob in Gillian Armstrong's **My Brilliant Career**, the contrast is clear. The feature film budget allows for enough extras to suggest a convincing crowd whereas the comparable scenes in **Outbreak of Love** (and **Lucinda Brayford**) have a decidedly skimped look. However, this is not a fault that can be laid at the feet of the adaptors, though it might perhaps have caused second thoughts about the advisability of the adaptation in question.

As I suggested earlier, the narrative voice of Guy Langton is one of the major assets of the first three novels in the tetralogy. It is a voice finely attuned to what seems Boyd's emotional and imaginative range, but that is not the same as saying Guy and Boyd are interchangeable. In *Outbreak of Love*, Guy's voice is less skilfully managed than in the two earlier novels, Boyd often making no attempt to explain how Guy knew what happened on certain occasions on which he was absent. Griffiths has chosen to retain Guy's commentary by the voice-over technique and begins with the novel's opening reflection that,

> Our minds are like those maps at the entrance of the Metro stations in Paris. They are full of unilluminated directions. But when we know where we want to go and press the right button, the route is illuminated before us.

The chief illumination of course is that of Diana, and after Guy's opening words, finishing with "this is the story of a lady who lost her head or perhaps regained it", the camera cuts to Diana and Russell, looking in separate shop windows and then recognizing each other after twenty years. At first, the slight stiffness in Tony Bonner's bearing seems apt for Russell, a sort of professional gentleman, and so too does Rowena Wallace's somewhat over-articulated formality as Diana, but as the serial proceeds it becomes clear that they have very little more to offer. Just as in the novel, their talkative affair is both central and rather tame. Whereas one might have hoped that the actors chosen would bring some of their own emotional resources to these roles, in the event the stiffness of Bonner's Russell does not reverberate with repressed emotional experience and, more damagingly, Wallace's somewhat statuesque presence lacks resonance and variety.

The deficiencies of the latter performance are the most serious flaw in this adaptation (apart from the presumably unavoidable results of an inadequate budget). In Boyd's novel, Diana is presented as ready for an opening out in her life; one responds to the attractive blending of the two heritages in her, to the "flair" which enables her to make "elemental things . . . elegant", and to the sense in which the circumstances of her life have thwarted the more exciting potential of her nature. One is made to feel that, given the occasion, Diana can emerge from the desuetude of her suburban backwater to provoke from Arthur Langton (Frank Thring) a remark such as ". . . is she meant to be Beatrice d'Este or somebody?" Wallace has enough beauty and distinction for the role but she has been

Would-be lovers, Russell Lockwood (Tony Bonner) and Diana von Flugel. **Outbreak of Love.**

encouraged to wear them with an unvarying, mask-like fixity of expression and to talk in a breathy monotone that, in my view (and I am aware of being on very personal ground here), alienates crucial sympathy. Only once — in her reconciliation with Wolfie, closely following the dialogue of the novel — is she moving, the very movement of the body pointing to an emotional involvement unregistered elsewhere. This is followed by a short scene in which she, with her hair down and sitting in a dressing gown at the kitchen table, is writing to tell Russell that she will not be joining him, and again she shows a touch of human warmth, the lack of which in most of her performance undermines the effectiveness of the adaptation. Even in the matter of costume, the role has been ill-served: if Diana's big public appearances, at Wolfie's concert or Josie's wedding, are to be really striking, and thus help to dramatize both her innate flair and the relative drabness of her everyday life, there needs to be a more obvious contrast in her appearance. This Diana is dressed stylishly throughout, not one of her many costumes looking as if it has ever been worn before.

If I have stressed certain aspects of this performance, it is because its limitations have a serious effect on the value of the adaptation. Griffiths' screenplay has been more or less literally true to Boyd's original in which Diana has seemed a much more resonant character than Russell. This lopsidedness in itself gives some interest to the relationship in the novel, but to have Diana matching Russell's poker-faced propriety puts the central relationship in danger of *rigor mortis*. One of the results of this deficiency is that the recurring conversations about coming or going to Europe, about the difficulties of living so far from one's cultural home, or about art and life, lack even the minimal dramatic effect the novel achieves by contrasting Diana's receptivity with Russell's too finished approach.

Apart from this intensification of a problem already there in the novel, Oscar Whitbread has in general created a lively sense of a network of relationships. The Langton twins (nicely differentiated by Susannah Fowle, as Cynthia, and Sigrid Thornton, as Anthea) parade their European erudition touched with colonial barbarity in a way that keeps the young Guy (John Higginson) in an amusing state of nervous apprehension. The dinner party given for Russell by their parents, Edward and Sophie Langton (John Lee and Cornelia Frances), skilfully conveys a good deal of narrative information. It makes clear the Edward Langtons' frosty dealings with The Enemy (Diana's branch of the family), establishes their half-affectionate, half-contemptuous exploitation of Guy, and gives Russell some idea of the social network into which he is cautiously picking his way.

Wolfie's relationship with Mrs Montaubyn is a comically effective visualization of some of Boyd's most entertaining writing. In her softly pink, flowered bedroom, they enact Boyd's simile, preserved in Guy's voice-over, as they dance about "like two large roses blown into contact by the afternoon breezes". The camera pans from her rigidly proper-looking late husband to these two indulgent creatures sensuously indulging themselves in bed, then cuts to Wolfie going home to Brighton by train, inspired by this encounter to finish his elusive prelude. The next cut reveals his hands at the keyboard, then his face smiling at his success, after which Whitbread cuts to Diana in the garden. As the voice-over comments on an ocean-liner steaming down the bay, Diana's thoughts of Russell and Europe are interrupted by Wolfie's jubilant calling to her that he has finished the prelude. The narrative moves economically and swiftly here, leading smoothly on to a lunchtime discussion about who will hear the music. He wants to play "before ladies with diamonds", but is afraid that, "People do not come largely to pianos." A brisk meeting with Diana's old friend Elsie Radcliffe and the party is arranged, the scene giving way to Guy and Aunt Mildy (Joy Mitchell) reading their invitations.

The relationship between Guy and Mildy is, perhaps inevitably, reduced. Its significance in the novel is thematic rather than dramatic, and indeed to be felt more intensely in the context of the tetralogy at large rather than in this individual novel. The filmed version tends to concentrate on those incidents and relationships that bear most obviously on the central pair, reflecting either by contrast (Wolfie and Mrs Montaubyn) or comparison (John and Josie) on Russell and Diana's situation. The deeper satisfactions underlying the comic surface of the Guy-Mildy relationship are, in the novel, usually intimated in the older Guy's narrative and as such acquire a dramatic colouring of their own. Though the voice-over technique is generally well-used in the serial, its function is to link and comment on those episodes which markedly advance the plot, and on this level Guy's progress in society is, if amusing, only minor.

If the big scenes suffer from a lack of appropriate physical grandeur, they nevertheless have their felicities. The *soirée* to launch the preludes has the merit of trusting in the music itself and giving a sufficient sample of it to warrant the occasion and the talk to which it gives rise. Lady Pringle, a caricature in the book, is played with appropriately gushy fulsomeness by Joy Westmore, who gives the role a dimension of reality that in fact takes it beyond caricature. As she reads a lushly romantic poem to introduce it, a cut to the twins' reactions indicates what the viewer is to make of her; and, as Wolfie plays, the camera keeps on him sufficiently to acknowledge him as the *raison d'être* for the evening, cutting in turn to Lady Pringle with eyes closed rapturously, to Arthur Langton looking sceptical, to Wolfie's image of Mrs Montaubyn brushing her long-flowing hair in soft-focus, to Russell prissily turning to Diana. John and Josie's relationship, lyrically unpersuasive in the novel, is given a little more substance by the presence of pleasing actors, as their appreciation of each other begins in this episode, prospers at the Government House ball, and culminates in their wedding scene. During the latter, as a cab-driver waits outside the church, he reads a newspaper on the back page of which a news item is headed, "Austrian heir shot", and a narrative link between personal and public affairs is unobtrusively made.

The penultimate scene at the theatre, well-staged so as to minimize one's sense of an undercrowded audience, achieves some of the melo-dramatic flourish Boyd gives it in the novel. It is organized as a birthday party for Mildy, given by Arthur Langton, not as in the novel by Guy's father Steven. (The omission of Steven and his wife Laura, who have no other part in the narrative of this novel, is a sensible economizing on characters. Whereas a minor character can be sharply sketched in a novel's paragraph, a fleeting, unexplained appearance in a film version can be merely confusing.) The routing of Mrs Montaubyn, aflame with patriotic ardour when she denounces Wolfie as he leaves the theatre, is effectively written and played. In a series of close-ups she has been shown singing "God save the King" lustily, and now there is a convincing look of confusion on her face as Cynthia Langton, rescuing Wolfie, calls her a wicked woman. A broadly drawn character has been given a momentary depth by the actor's understanding as reflected in facial expression.

Virtually no incident of any consequence has been omitted from Griffiths' adaptation, and Whitbread's direction seems bent on giving full weight to every scene. It seems ungrateful, then, to say that this is not enough. The two-and-a-half hours' running time of the serial has encouraged too dawdling a speed, and this has worked against dis-crimination between matters of major and minor importance. There has been a serious attempt to retain Guy's narrative voice but, though drawing closely on the words of the original in the process, the over-all effect is too measured. He remains a commentator, a device, not an integral element in the way one responds to what one sees. Above all, this careful, decently tasteful version of the novel remains no more than what Jack Clancy, writing of certain BBC serials, calls "a kind of pictorial sub-stitution"[7]. There is no sense of Oscar Whitbread's direction offering an interpretation or critique of the novel, in the way that some of the Aus-tralian feature films adapted from novels have done. The direction is invisibly competent but it is flavourless; what life the serial has is Boyd's rather than its adaptors'.

Behind the opening titles to the ABC's serialized adaptation of **Lucinda Brayford** is a series of softly blurred photographs of a beautiful, smiling face which belongs to the actress Wendy Hughes, playing the eponymous heroine. These introductory images may be taken as a sign indicating where the serial's centre of interest will be, and its strength is indeed in the actress' performance. The adaptation (by Cliff Green) and the direction (by John Gauci) work to keep Lucinda at the centre, in a way that is not wholly true of the novel. As suggested earlier, Lucinda's story tends to taper off in the novel and such unity as the latter aspires to is to be found elsewhere. It is, as Dorothy Green has noted, located chiefly "in the presence of an author who is himself the most interesting character in the book"[8]; this is what I had in mind when suggesting that "the third person voice in *Lucinda Brayford* also presents a major challenge to the film-maker" (p. 180). The adaptation in question, eschewing a narrator's voice, has not found an equivalent for the source of the novel's unity, but in focusing on Lucinda herself has extrapolated in a way that has achieved a more limited unity of its own. The cost has been considerable and the viewer is left with a more conventional narrative than the reader, privy to Martin Boyd's perceptions, had at his disposal. In fairness, though, it must be added that the serial's makers may have taken the only course possible in giving coherence to what is, in terms of plot, a somewhat rambling chronicle.

In placing Lucinda so firmly before the viewer, in making the television version almost exclusively the story of her life, what is missed is the sense of recurring patterns which Boyd so clearly sees as being at the heart of family history. Even in the two hundred minutes the serial takes, a great deal of selection obviously was necessary, but it seems a matter for major regret not to have included the opening scene at Clare College, Cambridge, or even a glimpse of Fred and Julie's drought-stricken days at Noorilla and their triumphant outcome.

Julie Vane (Carol Burns). **Lucinda Brayford**.

   To omit the first is to lose the framing symmetry of the novel which ends at Cambridge with Lucinda listening with a renewal of delight to the clear young voice of a King's College chorister, this hopeful note following the scattering of Stephen's ashes from Clare Bridge. The television version includes the Clare Bridge episode but loses the resonant patterning that would have derived from starting there. Further, instead of Lucinda's sudden access of joy in King's, which recalls Stephen's pleasure there, the serial offers not-very-revealing close-ups of Lucinda, Paul Brayford (Kirk Alexander) and Roland Roberts (Michael Boughen), Stephen's boyhood friend. They are presented perhaps as important influences on his life but the effect is too diffuse, and another aspect of the novel's patterning, important in so bulky a work, is lost — needlessly, one feels. What is moving is Lucinda's final grief as she contemplates Stephen's photograph, but compared with the novel's last moments it is not integrated into the over-all narrative pattern.

   The loss of the Noorilla section of the novel, one of Boyd's finest achievements as he recreates the sense of physical parching and the psychological equivalent in Fred and Julie's relationship, is more serious. Dorothy Green has written,

> The coming of rain and the rejuvenation of the affection [between Fred and Julie] result in the birth of Lucinda, the fruit of the one genuine moment of passion and harmony between them.[9]

To omit this section has a seriously thinning-out effect on the texture of the serial. For one thing, it lessens the viewer's sense of the rise-and-fall patterns in the family's history; it removes some of the motivation for Julie's social ambition, which includes the making of a "brilliant" marriage for Lucinda; and it undermines the sense of Lucinda's special qualities. As the serial manages things, beginning with a young people's dance at the Vanes' Kew house, whatever is special about Lucinda must derive chiefly from Wendy Hughes' performance.

   Lucinda is eighteen when the first episode begins and Hughes, perhaps a trifle old for the role at this stage, suggests at once a convincing visualization of that "composure and sensitive charm which had marked her as a natural artistocrat . . . Her physical texture, her hair and skin, were delicate and flowerlike" (p.11). One of the notable achievements of the serial is in finding its own ways of reproducing one of the strengths of the novel (and of Boyd's work at large): that is, the effect of a character's ageing, partly as a natural process, partly in response to the narrative's episodes. Green's screenplay selects the latter in such a way as to mark distinct stages in Lucinda's growth: for example, the scene on the rock at Flinders where she feels a special affinity with Tony Duff (Sam Neill), an affinity which may be love for all she knows, her serenity and easeful youth contrasting with Tony's edgy, truncated gestures and facial anxieties; a new, more confident poise in the way she dances with Hugo Brayford (Barry Quin) at the ball Julie (Carol Burns) gives at Tourella;

and the passionate love-making, against a vast background of Australian landscape, records a physical ripeness that makes convincing progression from the previous episodes referred to.

And one could chart this process of development, partly a matter of observable, external changes and partly a subtle shift of inner perspectives, throughout the series, but a couple of examples should make the point. In the second episode, Cliff Green pulls together Lucinda's observations of certain aspects of English country life in a discussion with Paul Brayford. As she asks him about the apparent contrarieties between his way of seeing things freshly and, in other matters, his rigorously traditional view of the aristocracy, dialogue and actress conspire to suggest a more mature thoughtfulness. Her life is no longer as straightforward as it was and it shows in the actress' face and bearing, in her function as an element of the *mise-en-scène*. The contentment she registers when, pregnant with Stephen, she moves into the dower house attached to Crittenden gives way to a feeling of comfortable imprisonment shortly after. In this later scene, as snow falls outside, there is a warmly lit interior with roaring fire, baby asleep in cradle — and Lucinda restlessly pacing the room. By now, the sheen has gone off the marriage. A little later, Hugo having been wounded in France, she sits anxiously at his bedside and there is a flashback, as she contemplates the bandaged face before her, to the time she first danced with him. This juxtaposition of shots, producing a slight shock effect, concentrates one's impression of how effectively the ageing has been managed.

By the end of the series, when Lucinda has gone through the difficulties of a wrecked marriage to which she is chained, of an unsatisfactory love affair with Pat Lanfranc (Edmund Pegge), of breaking up her brother's marriage to an English girl at Julie's urgent bidding, of seeing the life of her son Stephen (Stephen Oldfield) smashed first by a calculating wife and then by military imprisonment, she has settled into a tougher middle-age. Tougher, that is, because she has needed to bear with what seems like the continuing downward pattern of her life, and this is played out against a background of social change — of two world wars and the uncertain intervening years. This background is quite effectively sketched by the use of newspaper headlines, newsreels of soldiers marching, and talk of the Kaiser, Baldwin, Chamberlain and others around various bridge tables. It does, however, remain a background while Lucinda is kept firmly in the foreground. There are changes of hairdo and costumes (by Betty Jacks) which register fashions changing but, more important, contribute to the viewer's recognition of Lucinda's changing and ageing. The hair is rolled more severely, the dresses become more sophisticated; and they are of a piece with the increasing "smartness" and cynicism of her conversation, the incessant smoking, the more matronly bearing and posture. Hughes offers a very well-thought-out performance that responds to the suggestions of Green's screenplay and to Gauci's direction which places her in the frame and against the decor in ways that underscore her centrality. Whereas Rowena Wallace merely inhabits the role of Diana in **Outbreak of Love**, Hughes moves about and lives in that of Lucinda.

If Lucinda's development is the chief narrative element that has been transposed from the novel, and the serial's main strength, it does not take place in a vacuum. The film's *mise-en-scène* is variably successful in providing the physical aspects of Lucinda's world. The Australian scenes, perhaps inevitably, are a good deal more convincing than the English, not merely in physical verisimilitude but in helping one to understand the drama of Lucinda's life. (One wonders if it is a coincidence that these are also the most vivid scenes in the novel.) The Kew house, The Pines, has an aptly unpretentious charm against which Lucinda does appear a lovely flower in bud; the boarding-house annexe at Flinders where the family spends Christmas and the adjacent beaches create a relaxed openness that encourage Lucinda's flowering; and the Tourella ball (using the National Trust property, Ripponlea) has the right touch of grandeur for launching her into society and as a catch for Hugo Brayford. As in **Outbreak of Love**, scenes such as this in Australian television serials tend to suffer from undercrowding, but the effect is less damaging than when the story moves to London in the second episode. The boat-train arrives at Victoria Station where there seem to be no more than three people waiting to greet passengers and all of them are there to meet Hugo and Lucinda. It is a brief scene but it is wholly ridiculous from a realist point of view; ingenuity needs to be stretched further than this to overcome budgetary limitations. The English stately homes — Crittenden and Fitzauncell — are not really stately enough; they do not provide an adequate visual rendering of Boyd's descriptive accounts. In the case of Crittenden, this is an important narrative point, because Lucinda's response to it and what it stands for, and to its dower house, is one of the influential elements in her English life. As for the dower house, called End House, in which Lucinda and Hugo go to live, it looks almost *démeublé*, its sparse furniture neither good nor interesting enough to reflect Lucinda's taste.

The only other character whose story provides a clear narrative element is Stephen, and in this respect **Lucinda Brayford** follows Boyd closely. The final episode begins with the grown Stephen at Cambridge, meeting the chorister Brian who, as Boyd writes, "gave to his singing that absorbed attention which children give to work or play that interests them" (p. 376). The Cambridge setting is artfully suggested with a few cloisters, corners and a bridge that does duty for Clare. Stephen's undefined delight in life finds a focus when his cousin Heather Vane (Penelope Stewart) arrives in England with her father, Lucinda's brother Bill (Laurie Roberts), and socially ambitious mother, Muriel (Paula de Burgh). Stephen is too idealistic to notice the calculation just beneath Heather's radiant surface. The television version has worked at finding visual signs to convey the lyrical intentions of Boyd's writing. (In my own view, this is misguided effort since Boyd is usually at his worst on such occasions.) There are close-ups of water-lilies, shots of Stephen swimming in the reedy lake at Crittenden while Heather watches, not quite sure what to make of this simple delight in the natural nor of his romantic gesture of putting a lily in her hair as he kisses her. This is followed by the proposal scene in the Peacock Room at Crittenden, from which Gauci cuts to a shot of Stephen and Heather walking through the dappled light of the Crittenden grounds. In this attractive natural setting, Heather talks of Lucinda's "knowing everyone", while Stephen quotes, "Once a boy a wild rose espied." A premonitory dramatic tension is set up in their divergent responses, the visual effect and the dialogue, as well as the apt casting of the actors, working to prepare the ground for their subsequently disastrous marriage.

The scene in Lucinda's chic London flat where Stephen tells her that Heather has left him is another product of well-judged *mise-en-scène*. As Stephen sits somewhat gormlessly in the background, Lucinda, in the foreground, visibly older, needing glasses for the directory, briskly telephones Heather's lover. In the next shot she is still in the foreground, hair swept up maturely and in the fashion of the day, smoking and trying to think clearly, while Stephen mooches around in the background. The arrangement of the two within each shot, and against the discreet decor of the flat, makes its point about their lives and their relationship. The downward plunge of Stephen's life, from a Dunkirk rescue (remarkably free of the sense of battle, death, crowds and danger) to a refusal to obey military orders, to imprisonment and humiliation, and to death, is economically sketched. From a final, racked coughing fit, the camera cuts to take flowers on his coffin and then dissolves to Clare Bridge and the scattering of the ashes. In telling Stephen's story, the serial's visual signifiers evoke

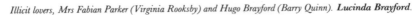

Illicit lovers, Mrs Fabian Parker (Virginia Rooksby) and Hugo Brayford (Barry Quinn). **Lucinda Brayford**.

with considerable fidelity the narrative "facts" and the tone of the original. Stephen is Boyd's vehicle for his pacifist concerns and for his final rendering of the gap between Lucinda's bright promise and its lack of fulfilment. The television production has realized this with touching accuracy.

In concentrating on Lucinda, and, in its last episode, on Stephen and relating Stephen's collapse to her development, **Lucinda Brayford** as an adaptation has achieved its own coherence. Boyd's philosophic concerns take second place to the depiction of more palpable *events*. Through the character of Paul, the screenplay preserves some of Boyd's reflections on issues such as the function of the aristocracy, the place of art in life, of patriotism in the face of a threat to a culture wider than national boundaries. Paul sometimes takes on the role of chorus, but the film medium (and perhaps especially the television serial with its unusual demands on audience attention, and the threats to this) is not naturally amenable to rendering this kind of discussion. Further, Paul's utterances need the "placing" commentary of Boyd's narrative voice for their full effect. One senses Boyd's endorsement of a good deal that Paul says but it is also clear that Boyd is aware of Paul's inconsistency. Lacking that narrative voice, the television serial is left with Paul as a character, with no reliable guide as to how far one can or ought to accept his point of view.

Despite these two conscientious attempts to film Boyd, audiences still await a rigorous film version of these and the other novels, uniquely attractive as they are in the annals of Australian fiction. Fred Schepisi responded to *The Chant of Jimmie Blacksmith* and Gillian Armstrong to *My Brilliant Career*, finding their own centres of interest in them and giving them a relevance to their own times. One hopes that some sophisticated and sensitive director may emerge to use the social aspects of Boyd's novels as a means to present his underlying concern for the way people are.

Notes

1. Brian McFarlane, *Martin Boyd's Langton Novels*, Edward Arnold (Australia), Melbourne, 1980, p. 55.
2. Martin Boyd, *A Difficult Young Man*, Lansdowne Press, Melbourne, 1971, p. 75.
3. Kathleen Fitzpatrick, *Martin Boyd (Australian Writers and their Work)*, Lansdowne Press, Melbourne, 1963, p. 18.
4. *Ibid*, p. 12.
5. Brenda Niall, "Boyd interprets his own past", Education Age, *The Age*, Melbourne, 9 November 1982.
6. Paul Kerr, "Classic Serials — To be Continued", *Screen*, Vol. 23, No. 1, May-June 1982, p. 6.
7. Jack Clancy, "The Film of *My Brilliant Career*", *Australian Literary Studies*, Vol. 9, No. 3, May 1980, p. 365.
8. Dorothy Green, "The Fragrance of Souls: A Study of *Lucinda Brayford*", *Southerly*, No. 2, June 1968, p. 113.
9. *Ibid*, p. 118.

Appendices

A: Australian Novels

1907 **Robbery Under Arms**
Dir.: Charles MacMahon
Based on the novel by Rolf
Boldrewood

1908 **For the Term of his Natural
Life**
Dir.: Charles MacMahon
Based on the novel by
Marcus Clarke

1910 **Thunderbolt**
Dir.: John Gavin
Based on the novel, *Three
Years with Thunderbolt*, by
Ambrose Pratt

1911 **The Mystery of a Hansom
Cab**
Dir.: W. J. Lincoln
Based on the novel by Fergus
Hume

1911 **Captain Starlight, or
Gentleman of the Road**
Dir.: Alfred Rolfe
Based on the novel, *Robbery
Under Arms*, by Rolf
Boldrewood

1911 **The Life of Rufus Dawes**
Dir.: Alfred Rolfe
Based on the novel, *For the
Term of his Natural Life*, by
Marcus Clarke

1911 **The Double Event**
Dir.: W. J. Lincoln
Based on the novel by Nat
Gould

1911 **Caloola/The Adventures of
a Jackeroo**
Dir.: Alfred Rolfe
Based on the novel by
Clement Pratt

1911 **Gambler's Gold**
Dir.: George Young
Based on the novel by Arthur
Wright

1913 **Moondyne**
Dir.: W. J. Lincoln
Based on the novel by John
Boyle O'Reilly

1914 **The Silence of Dean
Maitland**
Dir.: Raymond Longford
Based on the novel by
Maxwell Gray

1916 **In the Last Stride**
Dir.: Martyn Keith
Based on the novel by Arthur
Wright

1916 **The Pioneers**
Dir.: Franklyn Barrett
Based on the novel by
Katharine Susannah
Pritchard

1920 **Robbery Under Arms**
Dir.: Kenneth Brampton
Based on the novel by Rolf
Boldrewood

1920 **The Hordern Mystery**
Dir.: Harry Southwell
Based on the novel by
Edward Finn

1921 **The Blue Mountains Mystery**
Dirs: Raymond Longford, Lottie Lyell
Based on the novel, *The Mount Marunga Mystery*, by Harrison Owen

1922 **A Rough Passage**
Dir.: Franklyn Barrett
Based on the novel by Arthur Wright

1925 **The Mystery of a Hansom Cab**
Dir.: Arthur Shirley
Based on the novel by Fergus Hume

1925 **Jewelled Nights**
Dirs: Louise Lovely, Wilton Welch
Based on the novel by Marie Bjelke-Petersen

1926 **The Moth of Moonbi**
Dir.: Charles Chauvel
Based on the novel, *The Wild Moth*, by Mabel Forrest

1926 **The Pioneers**
Dir.: Raymond Longford
Based on the novel by Katharine Susannah Prichard

1926 **Hills of Hate**
Dir.: Raymond Longford
Based on the novel by E. V. Timms

1927 **For the Term of his Natural Life**
Dir.: Norman Dawn
Based on the novel by Marcus Clarke

1928 **The Romance of Runnibede**
Dir.: Scott R. Dunlap
Based on the novel by Steele Rudd

1928 **The Adorable Outcast**
Dir.: Norman Dawn
Based on the novel, *Conn of the Coral Seas*, by Beatrice Grimshaw

1936 **The Flying Doctor**
Dir.: Miles Mander
Based on the novel by Robert Waldron

1937 **Lovers and Luggers**
Dir.: Ken G. Hall
Based on the novel by Gurney Slade

1938 **The Broken Melody**
Dir.: Ken G. Hall
Based on the novel by F. J. Thwaites

1939 **Mr Chedworth Steps Out**
Dir.: Ken G. Hall
Based on the novel by Francis Morton Howard

1939 **Seven Little Australians**
Dir.: Arthur Greville Collins
Based on the novel by Ethel Turner

1951 **Wherever She Goes**
Dir.: Michael S. Gordon
Based on the novel, *Prelude*, by Clare H. Abrahall

1956 **Smiley**
Dir.: Anthony Kimmins
Based on the novel by Moore Raymond

1957 **The Shiralee**
Dir.: Leslie Norman
Based on the novel by D'Arcy Niland

1957 **Robbery Under Arms**
Dir.: Jack Lee
Based on the novel by Rolf Boldrewood

1958 **Smiley Gets a Gun**
Dir.: Anthony Kimmins
Based on the novel by Moore Raymond

1958 **Dust in the Sun**
Dir.: Lee Robinson
Based on the novel, *Justin Bayard*, by Jon Cleary

1959 **On the Beach**
Dir.: Stanley Kramer
Based on the novel by Nevil Shute

1960 **The Sundowners**
Dir.: Fred Zinnemann
Based on the novel by Jon Cleary

1961 **Bungala Boys**
Dir.: Jim Jeffrey
Based on the novel, *The New Surf Club*, by Claire Meillon

1962 **They Found a Cave**
Dir.: Andrew Steane
Based on the novel by Nan Chauncy

1966 **They're a Weird Mob**
Dir.: Michael Powell
Based on the novel by Nino Culotta (John O'Grady)

1969 **You Can't See 'round Corners**
Dir.: David Cahill
Based on the novel by Jon Cleary

1969 **Age of Consent**
Dir.: Michael Powell
Based on the novel by Norman Lindsay

1971 **Wake in Fright**
Dir.: Ted Kotcheff
Based on the novel by Kenneth Cook

1975 **The Great MacArthy**
Dir.: David Baker
Based on the novel, *A Salute to the Great McCarthy*, by Barry Oakley

1975 **Picnic at Hanging Rock**
Dir.: Peter Weir
Based on the novel by Joan Lindsay

1975 **Scobie Malone**
Dir.: Terry Ohlsson
Based on the novel, *Helga's Web*, by Jon Cleary

1975 **Ride a Wild Pony**
Dir.: Don Chaffey
Based on the novel, *A Sporting Proposition*, by James Alridge

1976 **Storm Boy**
Dir.: Henri Safran
Based on the novel by Colin Thiele

1976 **Let the Balloon Go**
Dir.: Oliver Howes
Based on the novel by Ivan Southall

1977 **The Getting of Wisdom**
Dir.: Bruce Beresford
Based on the novel by Henry Handel Richardson

1977 **The Mango Tree**
Dir.: Kevin Dobson
Based on the novel by Ronald McKie

1977 **Dot and the Kangaroo**
Dir.: Yoram Gross
Based on the novel by Ethel Pedley

1978 **Blue Fin**
Dir.: Carl Schultz
Based on the novel by Colin Thiele

1978 **The Irishman**
Dir.: Donald Crombie
Based on the novel by Elizabeth O'Conner (Barbara MacNamara)

1978 **Weekend of Shadows**
Dir.: Tom Jeffrey
Based on the novel, *The Reckoning*, by Hugh Atkinson

1979 **Born to Run**

1979 **My Brilliant Career**
Dir.: Gillian Armstrong
Based on the novel by Miles
Franklin

1979 **The Odd Angry Shot**
Dir.: Tom Jeffrey
Based on the novel by
William Nagle

1979 **Tim**
Dir.: Michael Pate
Based on the novel by
Colleen McCullogh

1980 **Manganinnie**
Dir.: John Honey
Based on the novel by Beth
Roberts

1981 **Puberty Blues**
Dir.: Bruce Beresford
Based on the novel by Kathy
Lette and Gabrielle Carey

1982 **A Dangerous Summer**
Dir.: Quentin Masters

Based on the novel by Kit
Denton

1982 **Monkey Grip**
Dir.: Ken Cameron
Based on the novel by Helen
Garner

1982 **We of the Never Never**
Dir.: Igor Auzins
Based on the novel by
Jeannie Gunn

1983 **The Year of Living
Dangerously**
Dir.: Peter Weir
Based on the novel by
Christopher J. Koch

1983 **Dusty**
Dir.: John Richardson
Based on the novel by Frank
Dalby Davidson

1983 **Fighting Back**
Dir.: Michael Caulfield
Based on the novel by John
Embling

B: Australian Short Stories

1911 **A Ticket in Tatts**
Dir.: Gaston Mervale
Based on the short story by
P. W. Marony

1911 **All for Gold/Jumping the
Claim**
Dir.: Franklyn Barrett
Based on the short story by
W. S. Percy

1912 **Strike**
Dir.: George Young
Based on the short story by
Casper Middleton

1915 **The Rebel**
Dir.: J. E. Mathews

Based on the short story by
James Bernard Fagan

1920 **On Our Selection**
Dir.: Raymond Longford
Based on the stories of Steele
Rudd

1921 **Rudd's New Selection**
Dir.: Raymond Longford
Based on the stories of Steele
Rudd

1921 **While the Billy Boils**
Dir.: Beaumont Smith
Based on the stories of Henry
Lawson

1921 **The Gentleman Bushranger**
Dir.: Beaumont Smith
Based on the short story, "A
Stripe for Trooper Casey",
by Roderic Quinn

1924 **Joe**
Dir.: Beaumont Smith
Based on the story
collections, *Joe Wilson* and *Joe
Wilson's Mates*, by Henry
Lawson

1932 **On Our Selection**
Dir.: Ken G. Hall
Based on the short stories of
Steele Rudd

1936 **Orphan of the Wilderness**
Dir.: Ken G. Hall
Based on the short story,
"Wilderness Orphan", by
Dorothy Cottrell

1957 **Three in One**
Dir.: Cecil Holmes
Based on the stories, "The
Union Buries its Dead" by
Henry Lawson and "The
Load of Wood" by Frank
Hardy

1978 **The Night the Prowler**
Dir.: Jim Sharman
Based on the story story by
Patrick White

C: Australian Poems

1913 **The Stockrider**
Dir.: W. J. Lincoln
Based on the poem by Adam
Lindsay Gordon

1913 **The Wreck**
Dir.: W. J. Lincoln
Based on the poem, "From
the Wreck", by Adam
Lindsay Gordon

1919 **The Sentimental Bloke**
Dir.: Raymond Longford
Based on the verse narrative
by C. J. Dennis

1920 **Ginger Mick**
Dir.: Raymond Longford
Based on the verse narrative,
The Moods of Ginger Mick, by
C. J. Dennis

1920 **The Man from Snowy
River**
Dirs: Beaumont Smith,
John K. Wells

Based on the poems of
A. Banjo Paterson

1924 **How McDougall Topped
the Score**
Dir.: V. Upton Brown
Based on the poem by
Thomas E. Spencer

1925 **Around the Boree Log**
Dir.: Phil K. Walsh
Based on the poems of John
O'Brien

1932 **The Sentimental Bloke**
Dir.: F. W. Thring
Based on the poems, *The
Songs of a Sentimental Bloke*, by
C. J. Dennis

1982 **The Man from Snowy
River**
Dir.: George Miller
Based on the poem by A.
Banjo Paterson